Dedications

I would like to dedicate this book to the three most important people in my life and the ones who have stood by me through thick and thin.

My Mum, Dad and Daughter. I can't express enough how much you mean to me and I can't thank you enough for the support and love you have given me since speaking out about my demons.

Without you three in my life I'm sure I wouldn't be here today sharing my true story with the world...

Love Stevie xx

Introduction

Hello everyone my name is Stevie and I would just like to thank you for taking the time to read my book, hopefully this will help many others in moving forward in their lives rather than punishing themselves just like I did...

You are about to go on a journey into the life of myself, explaining how one sick pedophiles depraved act destroyed the next thirty five years of my life. I am not looking for sympathy, attention or for anyone to feel sorry for me as if this was the case I would have spoken up many years ago. This book simply explains how keeping a thirty five year secret will only build up inside of you as you think you can deal with it but all you will really do is destroy yourself from the inside out. Secrets will always catch up with you in the end. I will cover many events in my life but unfortunately most of these will be about the darkness I have had to live through while hiding behind a mask, trying to take my own life on a couple of occasions, playing with death and blocking out everything with alcohol and drugs for a good twenty years, purely on self-destruct. Even to the point of breaking my neck and suffering a mild heart attack.

In this book I will also be covering Mental Health issues as I suffer from Borderline Personality Disorder due to a childhood trauma. I feel that not enough men are willing to take ownership of their illness as we live in a society where men struggle to talk about their feelings, also worrying what the 'so called' strong ruthless men out there will think about a man who shows any emotions.

STEVIE - BEHIND THE MASK

I really hope this book helps people in dealing with the above issues and also gives more of an understanding and insight to people that do not suffer as then maybe the ones that do won't have to keep it a secret any longer and can hopefully enjoy a normal happy and free life, not keeping any secrets. In my opinion it would not be appropriate for anyone under the age of sixteen to read this book as it will be very deep and I will be covering many situations and emotions in depth which I feel anyone under this age should not have to deal with until they have a full understanding of them.

So please sit back as you will now enter the journey of the little boy who lived behind a mask for many years hiding his true identity.

I'm STEVIE and here is my TRUE story.... FIGHTING FOR FREEDOM!!!

CHAPTER 1
LIVING THE DREAM

AGE: Born - 6 years old
YEAR: 1977-1984

I suppose if I am writing a story about my life, the best place to start would be with the gene donors: my mum and dad. It all started in the East End of London, Bethnal Green to be exact, it was March 1964. Dad was 14 years old and mum was 13 years old. Dad was attending Dansford Secondary School, but after a short time of not attending many lessons and deciding to get 'true love' tattooed on his knuckles, the school finally decided to expel him. On the other hand mum was a bit of a goody-two-shoes and attended John Howard Grammar School, to say she was a boffin would be an understatement! She managed to take every single exam and passed them all with flying colours, I myself would say that she was the teacher's pet. To say that these two were like Chalk and Cheese would be spot on, but for some reason they both fell in love and are still happily in love today.

The time came when mum finally left school and her and my dad's relationship was heading to the next level, stepping out into the big wide world on their own and both seeking employment. Mum got a job as a Personal Assistant to a Fabric Retailer/Property Developer and gave a hundred percent to her role, as she was focusing on saving for a house and marrying my dad. He managed to get into Tower Hamlets Council as a Gardner and also had a second

4

evening job, which was cleaning supermarket floors with my uncle just so he could get that extra bit of bunce money. He was also focused on saving for a house and marrying my mum. They both knew what they wanted and that was each other. Nothing was going to stop them from achieving their goals together.

They both spent the next ten years doing what young couples do best, working, socializing and saving for a better future. The day finally arrived after ten years together and having saved every penny they could, the day my mum had always wished for, it was the day they would finally get married.

Their wedding was in June 1975 at St James the Less Church in Bethnal Green and from what my mum tells me, it was a 'fairytale wedding' which went exactly as she had planned it to. Because she worked so hard and dedicated herself as a PA, her employer offered to take her to the church in his gold Rolls Royce and he gave them a fifty pound wedding present and a washer/dryer. It obviously paid off being the teacher's pet then! All of it was a bonus but from what I can tell the only thing she wanted was what she already had, which was my dad and nothing would ever change that. She worshipped the ground he walked on.

1975 was a busy year for my mum and dad as they moved into their new house once married. They moved into a three bedroom Victorian terrace house in Rixsen Road, Barking in Essex. The house was £4,500.00 which they got a mortgage for. Where they had saved so hard for many years, they managed to put a £500.00 deposit down as a lump sum, which in turn would bring their mortgage payments down. The house was not in the best condition as it had no kitchen, no wardrobe space and a few ceilings missing. It did have a new bathroom which mum was more than happy with. This didn't bother them at all as they both now owned their first ever house. After a good year of grafting in the house and my grandad (dad's dad) pointing the finger, it was finally finished and was now a much better home for them to live in so they could start to build a happy family.

In the summer of 1967 mum managed Reed Employment at London Bridge and dad was working as well. They finally both had what they wanted in life which was to own their own house and to be married to each other.

Then came their first Christmas together in their new home. A happy time of year, but this year would become a very special Christmas for my dad as my mum broke the news to him that she was now pregnant. To say they were both over the moon would have definitely been an understatement!

On the 27th September 1977 in Barking Hospital a baby boy was born, weighing 8lb 2 oz. This is where I enter the equation as that baby was me and on that day, I was named Stevie. As the story goes, according to my mum (but if ya want my opinion she is just being bias), on the ward where I was born, the nurses were coming up to the ward from other floors and asking to see her baby boy, that being me. Then other mums also started coming from other floors and asking to look at me as well, according to my mum, I was a good looking baby with light blonde hair and sky blue eyes. To some that would be a bonus, but one day that apparent gift I was given would come back to haunt me in the worst way possible.

Six months passed and the three of us start on a new journey, finally moving from the City to the country. They bought a lovely house in Welling in Kent on a lovely little place called Poets Estate, with two family pubs around either corner at each entrance to the estate.

There was also a church, two schools, a green and many open playing fields that surrounded the estate. The house was a two bedroom semi-detached with walk through drive at the side of the house going through to the back garden. The house was only eighteen months old and unlike the other house everything was already decorated and was located in a beautiful little cul-de-sac. Everything was just perfect about this house and being on this new estate would have been a dream for any family, even to the point that my Aunt (mum's sister) and her husband had lived here already for a while which made the move easier having their family and loved ones close by. Already their family was expanding and mum and dad were becoming more settled in their new house as time went on. From what my mum and dad tell me and from what I remember, I was an extremely loved and well looked after child. I was their first child and now they had to share their love with someone else rather than each other and that's something neither of them had a problem doing.

I had my own room located at the back of the house overlooking our back garden. I know I might be going a bit deeper into how cared for I was as a baby but I just want to give people an understanding of how loved, protected and safe I really was and how it can all change in the blink of an eye.

My bedroom had beige painted walls with an animal border going round, beige carpet and a beautiful white cot with matching animal bedding. Also, surrounded by as many cuddly toys as you could imagine. I (jokingly) thought my mum was 'milking it' trying to make herself seem like the perfect mum when explaining the start of my life. I've seen the photos and believe me I was a very lucky child at this time in my life. You could say everything was perfect and as a child I was 'living the dream'.

I suppose you could say I had the best start coming into the world and had two amazing parents who were willing to devote all their time to me, giving me the best chance they could at a bright and fulfilling future. Another sign of how lucky I was as a new born baby was my first Christmas. Just to let you all know, the first three years of my life I have no clue what happened as I was too young to remember, this is all down to facts from family and friends, I was no genius. So, Christmas morning arrives and as it was my first Christmas, I did really well with loads of cuddly toys, baby clothes and other stuff that babies get given. A teething ring was my best gift as we all know how much a teething ring means to a newborn child. I would say I was more than looked after as a child and didn't do too bad for a baby's first Christmas.

Then, after a lovely start living in our new house, the summer arrives and I am now 18 months old. I'm in the kitchen with my mum, she is preparing food and I'm being a weird child as usual and I'm playing with the back door and it's open. Like any child would do, I'm sitting there playing with the cat flap on the door and pulling it back and forth. Then I became more interested in the movement of the door, this then made me stand up as I could get a bit more involved with how the door worked. I then made the biggest mistake ever and put my left hand on the door frame to support myself. While doing that, I pull on the door with my right hand and 'bang'. I shut my finger in the door, taking the top of my finger completely off. There was blood everywhere within seconds and my mum started to scream and cry. She picked me up as quickly as she could and ran straight to the front door carrying me in her arms. Once outside the front of the house she would scream "please someone help me, my baby, my baby". Then, according to my mum, I just looked at her and said "don't cry mummy, don't cry". Mum was wearing a white V-neck jumper and she was absolutely covered in blood. She said it was horrific and she didn't really want to talk about it in depth when telling me the story. Finally, an ambulance came and I was taken to the Old Queen Elizabeth Hospital up over Shooters Hill. I had to have the top of my finger stitched back on and it was a very painful moment in my life as a child. Thinking to myself. 'I'll never do that again' as all I wanted was to be happy, not sad. I have never put my hand in a door frame since that day when using a door and I am not likely to do it ever again, that hurt.

Now approaching the terrible twos and getting even closer to doing my mum's head in around the house, my mum and my Aunt decided to take me out shopping to Marks and Spencer. Unfortunately for them, I'm not sure it was the nice relaxed shopping trip it was meant to be. Apparently, my mum and my Aunt were looking at clothes but then I decided to go wandering off which is something I would like to do. I suppose you could say I had no fear which is not a good quality to have in such a young child. Believe me, my mum had her eye on me throughout the day as I was a very hyperactive child, but as told by others in the family, one minute I was there and the next minute I was gone. Anyway, getting back to the story, my mum and my Aunt had come to the realisation that I had done one of my disappearing acts but really I wasn't that far away as I had left a trail of destruction leading to my destination. What I had actually done was dragged all of the hanging clothing from the heavy chrome rails onto the floor, I then decided to hide in the spot at the end of my trail of destruction! My aunt used to say to my mum whenever we went in there "I swear the lighting in this place affects his eyes and sends him crazy" what can I say, it wasn't me, it was the lights! Now my mum is really starting to feel the stresses of having a 2 year old running around. She even got to the point of calling me 666 and the devil child. This made her realise she needed to get me into nursery so she could have a break as what I didn't know at the time, she was five months pregnant with my little sister. Before you know it, my first day at nursery finally arrives in March 1980. Leaving the house with my mum pushing me in my buggy, we made our way to the nursery which was just around the corner from our house. We would go past the local pub on the right, then up past Shoulder Mutton Green on the left and then the nursery was up on the right hand side next to St

STEVIE - BEHIND THE MASK

Mary's church. I can't remember much of my first day at nursery as I was so young but my mum did tell me some things about my days at nursery. The entrance was at the side of the nursery and there were two big brown fire exits doors. The doors would open and a slim lady was stood there looking down at all me, smiling. She was wearing a white roll neck jumper with blue jeans a pair of white trainers with blue stripes, her hair was short and was in a side parting and to finish her look she was wearing a dinner ladies navy blue three quarter length jacket with bright blue material around the sleeves, pockets and around the collar. She wore red lipstick, which stood out more than anything as she would smile at me making me and my mum feel welcome on the first day. The one thing my mum did like to tell me about that was about how the lady took an instant liking to me. She knew her little boy would be safe, her name was Mrs. Kelly.

So, as I start to settle into my nursery, being looked after by the lovely Mrs. Kelly and feeling happy and settled, it's at this point I find myself getting my first memories of life. I suppose you could say I was having a good time and that is what memories should be, about the good times. Believe it or not, I can pretty much remember many events in my life once starting nursery, not that I want to remember but it was just a case of having to, as how could you forget such happy times. I remember walking through the main brown doors and on the right would be a place to hang our coats and stuff. That is where the boys and girls toilets were as well. Then there was a set of double brown doors and beyond them doors is where all the fun would begin. Once you walk through them doors there would be every child's dream, toys toys and oh yeah, I nearly forgot, more toys. On the left, there would be a corner full of spongy bricks of all shapes and sizes, I even remember the colours of them, red, blue, green and yellow. The idea was that with the bricks you could build camps, dens and pretty much whatever you like. Then on your right would be a huge hall with lots of other things to keep a child occupied, you could say I was in heaven. Then, while playing in the spongy brick section one day, I would end up meeting my first best friend. This friend would be my best mate all throughout nursery, infant and junior school, I think this friendship was meant to be as we were in every single class, session and outings that were arranged during schooling, right up until the end of junior school and our houses even backed onto each other. While attending nursery me and my best mate would spend every second, minute and hour with each other, whether we were building a camp, drawing things, making things, learning things, you name it, we did it together! This was according to both our parents. Anytime he or I were to get into trouble with anyone else at nursery, we would be by each other's side as quick as you like, defending one another no matter what the circumstances, as said by Mrs. Kelly to my mum. That's pretty much how things were for the next 4 months, me and my new mate cracking on at nursery, doing what kids do. The summer term was approaching which means our time at nursery would soon come to an end.

Now into July and times were moving on. Mum and dad decided to extend their house as they were looking to welcome a new addition to the family in the form of my baby sister but at this time in my life I didn't have a clue as I was too young to understand. The extension was built very quickly and we had loads of workmen coming in and out of the house and as a kid you just want to see what was going on. According to my mum, they were lovely blokes that were building the extension and always took the time to say hello to me whenever they saw me. Just like any other child, you always end up talking to the older people as that's what makes us grow and gain confidence. Then once the extension is nearly complete, mum and dad end up running out of money for the last and most important part of the extension. Yep, you got it, the roof! Luckily, they managed to lend the money off my Nan (Mum's mum) she wasn't shy of a few quid then.

Then comes the time that every first born child will probably dread, the birth of their little baby sister. She was born in a Hospital in South London July 1980 and it wasn't long before my mum and my new baby sister would arrive home. I was excited and happy as I now had a sister to share life with but also the feeling of being left out and having to share the love my parents with this screaming little baby who was now getting all the attention. As you can tell I was a little green eyed and jealous about the whole situation but I was just like every other child who had been in my predicament. I remember on one occasion when my sister was a couple of months old, my mum was in the bedroom bathing her in a small baby bath which was on legs as she was a newborn and couldn't sit in a normal size bath. Standing in the corner next to them was me. I was looking up at my mum thinking 'what about me? What have I done wrong?' I still have a photo showing exactly how I felt on that day. When my mum showed me the picture, she said I looked sad and she had no clue that I was feeling like that at the time, bless her. I was here first and if you see the look in my eyes in the picture, you will see that I really didn't like the situation and was looking up at my mum giving her an evil look, not intentionally, I might add, I was just a kid being a kid. As the weeks passed I find myself back at nursery with my mate and cracking on with my life, while my mum was at home with my sister, she was still a newborn and pretty much took up all of my mum's time and energy, just like I did when I was born but hey, that's life! It's not all about Stevie as there is now another child to care for, as well as me, that's something I just had to deal with but don't we all?

It's now coming up to September and I will soon be 3 years old and I am now thinking this is my chance to get my mum's attention, then my third birthday arrives. My third birthday was certainly one to remember as this was the first birthday I'd have since my sister was born. This meant that I would get spoilt so I wouldn't feel left out from the arrival of my sister into the family recently.

I can remember some of this occasion as I was a very lucky boy that year but had been lucky since the day I was born having the mum and dad I had. My Aunt (dad's sister) had bought me an aeroplane that I could sit in with wheels on that I apparently told her I wanted by looking at the sky and pointing at an aeroplane. As told by family, my auntie went all the way to Hamleys to buy it as that was the only place that sold them. My Dad bought me an electric battery powered police motorbike with a police siren and radio, which I was over the moon with. My Mum bought me loads of clothes as I was now at the age where she liked to treat me like a real life doll, not only taking pride in her own appearance but taking pride in mine too. Not a bad result having your own fashion designer at age three was it? To say I was living on 'cloud nine' would be an understatement, I was a very fortunate child. I had a dad that was working all the hours under the sun just to give me and my sister a lovely life. I suppose you could say we were spoilt in our younger times of childhood, not such a bad thing though is it? As time goes on, my sister starts to become more aware of her surroundings, having emotions, feelings and all the other stuff that we tend to do as we start to experience life. In turn, I started to bond with her, finally realising that having a little sister is the best thing in the world and was better than any present I could ask for. My mum would put her on a baby matt in the living room letting her kick her little legs and have a breather from her nappy, it was then that I would see her smile and giggle at me and it was in that moment that the bond become stronger. I would then realise that it's my job to protect and look after this little bundle of joy from now on, as the old saying goes, blood is thicker than water. Over the next nine months, as my sister grows, we start bonding even more and then comes the day my sister decides to start walking. She would follow me everywhere. Even if I needed to go to the toilet! Sometimes I would find it very annoying as I just needed space on my own every now and then, but thinking of it now, she just loved and looked up to her big brother and after all it was my job to protect her.

Now I had come to the end of nursery and was ready for the next stage of my life, moving on to infant school. I wasn't best pleased as I was happy at nursery and didn't want to leave my best mate and my teacher, Mrs. Kelly. They had both made me feel happy about my life. According to my mum, I said I loved them both to her all the time. After a cry and temper tantrum I was told by my friend and his mum that we are going to the same Infant school together, that being East Wickham infants, we were both over the moon. After a long six weeks summer holiday with my mum, dad and little sister the day would finally come that I would start what I liked to call 'big boys school'. I remember being outside the school on that first day and to say this school was big was an understatement as the infant's was on one side of the field then on the other side was the junior's. Both schools were on the same site and it was a big step from being in a little hall at nursery but nothing would hold me back on my first day. In the playground, that first day, was who? Only my best friend from nursery! From then on, nothing was a problem as we were both together again. My first teacher would be a lovely lady of medium build with short curly hair and glasses, her name was Mrs. Chittock. This made me even more relaxed on my first day as she actually lived three doors up from our house on our lovely estate. Her desk was at the very front of the room and as we all walked into the classroom for the first time, I made sure I sat at the desk right in front of the teachers' desk. I think this is where mum's genes must be kicking in as she was the teacher's pet as well! I remember halfway through the day I would start crying saying 'I want my mum' then, Mrs. Chittock would say something to me, I can't remember exactly what she said but all I know is she made me feel better and I continued with the rest of my first day. The best part of the day was yet to come when my first day finally finished and my mum would be there waiting at the gate for me with my little sister in her pram, smiling her head off. Then, on the way home every day we would have to walk past our local sweet shop, which we called Weekes'. This is where the long old day at school would pay off. My mum would buy me my first '10p mix' which were a range of loads of different penny sweets in a white paper bag, yeah, you heard that right, all for the price of 10p! After a couple of weeks at East Wickham infants I find myself settling into my daily routine, learning, drawing and playing games in the playground with my best mate. As it was September my birthday had finally arrived again and I was going to be 5 years old, not a big birthday to celebrate but as you will all know, every birthday was special around that age as it was that time for presents again. Yet again another great birthday and I was a lucky boy again, another good memory and a day I will never forget as they were happy times.

So, with Christmas approaching and already experiencing this occasion a few times before, it could only be the same as all the others, which meant presents and happy times with the family. I did well with presents that year, as did my sister, we would spend the morning at home playing with all our presents. Then in the evening, we would walk round to my aunts and uncles to see our cousins and show off our toys to each other. As you already know, my Aunt (mum's sister) and her husband lived on the same estate, ever since mum and dad had first moved there. My auntie had four children, two girls and two boys. The girls were older than me by a couple of years and the boys were just younger by a year or two.

With Christmas and New Year over, it's now January and I'm back at school. I am settling in better than ever, not depending on my mum every five minutes and was even giving the teacher a break from asking my normal hundred questions a day, which I had done for the last three months. What can I say, I was a child that wanted an answer to everything. I wanted to know what was going on and why it was going on, I suppose you could say I was just a nosey bastard that needed my brain to be occupied. Drawing probably became something that I was good at and took a big interest in. It was something that I put a lot of time and effort into in the classroom. I suppose I enjoyed it so much as at the end there would be a result whereas, with writing, it just looked like a load of squiggles on a piece of paper to me at the time.

There was a lady at our school who was the Head Mistress and her name was Mrs. Siggs. She was the only teacher I had my doubts about as her office was at the top of the stairs in the middle of the school. She always had a serious look on her face, that being angry and very scary looking to a 5 year old boy. In hindsight, she would be someone that was taking their job far too seriously but at my age, it would scare the shit out of me. I don't see why adults have to come across as scary when they should be protecting us. It wasn't just her look that scared me but also what she wore that made her look like a Sergeant Major and with that came authority. Her regular uniform she would wear would be a peach blazer with matching skirt, a cream blouse with a frilly bit running down the front, light tights and brown shiny shoes that you could see your face in. You could say she was a skinny version of Miss Trunchbull from Matilda, well that's how I saw her anyway. I wasn't sent to her office many times in school if I'm honest but when I was, it wasn't the best feeling and I certainly remembered it! So, just before the summer holiday I was sent out of the classroom by Mrs. Chittock and she asked me to go to the Head Mistresses office. I'm walking along the corridor until I come to the bottom of the stairs, I look up the stairs and nearer the top it just got darker and darker, then once I got to the top of the stairs I knocked on the door, I was shitting myself as I was knocking. I remember her eyes staring down at me and just before she could start to tell me off, I cried, hoping to pull on her heart strings, it didn't work though, not with this teacher anyway. I was now messing with the Head of the school and she took no shit in any way, shape or form. Thinking it about it now it was nothing but when you're 5 years of age you look at life totally different to what adults do. That's why we have to learn and retain, so that we can become stronger, preparing us for the big wide world. This is why it's so important for all children to seek pleasure and avoid pain. After all, a child that seeks pleasure and avoids pain, is a child that is happy.

STEVIE - BEHIND THE MASK

It's the summer holidays again and my mum and my aunt would take me, my sister and my cousins out on a regular basis. Always doing things together and just doing what families do best, making good memories and spending quality time with each other. When we were not all out on day trips together, us kids would still spend a lot of time together with other friends that lived on the estate but sometimes it would get very boring doing the same old thing week in, week out during the holidays. Plus, I think the Mums enjoyed the outings more than what we did sometimes. Yet again the summer holidays flew by just like they always did, time flies when you're having fun. So, it's now time to start my final year in infant school. My last teacher would be another lovely lady by the name of Mrs. Ransom. She was a tall slim lady, shoulder length black curly hair with what I could only describe as Michael Caine glasses and she always wore an all-in-one dress with long sleeves. I shouldn't take the mickey really as she was also a really nice lady who took a liking to me and just wanted the best for me. My mate and I were still close friends during school, we spent every break time together making sure we always sat next to each other at dinner time but sometimes too much time together could bring the worst out in each other. We were not nasty or bullies in any way but we just always ended up caught in situations that didn't concern us. I suppose we were trying to be the peacemakers when there was any trouble, when really we should have kept ourselves to ourselves and dealt with our own shit.

STEVIE - BEHIND THE MASK

September comes around again and my 6th birthday finally arrives. Yeah, you got it, its present time again. I won't bore you with what I got for my birthday but I did very well again, all thanks to my lovely mum and dad. My dad was always grafting and doing his best to provide for his family, what a geezer!

Now I am 6 and aware of my surroundings. I find myself becoming a little more independent and exploring more of the estate where I live. This was ok with my mum as we lived at one entrance to the estate and my auntie (mum's sister) lived at the other entrance to the estate. Back then kids could just roam free, well that's what I thought anyway. There was a main road running through the estate but my mums rule was 'no crossing the road' which wasn't a problem as the pavement went all the way around the outside of the estate without having to cross a road anyway. Most resident's on the estate would know each other or knew someone else that knew that person. Everyone knew whose child was who, and where they lived. You could say our estate was a bit like Big Brother, everyone was watching you. On the positive side we were all protected as kids which would be very satisfying for my mum and dad. Another Christmas comes and goes having spent quality time with my family and loved ones also celebrating and seeing the New Year in together as a family.

Now it's the start of 1984 and life couldn't be any better. The days were getting warmer and longer, I was coming to the end of my time at East Wickham infants as the days were dryer we would start to play in the fields at the back of the school during breaks and at lunch time. The fields were huge and ran all the way around the back of the school grounds joining into the junior school which were all connected. I noticed a big tree at the bottom of the junior field which had long branches that practically touched the floor, there was also an overgrown area, a mini play area with a red climbing frame and big concrete tubes that you crawl through. You're thinking 'why mention a tree?' but that tree would bring nothing but devastation to our family in due course. Getting back to my final days at this school my best mate and I, as you know, spent a lot of time with each other at break and lunch time. I remember this one occasion we thought, as we were coming to the end of our time at this school, we would push the barriers that were the school rules out and take a walk to the bottom of the school fields which was forbidden. We wanted to have a little look at the big tree that was on the junior side of the field. We knew we were not allowed to go there but we had already committed to it so we were doing it! We made our way into the junior playing fields, both fields were packed with kids and then I heard that noise that no one wants to hear.

A loud whistle going off and as we both turned around a dinner lady is steaming towards us pointing her finger and she's not in the best mood if I'm honest. We both looked at her innocently with me saying 'What have we done wrong?' Knowing full well what we had done and why the whistle had gone off. Both feeling sorry for ourselves we are now being escorted to that office that no child wants to go to, you got it, off to see Mrs. Siggs. While going through the dreaded wait outside her office we thought we would be smart and get our story straight, then I hear my name get called but only mine. I walk into the office holding back the tears and couldn't believe it, for once the Head calmly explained that what I had done was wrong and it wasn't to happen again. I was in shock and thought 'That went well', I had already mentally shit myself and could not deal with an angry telling off from Mrs. Siggs as I would of probably followed through practically If I'm honest. My mate got given the exact same calm telling off and we were both free to go, I couldn't work out why. Sitting here writing now, I have my own theory as to why we only got a calm telling off from Mrs. Siggs that day. My theory is because there were not many days left at school so she thought 'not much longer now, then I won't have to see them two little bastards again'. Only problem was, after that small grilling, lunch had ended so we had to go straight back in to class and join in with the lesson. No play time for me and mate that day.

The final day at East Wickham Infants had arrived and soon the summer holidays would arrive. I remember the last day being a shorter day than a normal school day as there was no lunch break and the reason I know this is that I didn't get into any trouble on that last day as I always did at lunch. All us kids were now about to have a nice 6 weeks summer holiday with our families, then we would take the next step in life and move into the juniors. Now it was time to say goodbye to all my school friends which was easier than at nursery as I was a lot older now and realised it wouldn't be long before we would all see each other again when we started junior school. Yes, the summer holidays are finally here, time to be with family and friends on and around the estate. Yet again I was 'Living the Dream'. Where my auntie lived there was a little square and that's where most of my mates lived. There was a see-through metal fence at the bottom of the square that would lead to open fields where we would often play. My auntie's house was in the bottom corner of the square and she and the other mums were always keeping an eye on us, not that we felt that they needed to though.

There was a big tree at the bottom of the field just off the mud path that my mates and I would always like to climb up and hang around. We named it 'dead man's tree' as apparently, someone fell out of the tree and died years before we were all born, that was the rumour that had circulated around our estate amongst us kids anyway. Being in the fields with my friends in the summer holidays doesn't get much better than that, building camps, making a fortress and god knows what else. We were just boys being boys and doing what boys do best.

Two weeks into the summer holidays and mum and dad start taking the suitcases from our loft which can only mean one thing, we are going abroad! We were going on a two week holiday to Marbella and things didn't get much better than that as far as mum and dad were concerned anyway as these two loved to sunbathe. Put it this way, If there was an Olympic sport for sunbathing, my mum and dad would win the gold medal every time. Mum would have her normal panic attack thinking that she would forget something, I wouldn't mind but she would always start to pack and organise things two weeks before we had to leave. So after many checks and making sure we had everything we needed, we start to make our way to the airport. We were being taken by dad in his cab as he had passed out as a London Black Cab Driver two years ago so you could say we were going in style. I would remember this holiday and most of the holidays we went on. Once we were halfway round the M25 to Gatwick Airport dad would say 'Sue, I don't believe it, I forgot the passports', she would say 'you ain't?' and then she would say 'I told you that you would forget, you silly bastard'. Then all of sudden there they were, in my dad's hands, he was waving them at mum and laughing. He just had to wind her up and she still falls for it today! Once at the Airport, dad would park up where he would leave his cab for two weeks, looked after by the Airport and it would always be ready for us on our return. My sister and I would sit in the departure lounge watching the planes landing and taking off, my mum and dad would be sitting with us drinking an alcoholic beverage while my sister and I were eating sweets and drinking orange juice from the Duty Free shop. I will say it again, things just couldn't have been better and I was as happy as a pig in shit being with my family, having fun in the sun, life was just perfect, even if I did have my little sister following me everywhere and annoying the life out of me. Finally, it was our time to board the plane. I dreaded this time as I hated flying, I just couldn't get my head around the situation. From the moment I boarded the plane I would go pale and start to feel sick instantly and we hadn't even taken off yet. The plane would speed up along the runaway then out came the white paper bag and I threw up everywhere. Once in the air, I started to relax more but even then I would sleep down in the foot well, laying under my mum and dad as I really hated flying.

You could say I was like B.A. Baraccus out of the A-Team, 'I ain't gettin' on no plane fool'.

Once in Marbella and my parents had unpacked everything, we all went down to the swimming pool. My mum and dad would sunbathe around the pool while my little sister and I would go in the baby pool but not before mum smothered us both in suntan lotion, bloody hated the stuff and I still do to this day. I remember anywhere my sister wanted to go whether in the pool or out of the pool I would take her, you could say I took my role as overprotective older brother serious at a very young age as I felt the need to protect her. At night they would have entertainment within the complex and my little sister would run here, there and everywhere, laughing her head off like a little looney. I would follow her everywhere and she loved it and was always playing on it as she knew no matter what she did, I would say 'it's ok' or if it wasn't I would make it ok for her as I adored her and wanted her to be happy. Mum would dress her like a little Spanish girl and she would go brown on day one in the sun. People would think she was Spanish, she was adorable and my dad was just as protective of her as I was and she knew that from a very young age. The holiday was the same every day and night, nothing but happiness and love being with my family. I'll say it again, life was perfect. At this point, I would just like to say that I wish more than anything in the world that if I knew then what I know now I can honestly say I wish we had stayed in Marbella and never came back to England. As you all know, we can never go back in time. The only thing we can do is go forward and try to deal with things the best we can, it's the only way.

Oh yeah, just in case you wanted to know, the flight home was just like the flight out there, sick, sick and more sick. Damn you plane!

We finally arrive back home in England, mum finishes unpacking then all of us walked up to the local pub, no doubt mum and dad wanted to show off their new sun tans. Dad went in to get the drinks while mum sat in the back garden with us kids as we didn't go in pubs back in the day, we spent most of our time in the back garden playing with the other kids, it's just how it was, we were all safe weren't we? Once done in the pub we walked home, as you do. The sun was shining, everyone was smiling and I'll say it for the last time, everything was perfect and I was happy, I had a mum and dad who loved me dearly and my little sister who loved me even more.

I was so happy and I was so free. I remember that night being introduced to Chinese food for the first time as mum wasn't going to cook as they were both still on a 'come down' from holiday and were both still feeling lazy. Dad took me in his cab while my little sister would stay with my mum, it was a lovely Chinese take-away, located near Plumstead Common and I remember it feeling like the longest journey home and my dad let me munch on some prawn crackers whilst sitting in the back of cab. Once home, I remember us sitting at the table and my mum being the boss of the kitchen as she always was. She was dishing up our food, my sister would have more food on her face and clothes than what she had actually eaten and I wasn't much better as I had a tea towel round my neck which looked like someone had actually thrown my Chinese at me. Mum would then bath me and my sister, dad would towel dry our heads and after that I would sit with my mum on the sofa while my dad would brush my sisters hair. Spending quality time together, watching television just like families do. Then it would be time for bed. Me and my sister would run up the stairs, go in the bathroom, brush our teeth, give each other a kiss and a cuddle and then say goodnight. I would then get into my cosy bed, cuddling my teddy with all my other toys around me. My mum and dad would come in my room, kiss me goodnight and say 'sweet dreams darling' then this happy boy would close his eyes and go to sleep having many a happy dream.

A few days would pass and everything was so good. I was living the dream and everything was just perfect. Then the day would come. The day my life would change forever...

CHAPTER 2
WHAT DIES INSIDE WHILST LIVING

AGE: 6 - 11 years old
YEAR: 1984-1989

I remember this day like it was yesterday and still thirty five years later there is not a day that goes by when this doesn't come into my head at some point throughout the day. As they say, 'time is a great healer' but if you want my opinion, I couldn't disagree more. Mind you, I did see the world totally different from what everyone else did from this day onwards, I suppose you could say that on that day I would become a 'Limited Edition' and let's face it, it's better than being called 'damaged' or 'crazy'.

So, I wake up mid-August on a lovely, hot summer's day with only a few weeks of the summer holiday left. Going down-stairs to my mum, dad and sister where we would all have breakfast together. I can't say I remember what they had but I had my regular fix of Rice Krispies with milk and sugar, I then asked my mum if I could go out to play on the estate where I was safe as everyone knew each other.

Mum finally said yes I could go out and she would dress me before-hand, she was like a fashion designer my mum, as she always had my clothes matching, top, shorts, socks, the lot. As I have already said, mum took great pride in her appearance and I suppose it was rubbing off on to me too. On this day, I was wearing a matching little set which I had worn on my holidays. It consisted of a white t-shirt with the sleeves being red with little red pocket on the front, red

29

shorts, white socks with two red stripes around the top and matching white Velcro trainers with red stripes on the side. My mum said I looked like a little Spanish kid as I still had my sun-tan from Marbella and I was wearing my little red and white number. She finished brushing my hair, gave me a cuddle, and told me stay on the estate and out the door I went. It was a very hot day, the sun was beating down on me as I am walking down the road and as I come to the end of my road, right would take you off the estate into no man's land, then left would take you down a little hill leading down to the square where my auntie cousins and friends all lived. Normally I would do a left to go and join my friends and cousins down in the square where we all hang out and play games, but that day I would end up making the worst decision of my life doing a right and putting myself straight into no man's land. Believe me, if I knew then what I know now, I would have been doing a left that day and not a right, even though I remember my mum saying 'Do not go off the estate'. I was the kid with no fear that just had to take it one step too far and just like all the other times, once I started something I was going through with it. I remember being a little bit scared as I was now approaching the main road which was always a no. Whenever I asked my mum, she would say 'no, you will get run over'. By now I knew there is no way that I' was going to try and cross this road myself, I'm stupid, but not that stupid! What I do is a left off the estate and then if I did another left I would be back on the estate again. Sticking to the pavement I start walking down the road then I see two brothers I know from school and around the estate but they are on the other side of the road. Being brave but also very stupid I did something that I said I wouldn't do and what most kids hadn't done and crossed the main road, where on the other side I would meet up and start talking to the two brothers outside their house. Their mum would come out and call them in, they asked me if I wanted to come in and play. Me being me, with no fear turned around and said 'yes', then into their house we went. I closed the front door and all three of us went into the living room, the brothers mum was in the kitchen and lingering around was a 'family friend' which I now know to be the brother's step-uncle. Looking at him, from a child's point of view, I would have said he was at least aged 18 to 21. He was a short bloke compared to my dad, he was wearing a white t-shirt, bleached blue jeans and had brown curly hair, not sure if he had blond steaks in his hair or it was just the sun shining through the kitchen window onto him. I remember him looking at me a lot and smiling and as taught by my mum, always be polite to adults back, so I would smile back at him. After being indoors for a while I would start to get hot and bothered, so I suggested to the two brothers that we should go onto the estate to the fields and build a camp. They asked their mum but she said 'no, you're not going over there on your own'. Then out of the blue the man that was standing in the kitchen said 'I'll take them', which lead to all three of us cheering in the living room and before you know it we are on our way to the fields to build a camp, well that's what I thought would happen. We would do that other left I was going to do earlier before seeing the brothers and was now walking back towards the estate but instead of going back onto the estate we would walk past the turning and down towards the fields where there was another entrance to the field that I hadn't used before. It looked a little cramped as it was a narrow dirt path with, what looked like, a forest on the right and an overgrown field on the left, then I saw Dead Man's Tree and I am now back on familiar ground. Sticking to the path, we walk a little more down the dirt path and then there is a gap in the trees on the right, not your usual gap but all the same we are with an adult and we are safe. Once we had walked through the gap there are trees on either side and I remember stinging my leg on a stinging nettle as it was that tight. Then it would open up into another little open space but with trees and bushes all around us. There was a big broken tree branch that went in a semi-circle and it's then that I noticed a brownish red armchair in the middle of this closed in area. I was happy as can be as this was the biggest camp I had ever been in and even had a brand new chair for the leader to sit in, it didn't get much better than this camp or so I thought. After a while, the oldest brother would be the furthest up the tree, his younger brother in the middle and myself at the bottom of the tree. The man who was with us was sitting in the chair which meant he was the leader of the camp, which I was happy with as he was looking after us so everything was ok. Then whilst we were sitting on the tree, the man decides to say who's going to be in the 'The Gay Gang' today. I remember thinking 'what the hell is that?' but I said nothing as I wasn't sure what it was. No-one answered so he started pointing his finger at us and from what I know now he was doing a dip, then his finger lands on me and he says to me, 'It's you Stevie, it's you', how did he know my name? I climbed down the tree and then I start to walk toward him, thinking to myself, 'Why is he sitting in that chair with his pants and trousers down with his penis in his hand?' Something didn't feel right but yet again I'm thinking 'It's ok, he's an adult and all adults look after kids'. He then turns to me, smiles and starts to take my clothes off. I am standing there, naked, with just my socks and trainers on. Being a kid, I'm thinking, 'This is just a game' but then things took a turn for the worst. He then faces me towards the two brothers and starts to lower me onto his lap, I start to feel him with force pushing his penis into my backside. The only way to describe it was constipation, times ten. He was pushing and lifting me up and down and I was in so much pain. I screamed and started crying, shouting out 'stop it, stop it, you're hurting me' and just like that, he stopped and said sorry to me and he didn't mean to hurt me.

Now he had stopped, the pain had stopped and I was just relieved that it was all over. Well, so I thought. He would then lay me across him, long-ways, where he would just rub his penis around my backside but wasn't hurting me as he wasn't inside me. He would keep touching my penis whilst doing the other thing. I had no clue what was going on but I wasn't in pain so I suppose I just let him carry-on as I was so scared. Then, he asked me to get on my knees in front of him on the chair where he then decides to put his penis in my mouth, while asking me to put my hand around it and rub up and down around his penis but like I said before, I was not in any pain at that time so I would have done anything to stop him putting his penis inside me again. Not realising that already I have been raped once and have also been physically and mentally abused by this man, making me perform sexual acts on him, I'm now realising they he was just trying to loosen me up, as just like that, he then put his penis inside me again and raped me for a second time. This time seemed a lot longer as when I cried and screamed he wouldn't stop. This dirty bastard was out to get his fix and nothing was going to stop him from getting what he wanted. Finally, he stopped. I was sobbing with all my heart but finally it was all over, I fell onto my knees on the floor, crying while still trying to put my clothes on. Meanwhile, the two brothers just sat in the tree watching as they were only kids as well and didn't have a clue what was going on either, it must have been very traumatic for them too. Just before I went, he turned around and said 'If you tell your mum or dad or anyone else, all them people will die and you won't ever see them again!'

Crying, I said 'ok' and couldn't believe I was free to go or was I? I wasn't willing to take the risk and sprinted as fast as I could. I didn't stick to any paths and ran straight through the field, including stinging nettles, mud and god knows what else was in front of me. I remember climbing over a little metal fence and cutting my arm as well but at this point I didn't care what or who was in my way, I was getting home and that's all there was to it! I wanted and needed my mum. I then ran up the hill and did a right into my Close, all I was thinking was 'I want my mum' and feeling dirty and in pain, plus I was feeling like a totally different person that had entered the woods mentally but I was finally home where I always felt safe. At the time, I thought it was just part of growing up and something we all go through, even though I was in silent pain. Like he said, no-one could know and that's just how it was.

I remember knocking on the door and it seemed like a lifetime for my mum to answer, this gave me just enough time to wipe my eyes and crack a little smile.

The door flies open and mum said 'where have you been? Look at the state of your trainers and what has happened to your shirt? You've stung all your leg darling'. Then she would give me a cuddle, it felt so nice, to the point I didn't want to let go. Then, I thought to myself 'From now on, when mum says something, she's saying it for my own good, so let's just do what she says from now on'. As we get in, she took my clothes off and takes me up to the bathroom where a fresh bath is run, only a shallow one as mum would leave me in the bathroom playing my toys and check on me every so often.

Not today, as today I wanted to clean myself and be as clean as can be. Even to the point of going down the side of the bathroom cabinet and getting out the bleach, I pushed the sides, as I had seen my mum do, then I squeezed some onto the sponge, I put the lid back on and got back in the bath and scrubbed myself as I saw how clean the bathroom would look when my mum had used it. Then it would be like nothing had happened as I had been bathed, had fresh underwear on and my hair brushed but I still felt very sore around my backside, I certainly didn't feel clean. Anyway, bedtime would soon arrive and I just didn't feel like I wanted to go to bed in the dark, I just couldn't do it, so I asked my mum if she could leave the hallway light on as there was a window above my door and the light would come through it making my room less darker. I don't remember falling asleep that night if I'm honest as I was pretty much exhausted after a draining day, mentally and physically. I certainly remember waking up a few times that night sweating and calling out for my mum, I would shout louder and louder as I was so scared, then the door would open and she would come in saying 'It's ok darling, Mum's here, its ok you're only having a dream'. She would then sit on my bed and the last thing I remembered was her brushing her fingers through my hair, then I must of fell back to sleep.

Waking up the next morning I remember my backside being more painful than the day before but I also remembered it was my secret and no one could know. After a week or so the time would finally come for me to start East Wickham junior school. I still had the memories of what had happened to me in the fields in the summer holidays rushing through my head every now and then. Trying to work out what happened and why was I having nightmares about this occasion so often.

A couple of weeks in to junior school and my mind is becoming more occupied as lessons would be a bit more advanced than the Infants, which was a good thing for me as didn't want to keep thinking about the same thing as I did for the rest of the summer holidays.

The first year in juniors was spent in huts at the back of the school leading straight out onto the school playing fields, I had my best mate with me again and we were in the same class again which was also good having someone you already know in your class, makes it that little bit easier. My first teacher would be Mrs. Butler and she was an 'ok' teacher but when she could get angry very quickly so the best thing to do was just keep myself out of trouble as she could make my life hell if I pushed her buttons too much. The problem now was that I trusted no adults, apart from my own mum and dad, which would start to become a problem for me regarding my schooling. All teachers were adults and there were a few male teachers within the school that I wasn't happy about either but it's not like I could tell anyone or do anything about it. As more time went on, I find myself changing and mainly at school, spending more time outside the class due to my disruptive behavior inside the class. I just couldn't seem to sit still or concentrate on what I was meant to be doing, even to the point of trying to be the class clown. I just felt like the teachers were out to control me and I wasn't going to let any adult do that again. I remember one time in lesson, everyone was concentrating and doing their work and I just couldn't deal with it all, so I farted and gave it that extra squeeze to cause full disruption to the class and get attention. Everyone in the class started laughing and so was I until Mrs. Butler stood up with her hand on her desk shouting out 'Stevie, outside the classroom, now'. Me thinking 'all that over a fart' then I walk outside the door and as I get outside the door I start thinking to myself 'what's that funny smell?' Yeah, you got it, I had farted with such force that, let's just say, I touched cloth. Then I start to panic as I can't let anyone know and

STEVIE - BEHIND THE MASK

I felt so dirty all of a sudden, so I ran to the boy's toilets which are just near the huts. Then get some damp tissues, lock myself in the toilet, take off my shorts then take off my pants. I clean my pants, put everything back on and run back to the hut. I must have been standing outside the classroom door for a minute then the door would open and out came Mrs. Butler, how I got away with that I would never know but I just had to get cleaned up as I hated that dirty feeling. She then asked me if I had calmed down and back into my class I would go.

From that point on I would spend the rest of the day avoiding people and keeping quiet, even a teacher would ask if I was okay. I suppose that was me putting my barriers up at a young age and pushing people away, maybe the start of having more than one personality or maybe a different side to me I didn't even know about. Very confusing for a seven year old.

The summer holidays are now approaching and it's another lovely summer for me and my mates on the estate. This summer was a hot one and we would start to spend more time in the fields as we were all now at junior school we were a bit older and wiser so we would all stick together. Most times we were in the fields, we would play down by Dead Man's Tree which everyone enjoyed apart from me as it was so near to where what had happened to me. I would then find myself getting angry and agitated as I didn't want to be there but that's what everyone else was doing, I couldn't say anything as I had this dark secret in me. I would then start an argument with one of mates and that would give me a reason to go home, it was better that way as I couldn't tell them I was scared, they would have all laughed at me. I remember wanting to spend more time at home with my mum and dad, I suppose I had no trust for anything or anyone, at least being at home I was safe and that's all that mattered at this stage in my life.

A new school year had started in September and I was still up to my usual tricks at school but keeping myself out of trouble and not pushing the teachers too far, you could say I was starting to learn my boundaries even though I had this anger and secret deep within me.

Then came the day where nothing but sadness and devastation would hit our family. A normal day at school, the sun shining and everyone at lunch playing in the fields. I was in the corridor, which is where you have to go and stand if you had messed around in the dinner hall, yep, you got it, I had answered a dinner lady back and she would always send me up last, I would end up with less time to play and end up with all the food that others didn't choose, all the crap. I am now standing in the corridor, after answering the dinner lady back again and I am not in a good mood as it is, then one of my friends comes running into the corridor shouting out my name. I turned around and he tells me 'It's your cousin, he has hurt himself, and he is down at the willow tree'. Totally ignoring what the dinner lady told me to do, I ran out of the corridor and onto the school field. Looking down at the willow tree I saw the teachers with my cousin and everything started becoming a panic for me, thinking 'what's happened to him, is he ok? Has someone hurt him like they did to me?' I then heard someone say 'Stevie, it's your cousin, someone has flicked a branch from the willow tree into his face and it's caught his eye'. With that, the final whistle for lunch went and we all had to go back to lessons, apart from my cousin who had to go to hospital as it was a lot more serious than a scratched face and knock to the eye. I felt sick for the rest of the day at school as I just wanted to know that my cousin was alright and for a while I didn't think of my situation as much. I saw that people got hurt in life and terrible things happen, maybe that man didn't mean to hurt me.

A day or two later the story comes out in school of what actually happened down at the willow tree that day. So, my cousin and his sisters were playing down by the willow tree and one of my female cousins had a mate with her that she had met at school but also lived around the estate. That girl decide to pull back a long branch with all her force then call my cousins name, as he turns around, she let go of the branch at speed hitting my cousin in the face. He then goes to the floor holding his face screaming as a twig from the branch had snapped off going through the center of his pupil and is stuck in his eye. I can't imagine what he went through that day but it would end up changing his life in many ways in the future. Once home from school, Mum sat me down and looked like she had been crying and explained to me that my cousin had lost the sight in his eye, he was now blind in one eye for the rest of his life and had only just had his seventh birthday.

The day came that my cousin would come home from the hospital. The day that he changed forever in my eyes, he wasn't the happy smiley cousin, he was quiet and looked sad as he had suffered a trauma. We would visit him often but after such trauma he would prefer to be on his own, maybe so he could process what had actually happened to him. He would spend a lot of time at home and I would still visit him many times whilst he was recovering as he was my cousin and we were really close as kids. Even though sometimes I would lash out at him, not meaning to as it was something I couldn't control sometimes as I was changing. Finally, he would gain the confidence to get out more and we could start playing out again. To this day I think he accepts the situation and cracks on with life but I don't think it's something he will ever get over as childhood traumas are the hardest to deal with.

Now all of us boys are back together on the estate and are spending more time down in the fields down by Dead Man's Tree on the mud path, which was part of The Green Chain Walk which was also the path that the brothers, their uncle and I had walked down that painful day. Since my cousin's accident, I found that I could deal with the situation better as I had got used to it now, so I thought.

We are now coming up to November and firework night is approaching. There was a big old tree in the middle of the field right near my auntie's house, we decided to build a big bonfire for firework night using bits of old wood from the field. Then firework night would finally come round and we would all meet up on the estate with my mates and all their parents, it would be a fun family night and my mate's dad would be in charge of lighting the fireworks. Normally me with, no fear, I would have found myself running around and enjoying myself with my mates but this night I was around my mum and dad more as there were many adults present that night and I just felt scared if I'm honest as I didn't recognise some of them. Thinking about it now, the trust issues I had going on were really starting to affect my life, as soon as there were a few adults that I didn't know I would start to play up, putting my barriers up and keeping myself safe. I would then get told off by my mum and then I had to stay inside for messing around but inside is where family and people I knew would be. Don't get me wrong, I am not making excuses for my actions and behavior, I take full ownership and to put it bluntly, I was a sod. Was it any wonder after what that sicko did to me? No-one could say that it wouldn't have affected them, unless they had experienced it.

Now I find myself not only changing in school but even more around my family and friends. I was now 9 years old and was already realising I was different but I went along with it. People might have known me as naughty but they didn't know my secret so it was good, as far as I was concerned. After all, I still had a loving mum and dad that looked after me and I wanted for nothing, nothing at all. They made my childhood so much easier and they didn't even know it.

After spending another Christmas and New Year with family and friends it would now be January and the start of 1987, a year when I found myself trusting two males that were friends of the family and also the start of me becoming a Millwall fan. My dad took me round to his friend's house, right near Welling train station. His two mates then greet me and we walked to the train station. Once the train arrived and we got on it was really busy and mainly full of adult men, all going to the game. I was totally dropped in at the deep end as it was a very scary experience for me but I had two of Dad's good mates with me. We then got off the train and made our way to the football ground, it was very loud and all the men would be singing and chanting songs.

I was so scared but I didn't show it, I just looked up at my dad's mates and knew I was ok, they were both walking either side of me so I felt safe. All the same, it wasn't the best experience but everyone has to go through that first time of doing something they don't like or are comfortable with. It was just all the men there, it made me feel sick as, to me, they were all like the other man over the field that day, that's how I was now made to feel.

We start to walk through a tunnel and everyone is singing Millwall songs, it was at that point that I hung on to my dad's friends arm, it was getting darker and darker. Clenching onto his arm it then starts to become light and open and I start to feel more at ease, I would see other kids all smiling and playing so I would start to feel better in myself. Then the game starts 'No One Likes Us' is what I'm hearing being sung and my dad's friends are joining in, then I join in shouting as well. I then start to have a feel good factor and I was in the moment, not living in the past. I was enjoying myself, doing what all big boys do and feeling, let's just say, normal. Then all of a sudden everyone was jumping up and down and I find myself three rows down as Millwall had just scored. The fear of being on my own was really scary as I'm now surrounded by men I don't know, I was starting to panic, I wave my arms and my dad's friend grabbed my arm and said, 'We scored Stevie, we scored!'. Both Dads friends are singing and so is the whole ground and this was my first experience of Millwall scoring a goal, scary as it was, it gave me that feel good factor that I was a big boy and no one could hurt me as I've now been to a Millwall match, I'm top boy. The final whistle blows and everyone starts to leave the ground singing and swearing but unlike 'scared me' that walked in, I'm now walking out, let's just say, like a lion full of confidence, joining in with the songs that other fans were singing. We get to the station and jump straight on the train back to Welling and then dad would pick me up from his mate's house and take me home. That day is when I felt I gained more confidence in myself but I was still hiding this dark secret and still couldn't understand why it had happened, that is just how it had to be as I couldn't tell anyone, the only person I could tell was myself every day. I was becoming more fixated with my secret and it was eating away at me slowly but surely. Now, half-way through junior school and I am finding myself getting into trouble more and spending a lot more time standing in the corridor at lunchtime as I couldn't control my emotions like the average child did. I put this down to what had happened to me as I was noticing more and more that I was becoming different. During time in the classroom I would find myself being a lot quieter in lessons as I spent too much time getting into trouble at break times and lunch. Then a boy in school would spend a while giving me grief and bullying me at lunch times. I mentioned it to my dad and he told me he would pick me up from school tomorrow and if the boy was there and he started on me or hit me I was to hit him back twice as hard. I felt like I was being controlled and I wasn't having that again as the last time I was, it brought me nothing but hurt and pain, no way am I feeling that like again. The next day the final bell goes and I make my way to the school playground, just waiting for the boy to come up to me and start, within five seconds he's walking towards me and my dad is watching the situation.

He starts to rough me up a bit and I can feel myself getting angry but I can't get into trouble at school again, it's all becoming too much. Feeling even more controlled, I walk towards the school gate and I'm crying, my dad gave me the dirtiest look and said if you don't get back in that playground and hit him, I will hit you. What dad was doing was cruel love and with that the tears stopped and the anger starts to kick in, turning around I have now hit the 'fuck it' button and am ready to explode. Walking towards him, I see that he is drinking at the metal round water fountain, half his face is in a metal bowl drinking water and now it was my chance to show him who's boss. Without no hesitation I went totally out of control, grabbed the hair on the back of his head, raised his head up and smashed his face into the metal fountain, then lifting his head up, I did it again. I had split his head open and there was blood everywhere, I didn't mean to but he asked for it as no-one would ever be controlling me again and that's a fact. Maybe it was harsh but I wasn't having anyone bully me especially when it had been going on for two weeks, what was I becoming? This wasn't the loving Stevie everybody knew, I had become a monster. All the teachers came out and even the Head Teacher, Mr. Champ, he was a big man with glasses and always dressed smart, wearing a tie.

As the teacher's calmed everything down, my dad enters the playground and comes over and explains the situation, then we all go inside where parents are informed and I believe the boy went to hospital and had stitches in his head.

A few days later my mum had to ring the boys mum and explained the situation, it went well as the boys mum said that he probably deserved it as he was no angel either and from what I gather he had had problems before with other kids. It turns out, a week later I went round his house to dinner and a few days later we become good mates, a friendship was made but in the weirdest way.

Then some weekends I would go and stay at my auntie's place who lived in East London. Me and my sister would go and stay with her for the weekend and it was at times like this that I would feel happy as I was away from Welling. When at my aunt's me and my little sister would get all the attention we wanted, this lady was a one off and was one of a kind as the moment we arrived there she would play with us for hours. Every time, without fail she would buy us one of every sweet from the shop and give them to us in a big paper bag, every little kid's heaven. It wasn't just about the materialistic things she gave me, she gave me what I needed more than anything and that was her love and attention. My sister and I would both sleep in my older cousin's bed and that was paradise and will always be a good memory in my mind and heart as his bed was so comfy and had loads of pillows and big thick clean sheets. Me and my sister had many good times there and this amazing lady made everything in my childhood so much easier, she was my auntie and I loved her dearly as she treated me like a son and made feel free whenever I visited her in East London. I worshipped the ground she walked on and she was always teaching me life lessons but what made her even more special, in my eyes, was the fact she would bath me every day when I was there. She would cut my nails and always made sure I was clean in general. Something that I loved to be was clean and she always made sure I was, the only bad thing was when mum and dad would come pick me and my sister up but even then I always knew there would be another time. This lady was my guardian angel and as long as she was in my life then things would be ok.

Now feeling like I'm gaining more confidence and realising I can protect and look after myself, I would start going over the fields with my mates. I would say I was feeling normal as I was doing what everyone else was doing and that's having fun, seeking pleasure and avoiding pain. We would walk down to The Dead Man's Tree and then one of my mates said let's go into the woods and build a camp, feeling more confident I agreed like everyone else did, then off into the woods we went. Then we are walking on familiar ground and all of a sudden we are in a big open space and I start to feel sick but I deal with it as I'm with my mates and they can't know. We walk through the open space and come to the back of Rose Cottage School, there was an old concrete block with a roof and a hole in the top where the drain cover was missing. Looking inside it was the perfect place for a Den for me and the boys, the only problem being is that it was empty and needed to be kitted out.

Starting to explore the woods we would look for things that we could put in the Den as this would be our meeting place, when not meeting on the estate. Then the worst thing that could have happened did, one of my mates shouted out I need help with this and when I saw it, I couldn't believe my eyes. It was the reddish brown chair that I was raped and abused on, everything was going well. Why did this have to turn up? There is no way this is going in the Den. One of my other mates came over and said that can be the leader's chair! I couldn't believe what I was hearing. Why was this happening? I started to feel myself getting angry but held it in. I said the chair is too big for the Den and we wouldn't have much room for other stuff, still debating they all came to an agreement that the chair stays and there was nothing I could do to change that. In turn, I then decide to have another argument about it as this chair brought me nothing but pain but they didn't know that. The mate who was the leader of our group I suppose, I had now argued with him, which probably made me look bad as why was I the only one out of all of us who didn't want the chair in there. I then walked off and went home as I couldn't deal with the memories that chair had brought into my life. I was crying all the way home as yet again I was the different one again, even though in my mind I was doing nothing wrong, just protecting my feelings.

It's at times like this that I would become clingier with my mum, to the point of doing her head in and standing next to her a lot. All the confidence I had gained at Millwall was now gone as all I was thinking about is what happened to me, thanks to the reminder of that evil chair.

Now it's a week into the summer holidays and it's that time again when mum starts to get the suitcases out of the loft, time for a holiday and it was perfect timing as I could really do with getting away from the estate. After recent events and what better place to be than in Tenerife for two weeks with my family, once we had checked in we would make our way to the departure lounge where me and my sister would get sweets and other treats for the plane, whilst watching them take off and land. I won't bore you with the flight as I'm sure you already know how I feel about flying. I now find myself feeling at ease and starting to enjoy myself with my little sister in the sun, we stayed in the Hotel Bitacora where there was a buffet breakfast, lunch and dinner, you name it they had it. The hotel had two swimming pools and a concrete water slide and waterfall, it was every kids dream and me and my sister were loving it, we wanted for nothing. Being more alert, due to my situation, I would watch my sister like a hawk and kept my eye on all adults that were anywhere near her, as I didn't trust anyone. I remember an evening we would play in the games room where all the other kids would play, then someone thought it would be ok to push my little sister onto a chair and I would walk towards him being that overprotective brother. My sister would look at me and say, 'Stevie I'm ok' as she could calm me down, she knew me better than anyone. We spent most of the days on the water slide and in the pool as my little sister was like a fish, she spent most of her time under the water which could be a bit worrying sometimes for my mum and dad. I was a totally different person when away with family, I suppose it was my break from the estate and reality, all I thought about was happy times and being just how a 9 year old boy should be. The rest of the holiday was like a dream but like everything, all good things must come to an end but at least we were fortunate enough to have such lovely holidays, sometimes twice a year.

Finally, back in England, it's now time to get back to reality. I was looking forward to seeing family and friends back on the estate but not going back to the memories.

Now back on the estate with my mates and we are all in the garages which lead onto the field. Today, we decide that we are going over the fields and are going to explore the farmer's yard which was situated on Shooters Hill. We all make our way through the fields and are finally at the back of the farmer's yard, it was a massive place, and we needed to be careful as the farmer would walk around the yard with his shotgun.

Then we all separated and took different paths getting into the barn where all the hay bales were stacked, the perfect place for us to hide and as the saying goes, it would be like 'finding a needle in a haystack', so that's where we needed to be as we couldn't get caught, well so I thought. It was a bit of a risky thing to do as kids but as far as I was concerned we were away from the woods so I was as happy as a pig in shit and had no fear. I found it exciting if I'm honest which is why I took the long way round with one of my mates rather than sticking to our plan, as I wanted to see what was in the other buildings.

STEVIE - BEHIND THE MASK

Me and my mate finally arrive at the other building and crawl in through an open door and we were in, it was full of all different animals and little workshops but no adults were about.

Then all of a sudden a gun shot was fired. The farmer was out and had obviously seen or heard something. We hear the main door open to the building and in walks the farmer saying 'who's in here?' Keeping as quiet as we could, my mate and I made our way to the back of the building where there was a back door, thank god it was open, we pushed through the door and ran into the barn where all our other mates were. There wasn't enough time to leave the farm so we all decided to hide in the hay bales, all finding different spots and everything became quiet.

I was near the barn door and all of a sudden I saw the Farmer enter the barn. In his hand is not only a shotgun but also a huge pitchfork! By this time all my other mates have made their way to the back of the farmyard by escaping through a hole in the building at the back. They are now in the field and are all safe, apart from me and another mate. The farmer then decides to start poking the hay bales we are both hidden in with his huge pitchfork, with that, I jump out the hay bail and start to run. There was no way I was staying with another man on my own, not after what happened the last time in the woods with that man. The farmer is hot on my tail and doesn't look happy and he is holding a shotgun, 'come back, come back' he shouts, I was thinking 'yeah, alright mate!' I sped up and finally managed to lose him, joining up with my mates in the field, including the mate that was stuck in there with me. Yet again, I had to mess things up by not sticking to what we all agreed and nearly got us all in trouble, all because I decided to change the plans myself and make things more dangerous. I suppose this was the mask I was now getting used to as no one would ever know about my dark secret, everyone thought I was fearless but little did they know. As we are running through the fields we are starting to get tired and stop off in the woods so we could go to the Den as the farmer was still in the fields looking for us and he wasn't giving up. Once in the Den everyone would be smiling as we had all just got away from the farmer, everyone was talking about what had just happened and how lucky we were. I was there but wasn't talking much as I was just looking at the reddish brown chair and thinking 'how can we get this chair out of here?' Then I start having flashbacks of what happened in that chair and feel myself becoming more angry, thinking to myself 'please let's just get out of here'.

Then finally my mate says 'it's all clear, let's get out of here' and we make our way to the Dead Man's Tree at the bottom of our field that takes us back onto the estate where we all go our different ways and go home.

Now at home and safe with my mum, dad and sister I find myself relaxing again and start playing games and drawing with my little sister in the playroom. For some reason, whenever I was drawing I could relax and be calm me. It just took me to a place of peace, which is why I would draw a lot I suppose, it was my release, just like writing this book is. Evening time would now be here and my sister and I had been bathed and were ready for bed, mum would kiss me goodnight and off to sleep I would go. I now find myself inside yet another nightmare. It's this nightmare that I still struggle with to this day, a complete repeat of what that person had done to me that day, in and out of the chair. I wake up crying, sweating and scared calling my mums name. My mum would come in and say 'it's ok darling, it's only a dream'. Any other time I wouldn't have minded but that night I wet the bed, which was a 'no no' for a boy of my age. No one knew about it, but all the same, I just felt like I was different again which was all down to him. I was looking at the world differently now and it wasn't a nice feeling as others were noticing me changing too.

Starting back at school and into my final year at East Wickham juniors we were now learning about sex education. This is where I realised that what happened to me in the woods that day was wrong and should never have happened. It all started in the TV room where me and the rest of the class would watch a video, my school mate and I were sitting next to each other. As soon as the video had started there was a man, a woman, a girl and a boy on a beach playing volleyball but they were all naked. Straight away I start to become uncomfortable seeing the little boy naked, this sets me off and I start to become disruptive during the video. The teacher had had enough and calls my name, followed by 'outside now!' this is exactly what I wanted to happen as I couldn't deal with what I was watching, it was wrong. Once outside in the corridor, I stand on my own thinking about what had happened to me that day. Then I start to blame myself as if it wasn't for me asking to build a camp, it would never have happened.

Also, if only I had done a left that day instead of a right. You would think that I would have learned my lesson and would do as I was told but I was damaged and there was nothing I could do about it as if I had told anyone, they would die. The video had now finished and everyone walked out the TV room and back into the class. My teacher followed me out and gave me a telling off and I started to cry, the teacher managed to calm me down and explained that I just needed to calm down more during class time but how could I? They didn't know what was going on in my head, no one did, it was like being in a prison, there was no way out! Now back in the class room with everyone else the teacher starts to talk about how women and men have sex and how they make babies and all that other stuff. I remember thinking to myself there is an adult man and an adult woman doing these things but there is no mention of an adult and a child doing those things so really it should not have happened to me, it was wrong. In turn, I now start causing trouble in the classroom again and only ten minutes after being sent out of the TV room I am now being sent out of the classroom. The lesson finishes and I now find that I am on my way to the Heads office, following my teacher there I realise this means trouble. I walk into the Head office and start to cry before they could say anything, I was in a terrible way and was even answering them back as they didn't get it, no one could see I was in pain. They just thought I was naughty and my mum had to come into the school and get me. She didn't tell me off but just cuddled me and that's all I wanted and needed as that's where I felt safe. This all happened on the Friday and by the time the Monday arrived I had already told my mum I wasn't feeling well, I was fine but I had just gotten to the point where if I wasn't at school I couldn't get into any trouble, it was a win win situation for everyone involved. I ended up having 4 days off with apparent sickness and my mum gave me the Friday off as well as didn't see the point in going back for one day, so 5 days off! I loved it as I was at home feeling safe with the people who loved me the most and I wasn't getting into any trouble, it was like living the dream again not having to deal with any teachers and just people in general, as I trusted no one!

The weekend passes and it's time to get back to reality and get back to school. Starting back with a stronger head I find myself calming down more in class and even getting sent up for dinner first at lunch time, which could only mean one thing and that was that I was being a good boy for once. I embraced the moment choosing a burger, chips, beans and chocolate sponge with custard for afters. I felt like a king as that's what most kids would choose. I knew this, as most times I was a sod which meant I would get sent up last and when you were sent up last there was none of that left.

At school I find myself on a roll and believe it or not, I start to do things for the teachers around the classroom, being what I like to call a good boy. I am being rewarded for it by not being told off and feeling like the odd one out all the time, even though I knew I was. Coming home that afternoon would be a blessing for me as my mate's dad would buy him a motorbike to drive over the fields. You're now thinking 'how's that a blessing for me?' Well, the way

I see it, motorbikes were driven on fields and not through the woods as there were no paths, which meant no more Den and no more chair.

That evening we would all sit around the garages with my mate and his new motorbike, it kind of took everything away for me as I was feeling more at ease, as I knew we wouldn't have to go to the Den and we were all moving forward into the next stage of our childhood, that being motorbikes. Finally, I wouldn't have to go in the woods anymore. It meant so much to me not having to go into the camp where I had to relive the suffering and so much pain, mentally and physically on a daily basis. Could I finally move on and get this sick individual out of my head? Only time will tell.

Things are now starting to get better for me as we are now all hanging around in the corn fields on my mate's motorbike and not the woods every other day, which would give me a rest from dealing with the memories that I got every time we went into the woods. I had the memory in my head every day which was hard enough, without having to keep visiting the place where it all happened.

At this point things are good, my mates and I were expanding our horizons by spending more time off of the estate and discovering more of the big wide world. This made me very happy, as I have already mentioned but I just want people to understand how much this bastard had changed my outlook on life and the damage that he had caused me.

Every now and then we would all walk up to Shoulder Mutton Green where we would all play football, then go to the shops at the top of the green, hanging out and thinking we were all the nuts and were all grown up. On this day I realised that the Spar shop had closed and the windows had been smashed so assumed it had closed down as there was stuff all on the floor so, me being me, decided to go and investigate around the back. Walking down the side alley I am now at the back of the shop and someone needs to climb through a little hole which leads into the back of the shop. I said 'I'll go first' as normal without any fear, well so everyone else thought but my mask was on so I was following this through, I wasn't scared. Once inside the old shop I would start to look around and from what I could see someone else had already beaten us to it as the good stuff had gone, cigarettes, money and all the popular sweets. When really I should have been thinking 'this place has been robbed and what are you, a young boy, doing smack bang in the middle of a crime scene?' but I didn't and that was just how I saw it. I was doing no wrong. Then a few other mates came into the shop via the back door and we all start gathering up food, drinks and any other stuff we can take with us. Now we are loaded up with stuff, we would exit the shop via the back door with our black bin bags full of the stuff we had taken from the shop. Not realising that I had just robbed a mini market after someone else had, I strolled across the green with my black bin bag of food and made my way back to the estate with my mates. Turns out a few days later the shop hadn't closed down and had been robbed just before we arrived, which means I'm now a thief and it didn't seem to affect me, if anything it was exciting, sad but true.

STEVIE - BEHIND THE MASK

Now I'm coming to final days at East Wickham juniors and have just taken and failed my eleven plus school exam, you would have thought that I had a chance of passing…not! It was multiple choice and I guessed pretty much every single question. It's not that I was stupid as I was far from it, it's just where I was so disruptive and naughty in class I didn't listen to what was being taught to me. Like I would listen and trust an adult, I trusted one before and look what happened then, as you can see everything changed after that day and it wasn't for the best. It would soon be time to move on to secondary school and I was still trying to process what had actually happened to me that day. After all, it wasn't part of growing up as growing up involves progression not devastation surely? My final day at juniors came and I would say it was an emotional day for myself as everything was about to change and I had no idea what to expect from secondary school, I didn't like change at the best of times and now I would dealing with a big one.

On that last day I wouldn't say that the teachers were sad to see me go but I bet they all went into the school hall at the end of the day and had the biggest Stevie leaving party ever. Probably doing the conga and the can-can after what I had put them all through. Some of the teachers were ok but all the male teachers hated me and I understand why as I made their time at a school a living nightmare but I didn't care as I didn't trust many any adults anyway, especially adult males and teachers that I felt were always trying to control me.

I remember walking out of the school door that day and looking at my mum, thinking to myself 'before I go to secondary school, shall I start fresh and talk to mum about my situation?' but then those words would enter my head, 'if you tell your mum or dad or anyone, they will die' and then I was back to square one again.

Wearing the mask and smiling at my mum like I was the happiest child in the world, I would give her a cuddle as when I cuddled her she knew everything was ok but if I didn't cuddle her she would know I had done something wrong. Walking home she asked me how my day had been and asked me if I was looking forward to starting secondary school, to make her feel good I would say 'yes mum, I can't wait' but really I was dreading it.

In turn, she would give me that smile, the smile that meant I'm so proud of you Stevie. If she only knew that I had walked off the estate that day and ignored everything she told me, would she still be proud? It didn't really matter as no one would ever find out, not even my mum.

The darkness was now inside of me and that's all because I was dying inside whilst living.

CHAPTER 3
GOT A REP TO PROTECT

AGE: 11 - 17 years old
YEAR: 1989-1995

The summer holidays had come to an end and it was time for me to take the next step in my life, moving on to secondary school and hoping for a clean, fresh start. Tuesday 5th September 1989 was my first day at Bexleyheath secondary school. I was anxious more than you will ever know. I started school with my cousin and my mate who lived on the estate and it would make it that little bit easier for me to deal with as starting a new school on your own is not the best way forward seeing as I didn't trust anyone. I remember getting ready that morning, the feeling of 'can I really face this big change in my life today?', but I had no choice, as today was the first day and I needed to make a good impression to all my new teachers. Even though I knew that there would be more male teachers present at this school than at Primary School as this school held over a thousand pupils, it was just something I would have to deal with sooner or later.

So, arriving at the school gate and seeing hundreds of people, my anxiety started to kick in and now it's time for me to put on the mask. Walking into the playground for the first time was doable as I had my cousin and my mate with me. Then the school bell rang but it was like a siren, just like the start of the war. Well, it was the start of a war for me in many ways as how are you supposed to fit in when you didn't trust anyone?

I hear my name get called followed by Drake House, these are the groups that we are put in and stay in until we leave school. My cousin and my mate were put into Caxton House and straight away we were split up, now I'm on my own and I start to panic. The only two people who I trust in this whole place have now gone.

Walking into my classroom, number 42, all of a sudden a funny feeling would come over me and my jaw hit the floor. I am smiling and looking at my new tutor, who is our 'go to person' and I was so happy as it was a lady. This was the start of my first adult crush, no joke! She was in her thirties and had brown bobbed hair, beautiful brown eyes, olive skin and was a French teacher, she was stunning! When she spoke, she sounded proper sexy, with this came a beautiful smile, white tight trousers and a fitted shirt with the collar up and a pair of Oxblood loafers. She was an absolute weapon. 'Hello Stevie, I'm Miss Lopez'. Happy days she wasn't married, perfect start for me.

I don't know what it was about her apart from everything I just said, I just felt very comfortable around her to the point of sitting right at the front of the class right next to her desk. Oh my god, I'm now the teacher's pet! It was all going so well, then there is a knock at the door. A male teacher would enter and straight away my barriers would go up. He was the Head of Drake House and his name was Mr. Carlos. He was smiling like a Cheshire cat but I wasn't having any of it. As far as I was concerned, any adult male smiling at me was after something. After all, once bitten twice shy and I wasn't taking any chances, smiles or not. Once he had left, I could start to relax again and could carry on with my first day.

We would get given our timetable of what lessons we had and who would be teaching those lessons. I would start to see male teacher's names cropping up but I just had to deal with it as it wasn't going away, just like my secret. The school was based on two sites, Church Road site and Graham Road site, the former being a base for first and second year pupils and the latter being for third, fourth and fifth year pupils. I was dropped right in the deep end now with many people around me and my trust issues at an all-time high. We would all spend the rest of the day sorting out stuff in our tutor room, books and all the usual organising and getting prepared for first lessons the next day. Then the final bell goes and I was free, meaning get me out of here. I had spent the whole day trying to work people out, I wanted to go home where I felt safe and could spend time with the people I know and trust. I needed a brain break.

Now at home, I get changed out of my uniform and put on my casual clothes and make my way downstairs to the kitchen. I can smell turkey burgers, chips and beans cooking, my absolute favourite. My mum would talk to me about my first day and asked how I found it. Putting a fake smile on, I would say 'I love it mum' as I knew it would make her feel at ease and happy that I was happy, little did she know. As long as my mum was happy that's all that mattered to me as I was getting used to the mask now. After five years of it, I became good at it and as the saying goes, 'practice makes perfect'. That night in bed, I would question myself. Can I get through this? Should I talk to someone? Will they believe me? What will happen to people if I talk? Will people think I'm crazy? Will I be in trouble? All the things that an 11 year old boy shouldn't have to deal with, it was hard enough dealing with my first day at my new school and getting used to my new surroundings.

As my week at school progresses, I find myself meeting two schoolmates who were in all my lessons and were on my level, one mate being in Whittle House and the other in Newton House. We would all sit near each other in class but this only lasted a few days as us three together was a disruption like no other! The teachers noticed this early on and nipped it in the bud straight away by splitting us up in the classroom. Not that it did much good as the classrooms wasn't exactly big. It was a pointless exercise in my eyes, just the teacher showing signs of control.

My first week at my new school was coming to an end and I felt a bit better in myself knowing I had met a few mates that were in all my lessons, the only problem was that I already had a few bad comments written in my school diary, I had received my first detention and it was only my first week! My mum was not going to be happy when she saw this as I was only one week into my new school and already the cracks are showing in my behavior. So much for a fresh clean start. Luckily mum didn't ask to look at my diary when I got in from school, which was a result as it meant I could go out at the weekend because as far as she was concerned, I was a good boy on my first week at school but little did she know. Now into my second week at school and I am starting to find my way around the school without getting lost or being late for a lesson.

The older kids would run things and with age they became more confident, showing off and giving the teachers grief, shouting names at them. It was on this day I would come to the conclusion that what happened to me that day in the woods was totally wrong and should never ever taken place. One of the teachers was telling off a pupil and then others walked past calling the teacher a 'peado'. I had never heard someone call a teacher that before, what did it mean? I asked someone what it meant and they said 'it's when older men and women touch and play with kids, you know what a peado is, don't ya mate?' I felt sick and couldn't believe what I was hearing, running to the nearest toilet, I locked myself in, and I felt my eyes well up but couldn't let anyone see. Now I am thinking there is a 'peado' in school, I became angry but I still had lessons I need to attend, wiping my eyes and sorting myself out I make my way to my next class thinking about nothing but what had happened to me in the woods. I was trying to process it as I was trying to move on from it but how could I when I now knew exactly what a pedophile now was? I pretended to listen in class but I couldn't concentrate for long enough and I am now back to square one again. Is this how it's going to be from now on? I was so confused, I just wanted to be like everyone else. This is all my fault, I asked to build the camp and now, because of that, I see the world totally different to others.

STEVIE - BEHIND THE MASK

Once home and in the bath, I locked the bathroom door, then out comes the bleach and I find myself cleaning every part of my body. Realising what I had been through when I was 6 years old, feeling dirty and it wouldn't go away. Sad really, that a child feels the need to clean with bleach to feel normal. I remember slowly crying in the bath, making noises with the water so no one could hear me. By now, I pretty much knew nothing would happen to my mum and dad and that was his way of keeping me quiet and not telling anyone. I would always end up thinking, it's done now and I can't say anything otherwise mum would say 'why didn't you tell us sooner, when it happened?' Would she even believe me? So many thoughts ran through my mind but as usual I kept it quiet. After all, as far as I was concerned if someone told you a secret, that's how it stays, a secret.

The more time that went by at school, the more frustrated I would become which would then show in my behavior. I was in the first year at secondary school and was spending more and more time getting into trouble, answering back most of the teachers plus visits to the head's office on a regular basis. I suppose I had hit the 'fuck it' button again as I just didn't care what people thought of me. As long as they didn't know what had happened to me, it was all good. All I was doing was becoming better with the mask, making everyone think it's all fine, not realising the damage it was doing to me mentally. I didn't care, I was doing what I needed to do to make me feel, let's just say, 'normal'. In my eyes, being naughty would be a good way of releasing my frustration and anger but also I felt that teachers would not come anywhere near me, keeping all adults at bay. Some days I was happy to be out of the classroom, away from people, as I still had trust issues.

Now the Christmas holidays are approaching and school will finish until January. It was a break that was well needed after my up and down start at my new school. I just couldn't wait to be surrounded by people I love and trust, my mum, dad and little sister. It's Saturday morning on the first weekend of the Christmas break, it was a good day as it was time to go get rid of all the anger at Millwall with my Dads two mates. Now used to my surroundings in the terraces, I would feel a lot more confident as I had been coming a while now and was introduced to other people through my dad's mates. Still keeping my barriers up as I wasn't willing to trust any of them. The best thing about going Millwall was that's where I felt I could be myself and have a brain break at the same time. Shouting and singing in the terraces was just the best way to release all my anger. I felt good in my surroundings as there were other kids my age and we all stuck together. We thought we were the next up and coming Millwall firm, we were only twelve.

After a nice burger and chips from the burger van we would make our way to the station, then we would finally be back at Welling and back to reality. Things were not always so bad, don't get me wrong, I still had good times but that was mainly with the three people I loved and trusted.

So, just before Christmas, my mum, dad, sister and I would go up to London in dad's black cab to see the Christmas lights in Regent Street and then visit Hamleys. Something we did most years in my childhood. The moment I walked through the doors there were just toys, toys and more toys. I was in my element and it was very busy in there, which only made me want to follow my mum and dad everywhere. All the same, I was lucky to be there as it was most kids dream to visit that place and we went every other year. My sister and I still got a treat and this year it was a tube of sticky stuff and a straw, you would put the sticky stuff on the end of the straw and blow in the other end making your own balloons. The stuff absolutely stunk and would get most kids high if they smelt it enough, well that's exactly what I did as I always took things one step too far. It's finally Christmas Eve and we would either go to my auntie's house or they would come to our house, where the adults would exchange presents in secret. The adults would like us to think that Father Christmas had all the presents in The North Pole and if we were good, he would deliver them all tonight and like a wally, at twelve, I believed it. Waking up Christmas morning, my sister would burst into my room and say 'Stevie, Father Christmas has been, quick hurry up!' We would walk downstairs and the smiles on our faces were from ear to ear. The whole living room was covered in presents and it would be at times like this that I would think that even though I had trauma in my childhood, I was still very fortunate to have the family and surroundings that I was in.

Now into the start of 1990 and I was becoming really worried about myself as my bad behaviour was increasing at school and I was becoming out of hand. I was also having more heated arguments with teachers and felt myself spiraling out of control.

STEVIE - BEHIND THE MASK

One of the struggles I had was P.E but I suppose that was going to be something I struggled with due to the lessons being taken by male teachers. It was a shame as I really thought I was an all-rounder when it came to sports but yet again my secret would involve my mask going on as I wasn't trusting any male teachers and that's all there was to it. It was during P.E that I would say that I was at my worst and didn't really feel safe as at the end of the lesson we would all have to get naked and share showers. For someone as clean as I liked to be, I would miss showering sometimes as I just couldn't deal with the situation. I would rather stay dirty than spend time in a room full of naked men and male teachers walking in every five minutes to check on us. I remember one occasion just before the Summer Holidays where I would disrupt the class during P.E, I totally lost it and my anger was not acceptable. We were all playing football and a male teacher was the referee and the game was becoming a bit heated, the referee/teacher was doing nothing about it and the moment came where I was harshly tackled and I was having none of it. Myself and the other boy involved squared up to each other with both our heads touching each other, with that I pulled my head back and head butted him straight on the nose, might seem harsh but this little shit was taking me out every two minutes and the teacher was doing nothing about it. I was being controlled in my eyes, bullied, I wasn't having any of it. The teacher saw this and came over to split us up and pull us apart, 'Get your hands off me you dirty fucking peado', where does it say in school rules you can touch a pupil? I was so angry and so was the teacher as there was no way I was backing down. No one bullies me and no teacher, male or female, will ever touch me, it just wasn't happening.

I was sent in to cool off, with the teacher smirking at me as I left the field, 'what are you fucking smiling at, you mug, you touch me again and my dad will come up here and bash the shit out of you, you won't be laughing then will ya, you prick?' I had snapped and I wasn't calming down anytime soon as no adult will touch me, I don't care who they are, once bitten twice shy. Once in the changing rooms I had a shower to cool down, it was only me in the shower so it wasn't a problem for me. Then the teacher entered the changing room and he didn't look happy, he looked extremely angry. He was saying my behaviour was not acceptable. My reply was 'I don't give a fuck, you touch me again and next time will be worse. Get out of this room whilst I'm getting changed. What's wrong with you? Do you like boys?' That was the final straw, the teacher had had enough and asked me to go to the office when I was changed. The answer was 'no, leave me alone' and I just walked out cool as a cucumber and nothing more was said. I hate bullies and that's all there is to it, if the teacher couldn't see that, then that's his problem, not mine.   If I was in the wrong, I would take ownership but If I wasn't, I would never back down and that is just how I saw things or was made to see things.

That teachers cards were marked from that day onwards and that wasn't the end of it, not by a long shot!

I would spend many occasions that year missing P.E, saying that I had forgotten my kit as it was easier than having to share changing rooms with a load of naked people and male teachers walking around every five minutes. I remember thinking to myself 'why not have single changing rooms, just like they do at swimming', this was all wrong in my eyes and just didn't feel right.

If I was really struggling I would get into trouble in the lesson before, that way I would have to go to the office which meant, chances were, I would miss P.E while waiting for the Head to see me. This is something I struggle with to this day and something that I will never feel happy or comfortable about, we wear clothes for a reason and that's to keep us covered. Not only was I struggling in P.E but also other classes and these were where I had male teachers and I wasn't willing to trust any of them. Even some female teachers I didn't like as they were trying to control me and I just couldn't let any adult control me, that's my mum and dad's job. Detentions were coming through thick and fast and I couldn't let my mum know this as it could lead to her finding out my secret. I became very sneaky and stole a spare diary out of the stationary cupboard at school, the crazy thing was that I stole it while waiting to see the Head for another time that I had got into trouble. I was becoming pretty ruthless but would do anything so my mum and dad didn't know about my behaviour which could lead them into finding out my secret. I refused to let that happen, I had come too far and would do whatever needed to be done as no one could know. With the stolen diary, I would copy out all of my timetable and this is the book I would give mum to look at. The diary that had detentions and bad comments, that would get given to the teachers. Genius idea, if I do say so myself, as the teachers would fill out detentions and bad comments in one dairy, then all the good stuff into another one which is the one my mum would see and sign. That way everybody was happy and mum wouldn't think her baby boy was a complete arsehole. That's the way it was going, it was my mask and I thought it was working fine. I even learnt my mums' signature and would sign the bad diary so the teachers would think she had read it and signed it. Already, I was creating two personalities which, thinking about it now, was the start of my Mental Health issues but I didn't know this at the time as I was just a kid. I now know that I was dealing with Borderline Personality Disorder, due to childhood trauma but didn't know at the time. As far as I was concerned, I was just hiding a secret, not realising the damage it was causing.

I won't bore you with the second year at school, it was the same as the first year.

Detentions, being sent out of class, answering teachers back and all the other shit that comes with it. If you want to know what the second year was really like just read the first year again as it was pretty much the same, apart from the fact I was getting worse and I was becoming a teenager. I was now changing from a boy to a teenager and with that comes a change in feelings and emotions, plus the realisation that my secret would start to affect me more and I would become even more aware of what happened that day and how it wasn't right.

I was 13 and spending more time around our estate and in the field on my mates' motorbike. I find myself arguing more and more with my mate who owned the motorbike as I was blaming him for us always being over the field when really he was doing nothing wrong. In my eyes, neither was I as all I was doing was protecting my feelings but he didn't know that. We were always disagreeing with each other or maybe I was blaming someone else for my problem as I didn't know myself how to deal with it all, I just hated being over the field. My mates didn't know about my situation, it wasn't any of my mates fault, but I took it out on them many times during our friendship as I just couldn't let anyone in and get too close to me, just in case they found out my secret. Like I said, I was no angel but I took ownership of it when I needed to. I knew I was different and I knew I could be nasty at times but I just couldn't help it, I was angry and could explode at any time. So would anyone else that was living a lie and hiding behind the mask, not being able to be like other kids and seeing things differently. Is it any wonder that I was so angry all the time? That 'peado' had changed me and changed my outlook on life by doing what he did to me that day in the woods. That's just how it was and it had been done and I couldn't do anything about it. Just maintain the mask and everything will be ok, or so I thought.

I would see the two brothers that was there on that tragic day quite a lot as they lived just off the estate. I never stopped long enough to get into a conversation with them as I didn't want anyone to know about that day so I would just nod my head at them, they knew, but I couldn't say anything to them as I was always with my mates. The younger brother would always look at me and then look down, he knew what happened that day and so did his brother. He was about two years older than his brother and at this time, I didn't want them to say anything. It was like a three-way secret that no one wanted to talk about. This suited me to the ground, knowing they would never say anything but it still made me angry. Every time I saw them, I thought 'how could they let him do that to me?' Not realising that they were only kids themselves and didn't know he was doing me wrong. Now a week or so into the summer holidays and me and my mates would go over the fields at the back of the estate on his new Motorbike, that being a KX100, it was an absolute speed machine for a 13 year old at that time. My mate would let everyone have a go on his bike and when I had a go, it was like a release for me, concentrating on what's ahead but hitting speeds that just made me feel free with the wind blowing in my face. Turns out, that day something went wrong with his bike so it had to put in his garage, I wish now that had never happened as the events that follow would end up scaring the shit out of me and my behaviour would take a turn for the worst. We all decided as there was no bike in action we would all take a walk to the petrol garage through the fields onto Shooter Hill to get some food and drink. It will be ok, it's not like anything can go wrong, walking with mates for a bit of a munch. Once we arrived at the garage we all steamed into the petrol garage, grabbing food and drinks and paying for them at the counter. Well, some of us paid and some of us didn't. We then did a right onto Shooters Hill and then another right where there was a path leading back into the fields, for some reason, one of my mates had some wet tissues from the petrol station and turned around and threw it towards the main road and hit the side of a car. Then the seed had been planted and everyone was getting wet tissues and throwing them at the side of cars, only little bits but all the same, still dangerous and not the right thing to be doing. By this time, I'm thinking 'don't be a wimp, put the mask on and have a go. It will be ok' I now do what I normally do and take things one step further, being a child that was just generally angry at the world, I walk into the petrol station and grab about ten bits of tissue and drench it all in water and make my way back to the field. Everyone is doing one bit of tissue but I decided to put the ten bits together. Before doing a right onto the path I see a clear road but a red mini Bedford van is coming down the hill and looked to be going slow. Now's my chance so I run and throw this big lump of wet tissue hoping to hit the side of the van, I don't know what I was thinking at the time but I threw it too early. Thinking nothing of it, just like a kid would, I turn around and start to walk off. As I do this, I hear the loudest skid ever, then a pause, then the loudest crashing noise ever. Not hanging around to see what's happened, me and my mates all ran. One of my mates was nearly six foot and I ran past him, faster than anything, making our way back to the estate. As I was running, all I could think was 'what have I just done?' its ok having a laugh as kids but this was no laughing matter. The feeling I had was like running home that day from the fields after what had happened to me, feeling sick and panicking, thinking 'please don't be dead, please don't be dead, what have I done?'. I left all my mates and got to the front door,

putting on a normal face and smiling, I knock on my front
door and my mum comes out and says 'you're home early
and my reply was 'I don't feel well mum', she felt my head
and said 'you don't feel hot, go and have a lie down in your
bedroom'. Just what I wanted to hear, I then ran upstairs,
put my pajamas on and got into bed, shitting myself at the
same time, metaphorically speaking of course. An hour
passes and there is a knock on the door, panicking I answer
the door and my mate is stood there and explained what had
happened. By the time he had finished, I felt relieved but
also still very worried.

What happened was, I had thrown the wet tissue too early
and it ended up hitting the windscreen of the red Bedford
van and spread across the front of the van. This had
stopped the driver from seeing out of his window so he
slammed on his breaks and skidded into the petrol garage
wall. Luckily, the wall was there otherwise the van would
have crashed into the actual garage and probably caused an
explosion after hitting a petrol pump and killed the driver
and others in the garage at that time. My friend said no one
was hurt but all the same, I can't believe the destruction I
had caused, yet again. The man came round to the estate
every day for a month looking for me as he had already
collared my mates but they wouldn't 'grass me up' and just
stayed indoors for a whole month.

All I can say is, I'm so sorry for putting his life in danger
that day, I was just a little kid that was dealing with a lot of
stuff and I wasn't well. I didn't know what I was doing. I
ended up staying in a lot more as whenever I was out, there
was nothing but trouble. I dread to think what all my mates

actually thought of me at the time as not only was I was nasty to them sometimes but I was now getting them into trouble.

The rest of the holidays dragged like you wouldn't believe but finally it was time to go back to school. I would be starting the third year at school and me and my mates would get a bus from the top of Shoulder Mutton Green towards Bexleyheath Clock Tower. This would be a good day for me as it would be the day me and my mates would meet a couple of girls. They would be at the bus stop on the other side of the road, going towards Blackheath. They had recently moved into a house in a road that was just off the green that we walked up most days to get the bus to school. It was the first time me and boys started socialising with the 'other side' as in 'girls'. I would put the mask on and walk over with another mate and we started to make conversation, we asked them where they lived and just the usual shit that boys say and do. We then arranged to meet them on the bench on the green after school and that would be the start of our friendship with the two girls. A bigger bonus for myself as we would now be meeting and hanging around the green instead of the poxy woods and fields. It's something that I had always wanted to do, move away from 'hanging around' on the fields and now it was finally happening. I would start to let go a bit of all the trauma I had been through, nothing could be done anyway and no one would find out. The start of the third year got off to a good start and things were going as they should, my mate and I from Whittle House would be up to our usual tricks but keeping low key as I had just had enough of standing outside the Head's office. I was doing ok in P.E, in my eyes, as I was avoiding taking part as much as possible, it was just all too much drama so I came to the conclusion that if I'm not taking part, I'm not getting into trouble. What I was starting to do was avoid things for a peaceful life and let's face it, if you were me you would have done the same. By now you're probably thinking 'why doesn't he just tell someone?' Believe me, I wanted to speak up so many times, as you will read further along, it just wasn't that easy.

Getting back to my third year at school. I was now based on the Graham Road site of the school. It was at this point in school that pupils could go out of school at lunch to grab some food and have a break from the school. Something that a lot of pupils did but something I didn't do as on school grounds I felt safer than I did around the shopping center, just another way that I see the world after my childhood trauma. It wasn't so bad staying in school at lunch times, well it wasn't for me as I loved a bit of school dinner. Plus, I had a regular little scam going on with one of the pupils at the school, his mum was a single parent so he was given a token every lunch-time as a subsidiary for his dinner. The token was worth £1.30 and I would give him 70p for it, which meant, with my own money I would eat like a King in the canteen most days. I still remember my order from the canteen today, it consisted of: two hamburgers, chips and beans, then for afters, it would be chocolate sponge with chocolate custard and a strawberry milkshake and I would smash the lot of it. Then one afternoon after lunch it would be P.E and as you know, I didn't have my kit with me as I hated the situation of all sharing showers, plus male teachers would walk in every five minutes. So after informing the teacher I wasn't doing P.E today, he looked at me and said 'why are not doing P.E? It's something you're good at and it's a complete waste'. Sad, but true. The first thing that entered my brain was 'why is it so important to you that I do P.E? Do you like seeing me getting changed or getting in the shower? The more I thought about it, the angrier I became. Now I'm in defense mode and shout out 'I don't want to fucking do it and you can't make me', pointing my finger up at his face. I then walked out of the room saying 'you ain't controlling me', followed by 'you're a bully arsehole'. The worst thing I could have done. That was the last straw and the teacher had just about had enough of my behaviour, off to Mrs. Jones office I went, thinking 'is this how it's always going to be?' But, it was worth it rather than anyone knowing my secret.

Now in the corridor, I am waiting for my name to get called to see what the latest punishment was, my name is called and into the office I go. I've lost count of how many times I had done this journey. To say I got a grilling is an understatement, then I hear the words 'report card', this was punishment for the naughty kids and wasn't your everyday thing. It was a folded card and you would have to attend every lesson and couldn't get any bad comments otherwise you would stay on it again, it was a very bad thing. This would be an extra bad thing for myself as my mum would now find out that my good boy persona at school was all lies. I panicked about it as I would now have to talk to my mum and I didn't want her knowing why I was different and why I couldn't control my personality sometimes. I ended up being grounded that weekend and mum wasn't happy. I would get the same old telling off, followed by 'I don't know why you do it. You're clever, not stupid, you're my son and I love you but this stops now'. Rather than argue and say I can't help it mum I would just agree and cry, then go up to my bedroom where I would try and process everything my had said to me.

A few months on and I am off report card and it's now January 1993 and I am 14 years old and seem to be maintaining a bit of stability at school. I thought this was due to me now spending more time on the green with my mates and the girls, being off the estate and away from the fields and woods. I was no longer having a constant reminder of my secret which seemed to help me cope with the situation more, even though it was still on my mind all the time. As we start to hang around on the green more, the group would start to get bigger, which would be a good thing for me as the more of us there was, the safer I would feel. We were not a nasty lot and respected all the older people that would walk down the green as we might of looked intimidating to the elderly as there was quite a crowd of us but we meant them no harm. After all that was someone else's nan and grandad so respect was needed for them all as me and my mates all had our own grandparents and that's how we all saw it, 'treat the elderly like one of ya own'.

Then we would meet the girls who we met at the bus stop, they came onto the green with their neighbour one day, another girl, and this girl would end up being my best friend. She would be the one that I would talk to often as she wasn't part of my past, she just seemed to understand me, even when I was that angry person hiding behind the mask. My other boy mates would bring other girls they had met, making our group even bigger. I would say there were at least thirty of us on the green all passing time and socialising, doing what youngsters do.

March came and after spending the weekend with all my mates on the green, it would be Monday morning and time to go to school again.

My mates and I made our way to the bus stop at the top of the green, it was quite a sunny day and then the bus would stop at the top of the green. We made our way upstairs and sat at the back of the bus thinking that we owned the whole back seat. I got to the top of the stairs, turned around, looked at the back seat and at the back of the bus there sat the most beautiful girl I had ever seen in my life. I froze, like a little boy as I had the funniest feelings running through my body. What was happening to me? I couldn't tell you but I didn't give anyone the chance to see how I was feeling and the mask went on. Looking back at her, I smiled but didn't give too much away as I still didn't know her so the barriers would stay up. All my mates followed me towards the back of the bus where we would normally sit, not only was there a beautiful girl on the bus but she was sitting in my seat and wasn't moving anytime soon. Who was going to back down first, well I can tell you it was me and that was a rare thing for me to do, this girl had me hooked and only one minute had passed what was going on?

As she wouldn't move I would sit bang next to her where I would get a cheeky little grin from her and that would be followed by a smile back from myself. She was only tiny, a tiny little thing, bless her, but as my mum would always say, 'good things come in small packages' and on this occasion, she was spot on. This girl looked pristine and took great pride in her appearance, even though she was in school uniform, she had shoulder length blonde curly hair, a face like a doll and she just hit every button as far as I was concerned, she was absolutely stunning.

Half-way through my bus journey, she would get out of her seat and make her way to the stairs as she was getting off the bus. Before walking down the stairs she would look towards the back of the bus and smile as she walked down the stairs, me and one of my mates would start arguing about who she smiled at so I asked one of the younger boys to go ask her who she was smiling at before she got off the bus. The younger boy come running up the stairs and said 'Stevie she was smiling at you'. I look out of the back of the bus window and she is walking along. I smiled to myself thinking 'that pretty girl likes me', then she turns around and gives me a smile. I had fallen for someone I had never even met or seen before. Plus, she wasn't from the estate so she wouldn't know about my past, every box had been ticked. Would I ever see her again?

I spent the whole day at school and only got told off once for laughing, that was a good day for me at school just in case you were wondering.

STEVIE - BEHIND THE MASK

Now I find myself at home thinking about this girl on the bus and wondering if she will be on the bus in the morning. I was feeling really relaxed and wasn't battling with my brain and found I was smiling like a Cheshire cat. I felt different and remembered my mum saying 'sometimes love is at first sight'. Was it or was it just because she was a female and was someone that wasn't too close to home? I just didn't know. Morning time came and I had a bit of a spring in my step and was feeling fresh and ready for the day. I walk into the bathroom and spend that little bit longer in the bathroom making myself look fresh, hoping that lovely girl would be sitting at the back of the bus again. Bit of dad's aftershave on, teeth brushed, gel on and I'm ready to go. Meeting my mates at the end of the road we make our way to the bus stop and pop over the sweet shop where I buy some chewing gum. Mr. Smooth is kicking into action and preparing what to say if she's on the bus. The bus pulls up and I steam on first and walk up the stairs, turn around and there she is looking a little bit more dressed up and prettier that the day before, from what I can gather, she was thinking the same as me the night before. Then I said it 'alright?' She looked at me and said 'alright', happy days, the conversation is open. We didn't say much to each other but the eye contact and smiles were telling me this girl liked me. Again, the time comes for her to get off the bus, I remember saying 'see ya later' and she replied 'yeah maybe', now she was playing hard to get and I'm thinking how do I reply to that, so I said 'yeah maybe' and off the bus she got. I played the 'hard to get' card and didn't look out the back window this time, but I got one of mates to look to see if she was looking back as now I was playing her games, but this game was fun as I was seeking pleasure and avoiding pain. Finally someone who could help me move forward and help me in starting to lead a normal life, well that's what I was hoping for anyway. After seeing her many times on the bus I decided it was time to meet up with her, so me and my mate met her and her mate on Welling corner where we arranged to go to Shoulder Mutton Green the day after.

Then that day came and I made sure I was extra smooth looking, wearing all my best clobber and my fresh white trainers and aftershave as this was my chance to get into my first relationship. Hopefully taking my mind off my trauma and moving on with this little stunner, who for some reason, liked me. We all met up the green that day which was a routine thing to do, there was quite a few of us, a mixture of girls and boys, all doing what little crews do.

Me and my mate was at the bus stop waiting for the girls to get off the bus, my idea as I knew all our other mates would take the piss out of me, which they did anyway. As the girls got off the bus, my mates all started shouting which, in turn, made me go as red as a beetroot, great start to our first meeting. After a while, everything would settle down and the girls would start to mingle in with everyone else which would make me feel a bit more at ease. I couldn't stop looking at her but I wouldn't let her see me looking as I was playing it cool plus, didn't really know her yet.

She was wearing black tight leggings, high heeled black boots, and a tight white fitted top. Her hair looked perfect, her eyes looked perfect, her smile was perfect, this girl was just perfect in every way and I had hit the jackpot. That's the feeling I got every time I looked at her, like I had won the Jackpot on a fruit machine, the best way to describe her would be like baby out of Dirty Dancing, height, figure, looks, personality, everything. Then the time came for the girls to go and I would walk over to the bus stop with my mate and the girls while they waited for a bus, then for some mad reason I went in for the kill and by that I mean a kiss. I don't know what came over me but I did it, luckily she liked me and had no problem in giving me a kiss too. Once the girls were on the bus, I jumped on my mate and said 'get in there!' with the biggest smile on my face. He said sort me out with her mate please Stevie she is really nice and my answer was no problem, having a mate there when you first start dating just makes it all the easier as you could bounce off each other in and out of conversation.

I'll be honest now, it was the weirdest feeling kissing her but it felt nice at the same time, did I like her or was she just a distraction from my secret? I didn't know so just went with it as I was happy, she was happy and that's all that really mattered. I was still holding in this dark secret and wasn't sure what I should do regarding this but then my brain starts to go and I think to myself if I tell her we might fall out and she will then tell everyone. So within seconds my answer was no as no one could know but this wasn't a problem as I had been living behind a mask for eight years now and it just wasn't getting any easier.

Me and mate would meet up with the girls a few times just like double dating which made things easier as me and my girlfriend was still getting to know each other, my mate would always try and be Mr. Smooth around the other girl which just had me in stitches as he would always play the tough guy as he had a motorbike. He reminded me of one of the T- Birds in Grease. The other girl liked him as he had a motorbike which was the reason we ended up meeting the girls a few times, going over the fields, taking the girls on the back of the bike thinking we were proper little geezer's.

Whilst over the fields I would manage to get a bit of time with my girlfriend, laying on the grass and having a kiss and a cuddle, but that's as far as it went as this girl was no slapper, which if I'm honest, attracted me to her even more. My mum was right that good things come in small packages as this girl just seemed too good to be true and I was starting to build trust in her and I didn't trust anyone. We would get closer and closer as time went on, doing things that new couples do, buying each other Christmas presents and going to family gatherings. Over Christmas my Nan had a family gathering so I invited my girlfriend to come along with me, as things were good between us and it was the right time for her to meet other family members. I remember opening my nans front door and she stood there in the porch wearing all the stuff I had bought her for Christmas, she looked amazing and was even wearing the bottle of Giorgio perfume I bought her.

I just couldn't wait to show her off to the family, everyone was saying how beautiful she was and I was a lucky boy to have her, they fell in love with her bigtime and everything was so good. I was really enjoying spending time with her.

STEVIE - BEHIND THE MASK

We would meet up many more times and things were all going so well but then, just like that, things would start to change. I would find myself doing my normal thing and slowly but surely started to push her away. She hadn't done a single thing wrong, she was absolutely perfect but she was just getting a little too close for my liking and that's something I couldn't deal with as letting someone in would make me open up and I just couldn't afford to let that happen. I would find myself being nasty and putting in little digs, I was an arsehole and believe me, I didn't want to be but I didn't know what else to do as I needed to protect myself and I had no idea of the pain I was causing her. I was just so obsessed with my secret and myself if I'm honest. Then the day came that I would end up regretting, how low can someone be to call up his girlfriend and dump her over the phone without an explanation or anything. My Mum didn't bring me up to be like that, but all that went out the window as I needed to protect me and my secret. She was really upset and I felt terrible but at this point in my life I just couldn't deal with being in a relationship and anyone getting too close to me. I got off the phone and regretted it big time, believe me but I put on the mask straight away and went out with my mates acting like nothing had happened.

Now into my final year at school and no longer in a relationship, the guilt would start to settle in and I would find myself rebelling, yet again my happiness taken away all due to this sick peados actions.

Instead of playing up in the odd lesson, I would now find myself playing up in most lessons and giving the male teachers more stick than ever, to the point of not putting me on report card but now on report book! This was no weekly thing, I ended up being put on this for three months and it was all down to many things I had done wrong in lessons over a period of time.

From throwing pritt stick on the ceiling, shooting a paper clip at the blackboard with an elastic band to scare the teacher, setting the gas tap on fire in the science lab and nearly blowing it up to sticking chewing gum under my desk, eating in lessons, back chatting teachers and many other things that I needed to be punished for. All the punishment in the world wasn't going to change me I was a loose cannon and just blamed everyone for what I had been through. No one could tell me otherwise as they weren't dealing with what I was.

I just couldn't wait to finish school but before that could happen, I would have to take my GCSE exams, it wasn't that I wasn't clever because I was but at this time in my life I just didn't know how to put it into action as I was dealing with maintaining my secret on a daily basis and maintaining the mask. I can't believe I managed to sit through all my exams but I wasn't expecting anything if I'm honest after the way I behaved in the last year at school I was expecting to fail them all.

I would go to the school for the very last time and collect my results, not feeling nervous one bit as I knew what was coming, opening my results to see the letters D, D, D, D, E, E, F, G and a U for ungraded which was computers but that was understandable as I got sent out of the room during the exam. My two best grades were a D for Geography and a

STEVIE - BEHIND THE MASK

Merit for R.E, the reason for a Merit had nothing to do with me being good at Religious Education, I was just good at retaining things that were on TV and this lesson was mainly videos to watch which was the only time my brain would be occupied at school. Sitting on the bus on the way home I would try to think about how I could get out of this as my mum was expecting a lot better from her son, well according to the fake diary she had been signing all year round anyway. Walking through the front door, I found myself concentrating on the two best grades, then walked straight into the kitchen and said 'I done ok mum', she said 'what did ya get?', my reply was 'yeah, I got a Merit for R.E and a D for Geography'. Her reply was 'what ya gonna be? A fucking travelling vicar?' she was not happy at all and when she saw the rest of the grades she was even angrier. The reason she was angry was because she knew when I was at home, I had no problem with anything homework related and knew I had a brain, scary time for me as she would question why was my grades so bad and I couldn't let her find out my secret. After a grilling from my mum and me feeding her a load of old shit about how I will go to college and make up for it, I was finally allowed to go out up the green with all my mates as now would be the time I would start to feel like I needed to tell someone about my secret as it was eating away at me slowly but surely.

I had started to form a great friendship with one of the girls on the green and she lived right on it, she was someone I hadn't known that long but she was a girl and I felt I got on with girls better than I did boys at that time in my life. She had her own living room in her house and we would meet up and hang out with each other a lot, she got me and whenever I felt alone in my head which was often she would listen to me and was just always there. There was no physical attraction, even though she was a pretty little thing bless her but we just enjoyed each other's company and was always there for each other, a bit like brother and sister as I felt like I had known her for years. She was my best friend. I remember one night sitting in her house preparing everything in my head about how I'm going to tell her what happened, then changing my mind thinking she will think I'm gay if I tell her and what if she tells the boys then what will I do so I decided not to tell her. Believe me, I wanted to and wished I had but then all the 'what if's' entered my mind and I decided it was better to do what I had done for many years already and that's to tell no one and maintain the mask it was easier than telling anyone.

She must have wondered why I was different when I was around my boy mates than when I was with her but she probably thought what most girls would of thought and that's boys just being boys but little did she know.

I was now 16 years old and becoming even more knowledgeable about what had happened to me, I find myself lashing out and becoming nastier to my mates, the closest people to me. I started drinking alcohol on a Friday night with a few mates, they would only have one but me being me would take it to the max by having two or three, sometimes four. That would be the best thing I have ever done but also the worst thing I had ever done. The reason for it being the best thing was I felt great, I felt unstoppable, my problems had disappeared, and I didn't have a care in the world. The reason for it being the worst thing was, I wasn't nice company, I became a pain, and I hurt the people close to me, my close mates. I pushed people away and was becoming this angry person, how my mates still stood by me I will never know. I was blaming everyone as well as myself and in the meantime that arsehole was living a normal life, after destroying mine. Now thinking more about the situation, I find myself having a drink on the green on a Friday night, then on a Saturday night, not the regular thing for a 16 year old to do at weekends. Well it probably was but not as much as I was drinking compared to everyone else, but it was blocking out my demons. So, if I'm honest I didn't care as I was happy for a few nights a week and didn't have to maintain that poxy mask all the time. I would meet up with a girl that was two years older than me by Aye Gees motorcycles in Welling Way, where we would get alcohol, as she was 18 and had identification, she would get four diamond white ciders and a couple of K ciders as well. We would go to the blue bridge over the railway and sit there talking whilst drinking and having a kiss and a cuddle. I suppose it made me feel like a normal young man, it was mainly on a Friday night so it wasn't anything too serious which suited me down to the ground as I didn't get time to get too close and she wouldn't find out anything about me. The problem I now had was that alcohol was now becoming a brain break for me, a release from everything I had to deal with. After all, this 16 year old boy was becoming a young man and now had a rep to protect.

CHAPTER 4
IF IN DOUBT BLOCK IT OUT

AGE: 17 - 23 years old
YEAR: 1995-2002

With school and my GCSE's out the way, it was now time for me to enter the big bad world and look for a job. I wasn't looking for anything with good pay as my grades wouldn't allow me too. Yet again, another thing that was stopping me from moving forward but that's just the way it was. After all, I would need money as I had discovered that alcohol wasn't cheap and it wasn't going to pay for itself. I would need it as it was my brain break and could help me move on with my life, well that's what I thought anyway. I ended up taking a job in Crayford working for a plastic company on a machine. The most boring job anyone could have had, working on the same machine all day making plastic parts of all different shapes, sizes and colours. It paid a weekly wage and was enough for me as I would get money once a week, enough to live on and I could have my little brain break twice a week.

I found it very awkward working there as I was working with three other men, all older than me and they all knew each other. They were nice enough blokes but at the time I just couldn't seem to trust or get involved with them so I kept myself to myself. I found the job so boring as I had too much time to think and I was thinking more and more about my secret as the week went on.

STEVIE - BEHIND THE MASK

Friday finally came and I couldn't of been happier as I had got through the first week at my new job but even happier as I would not be controlled all week by another man, my boss. He would come in and say 'it's time now mate, we are finished for the weekend', my face lit up! I got my stuff together and ran out of the building, finally freedom for two days. As soon as I got back to Welling, I would go home, have a bath, spruce myself up, throw on my clothes, my fresh white trainers and meet the boys and girls up Shoulder Mutton Green. Now with money in my pocket I'm feeling good and I am in a good place as now I know it's time for my brain break. The good thing about it was, one of my mates got on well with the off licence bloke so identification was no issue and we had alcohol whenever we needed it. I remember buying a few Fosters and a couple of Diamond White Ciders so I could mix them together and get the full effect. Once on the green with all my mates we would sit in the middle of the green in the dark, all drinking and doing what all youngsters do, having fun. Even at the age of 17 I find myself being scared of the dark and you would never see me walking through the woods on my own, it's just something I couldn't do, ever since that day in the woods when I was a kid. If I was with anyone else or under the influence of alcohol I wouldn't give a shit but I just couldn't deal with them things on my own or with a clear mind. I would knock the drinks back like no one's business that night and found myself becoming a bit out of control. To the point where I would walk off over the green and go sit on the bench. Within five minutes my best girl mate would come over and sit next to me and ask me if I was ok, I would change instantly give her a smile and say 'I'm ok thanks mate'.

She would then say 'you're drinking a bit too much, maybe ya need to slow down a little', I'd put my arm around her and give her smile and say 'it's all good mate, thanks for being there'. Really, I was masking how I was feeling as even though I trusted her, it still wasn't enough for me to open her to her. Even though I had wanted to tell her many times before, I just couldn't bring myself to do it. Knowing that she would always be there whenever I needed her would bring me great comfort, she never knew that as I would always put on the mask. I think she had an inkling that something wasn't right as I was a bit crazy but that was just the frustration I was holding in, due to my secret. Every now and then I would just lash out and push people away.

She would get the brunt of it sometimes as she was one of the closest friends to me, she was my best mate and was always one hundred percent there for me.

Saturday morning arrived and a letter arrived through the door, it was a letter from British Telecom as I had applied for an apprenticeship. I opened the letter and there was an offer for me to work for them but because I had done rubbish in my GCSE's they said if I attend a college course and get a qualification that equalled to four C grades and above, then the job was mine. This meant I would have to start college in January, complete the course by August and start for BT in the September 1996. My mum got on the phone to her sister and explained the situation so she could help find a course for me. Within a week my auntie had found the course, it was starting in January. Even better, I would be attending the same course as my cousin, the one who had lost his eye as a kid, so straight away I felt at ease knowing my cousin would be with me and we could work through it together.

The start of December is now here and I am no longer working for the plastic company as I had given in my notice, that job was not good for me if I'm honest as I had too much time to think and I needed to be active. I felt that I was worth more than that, even though I found life a struggle sometimes I still wasn't going to end up in a dead-end job like that. I needed a company with prospects, somewhere I could work my way up so no one would know what I had been through and I could try to make something of myself.

Christmas Eve came and everyone is in the holiday mood. To me, it was the best time of year as everyone was celebrating which involved alcohol and that was my brain break right there, bring it on!

At Christmas I would attend family gatherings where I would have a sneaky beer as I was still only 17 and my mum was very old school, in the sense that she said rules are there to be obeyed and as far as she was concerned no alcohol until I was 18. Little did she know that I was having the odd session out with the boys and it wasn't that hard to hide from her as I was becoming so good with the mask, it was now actually part of me. By the end of 1995 and after a few uncles saying to my mum 'let him have a beer' at family parties, she was now realising that her baby boy was becoming a man and she was starting to accept me drinking alcohol so the mask wasn't needed as much in that respect. That New Year's Eve I would go to a family party with my best girl mate, I didn't have to worry about my surroundings as I had known her family a while and got on well with them all. The only time I struggled is when going to parties and not knowing anyone. As you already know, I found it so difficult to trust or get to know any man that was older than me but with anyone my age or younger, I was fine. As far as I was concerned, any man older than me that I didn't know was a wrong'un and was not to be trusted.

The start of a new year was here. I was still struggling but I had more of a positive outlook on my life as this year could be my year. If I got my head down and focused on passing my course, by September I would have an apprenticeship with the biggest Telecommunications Company out there. It didn't get much better than that for security, pension, education, company van, private healthcare, the lot. The world was my oyster and it was only me that could spoil it. Finally something to look forward to and hopefully I would forget my demons and move on with my life. After all, living behind this mask was starting to take its toll on me as it could be so draining maintaining the smile and letting everyone think that I was ok.

As far as everyone was concerned, I was just a crazy bloke that was always up for a laugh and always smiling, making everybody else laugh and just generally being the clown of the group. No one had any clue what I was dealing with.

STEVIE - BEHIND THE MASK

At this point, I had thoughts of him going round in my head every day. Who he is? Where is he? I wanted to kill him, look what he has done to me! Should I speak to the brothers? I would fight it still, not realising that I am starting to change in many ways, becoming harder, more nastier, more angry and more against society in general. In my eyes I was doing the right thing, protecting myself and my feelings. After all, as far as I was concerned, no one cared about my feelings, so it was down to me to protect them.

Now into January 1996 and a fresh year. The first day at college is finally here and my cousin and I start our course at Woolwich College.
The course me and my cousin were on was for NVQ level 1-2 in Electronics, Engineering and Information Technology. This was serious shit and there was no way I could fail this. I fitted in nicely with the course as my cousin was in every lesson so meeting new people wasn't an issue. The only issue I had was that most lessons were taken by older men, which I knew I would struggle with. Now older and becoming more angry with my situation and the realisation of what happened to me, I start to struggle with the male teachers. They were different to school teachers and would have a bit more of a laugh and banter with students which I would take totally the wrong way and get into arguments with them. People in the class must have thought I was a pain in the arse and was crazy, well they would be right as I didn't care. To me I was just protecting myself from the older male teachers, I didn't

expect people to understand but at the time I was doing what I thought was right and maintaining the mask.

Then comes the day at college that things would start to become more easier for me as during break on that day I would be introduced to 'solid' for the first time and for all the young ones out there that's puff, cannabis, pot or whatever you call it nowadays. A solid little brown block that you would burn with a lighter then crumble into a rizla with tobacco to make a joint. Then you would spark the joint, take two lugs on it, pass it to your friend and by the time it gets back round to you, you are in a world of your own. It was more than that for me. It was a break from my thoughts, my fears and every other negative thing going on in my life. It made me feel happy and focused. To me, it was the best medication in the world. I would go back into class like a new person, laughing, joking, concentrating, focused, working and getting on with the teachers. What was going on? I felt free for the first time since 'my secret'. If life could be like this from now on, then I'll take it. I already had a brain break with alcohol every now and then and now I had puff that made everything go away as well. That's two things to help me get through the struggles with my demons. It looks like this year is going to be my year for sure, I felt as happy as a pig in shit.

I spent the next four months getting my head down at college as this was my only way to move forward and get into BT. Over them four months whilst at college I would notice that my alcohol and puff consumption was increasing, which would block out my secret and help me get through and pass my college course. Everything was going so well and I was finally coming to the end of my college course and I was now due to start my final exams. When taking my exams my mind would just go blank which is something that I didn't need to happen as these exams were my golden ticket to a new start, a career and hopefully a normal start in the big wide world. There was no way I was failing this course as I knew I could do a lot better than working in a plastics factory so I found myself copying whoever I would sit next to in my exams. Call it cheating, call it what you want, I called it desperation as I would have done anything to pass that course and nothing was going to stop me from doing that.

My last day at college arrived and the boys and I would go to the local pub near the college. We would go there most lunchtimes, just for one beer but today was the final day so we all tucked into the beers and celebrated.

Now into August 1996 and my certificates would finally arrive for my course that I had completed and passed! I could now start my apprenticeship with BT in September and everything was flowing nicely. Once I looked through my certificates I called them up and they asked me to send my certificates to them. Once they had seen them, they would give me a start date. On the Saturday morning I went round to my best mate's house and told her the news about getting a new job. In turn, she informed me that one of our mates was going to be the DJ at a House and Garage night called 'Windsor's' and asked if I was up for it. Some of my other boy mates were going, what a perfect time to celebrate my new job than with a brain break and a night out with everyone. My girl mates Dad was going to take us and drop us off there. This all seemed too good to be true but all the same I was 'on it like Sonic', party time here we come! That afternoon we would all leave the green early and go home to get ready for the party. I went straight home and was on at my Dad for ten minutes asking to borrow one of his shirts I like so I could look the part for that evening. Once I was ready I would make my way up the green earlier than everyone else and necked a couple of beers so I could feel relaxed and not deal with my head today as this was going to be a good night, a night I would feel free in my mind. We would finally all be on the green near my best mate's house and her dad would fit us all in his Land Rover and take us to the party.

I was already pissed and everyone else was on, what I like to call, a boring normal level. I was the one in the wrong but thought everyone else was in the wrong as I was doing what I thought was right for me. That was to have a numb brain which would help me get through the night and not have to deal with trust issues and my own thoughts. Once we had arrived outside the party, I was already feeling the strain as I had taken things too far again and already I'd had more than enough alcohol in me. If I'm honest, I didn't need any more and could have enjoyed myself for the rest of the night, but not me, I wanted more. I wanted the biggest brain break ever.

The music was thumping and I was in the zone as I had got an ecstasy tablet off of one of the older lot which I had taken 30 minutes previous and it was my first time. With the alcohol as well I was where I needed to be, happy and carefree. I felt like I was dreaming as I had a mist around my sight, everywhere I looked people were smiling and dancing.

Then the pill proper kicked in and I started swaying. I made my way to the toilet where I threw up for about 5 minutes and then I made my way to the exit as I was in a bad way and struggling to catch my breath. Once outside I walked along the dual carriageway and collapsed on the grass. I was in and out of consciousness and was in a really bad way. At one point, I remember choking which woke me up, luckily, as I was laying on my back and choking on my own sick. I don't know how but I managed to turn my head to the side to carry on being sick, which probably saved my life if I'm honest.

All of a sudden I heard one of my mates shout out 'there's Stevie'. What had happened was all of my mates thought I had gone home but I had been laying on the carriageway for the last four hours. Choking on my own sick every now and again. I mean, how lucky was I to still be alive as many people die from that? My mates Dad pulled up in the car and my mates picked me up and put me in the car. I was in a bad way but the pill was still kicking in with force and I just wanted to get home, to my bed and hopefully sleep it off as my head was all over the place. I felt numb and wasn't dealing with any thoughts, I just felt free, and well that's what I thought anyway. I would say that I'm like a cat with nine lives and I think I just used the first one for sure!

Into September and I started my first day at BT, I remember it like it was yesterday. I made my way to 81 Newgate Street in London where I would have my induction for my apprenticeship. I walked into a room full of people and just froze as it was full, mainly of men. Then the mask goes on and I introduce myself, being that cocky, funny guy that everyone thought I was. I was introduced to my manager who was my mentor through my apprenticeship, yet again another man which straight away got my back up. I realised the field I was working in was predominantly male orientated.

After a while at BT I would get given my own van and all the stuff I needed to become a telephone engineer but I would assist qualified Engineers so I could learn the trade. The best thing about it was that I would finish by two o'clock most days and would be home in Welling within an hour. To me, it was a bonus as I could get to the pub by three o'clock and have a cheeky beer but as most men know, there is no such thing as one cheeky beer. I had my local pubs that surrounded the estate, but I didn't really like being in them unless I had to as I didn't want to bump into the brothers who were there that day, I didn't want my secret coming out and I didn't need a constant reminder of what had happened that day. I was already reliving it in my head and even into my dreams and nightmares as well.

Friday afternoon came and work had finished for the weekend, my brain break was needed and today would be the day I would find a new pub, I called it 'The Office' many called it The Moon And Sixpence. This place was about a ten minute walk from my house and was situated right at the top of Welling High Street, right near Welling train station. I would find myself here most days after work or at weekends. I could hide my van in the back roads and have a couple of pints without anyone knowing.

That Friday, I would stay in my uniform and end up being out most of the afternoon and night. The beers were going down a treat and all the fear and trust issues I had were slowly getting numb due to the amount of alcohol in my system. I made my way to the toilet where there is one of the older lot tucking into some cocaine, I remember asking why does he do it, his reply was 'to get me through a week'. Then I would make yet another bad decision as the other bloke passed me the cocaine wrap, I opened it, pinched the biggest amount that I could, raised it to my nose and sniffed as hard as I could. The feeling I got was immense, the combination of alcohol and cocaine made me feel let's just say 'normal'. All of my thoughts and feelings had disappeared, I felt like Darth Vader and I felt unstoppable. As soon as I walked out of the toilet the music was playing and I made my way straight to the dance floor. I felt so free and full of energy and if I'm honest, I felt amazing. My confidence was flying and I was talking to the ladies, no problem at all. I would end up spending the rest of the night in the pub, feeling as free as a bird and drinking and sniffing as much alcohol and cocaine as I could. I had now discovered my new fix and that was a combination of cocaine and alcohol. What I was doing was self-medicating, but no one would be able to change my view on the situation as it was blocking out my past and in a way I felt normal. At the end of the night I walked home from the pub and left my van parked in a back road as I was in no fit state to drive. I couldn't risk losing my job as I had only just got it and needed it to pay for my new self-medication.

I would also drink in another local pub at the bottom of Shooters Hill. I liked to move around to different pubs as all of a sudden I found I was more confident and wanting to interact with people that were on my level. By that I mean people that took cocaine and drank alcohol, they were the people I wanted to be around as I felt they understood me on many levels.

I was totally wrong in the way I was thinking but at the time I was doing what was good for me and that's all that really mattered. All I wanted was a break from my demons and the way I was doing it was working so, 'if it ain't broke, don't fix it'.

After a few months of the same routine, going to work, going to the pub and getting wrecked most nights, I find myself getting into the drugs more and more as my new medication was working a treat. I would still hide behind the mask anytime I wasn't drinking but when I was out, getting messy, I could be the free Stevie and if I'm honest, I loved it. I would also find that I was changing personality wise and starting to become an arsehole around the people closest to me, pushing them away for a few reasons. The first being that I had always done it anyway as I didn't want anyone knowing my secret and secondly, the fix that was blocking everything out was taking its toll and I wasn't getting much sleep, so I was becoming more moody and very impatient with friends and family. Sometimes I couldn't tell if people were joking with me or being serious but even if someone did the slightest thing wrong to me, I would totally change from a fun loving bloke to a monster. I wouldn't let many people take the piss and one of my mates felt the full wrath of my anger on this day as I feel he took the piss out of me big time. Seeing that this was my best mate and we pretty much did everything together, the more I write about this situation, the more of a piss take I see it being. We were all in the pub and I don't know how but I ended up pulling this right pretty little blonde girl in the pub and saw her on a few occasions at my mates house parties where we would get to know each other and had a snog a few times but nothing too serious. I was quite happy that things didn't go too far, as I know that when they did, I would just walk away.

Anyway, back to that night. I would end up having an argument with this girl which I will take full ownership for as I was pissed and sniffed up and was acting a complete prick. We ended up calling it a day as I was in no state to be with anyone and I wasn't giving up coke and alcohol for anyone. A couple of hours later once I've started to come down off the coke, I notice that my best mate is missing so I go out the back for a cigarette and get the shock of my life. There he is, standing with the girl that I was with just 2 hours ago and they looked very cosy together, if you get my drift. I walked towards them both and said 'call yourself a best mate, you fucking arsehole', his reply was 'well, you ain't together no more'. Correct me if I'm wrong but my best mate has just disregarded our friendship for some girl he has known for five minutes. I wasn't having any of it. I started shouting at the girl and he in turn stood up to me and that's the worst thing he could have done. Coming up in my face like I had done something wrong, plus he's now in my personal space and only one person had come in my personal space and it wasn't about to happen again. With that, I pulled my head back in anger and head butted him straight on the forehead and all hell broke loose. All my mates run out and split things up and because I made the first move I noticed most people backing him. Yes, I was out of my head but that still don't give my best mate a pass to taking the piss out of me, I would then lash out at everyone as I struggled to calm down. I had lost it. I take ownership and I could have dealt with things in more of an assertive way but that didn't enter my mind as he took the piss and that's all there is to it. Once things had all calmed down he said 'sorry', my reply was 'a bit late now ain't it ya mug' walking off as I was not sure if I was going to go off again.

I remember walking across the road and straight into The Plough And Harrow, the worst place I could of walked into if I was in a bad mood, but I had already hit the 'fuck it' button and the only thing on my mind was alcohol. Already I was taking the easy option out which was rather than deal with things is to block things out.

A week later and I would be in the pub again. Early as usual as my manager was so busy hitting targets and stats that I was free to do as I pleased, as long as I was doing my coursework and hitting my targets he didn't really care where I was. That day I even had time to go home and freshen up. Meeting my dealer at the end of the road I would pick up my wrap of cocaine feeling complete and made my way to the Moon and Sixpence.

I met a few mates in the bar and then made my regular trips to the toilet, opening my wrap before I had even entered the toilet. Within three seconds, I had my first line and my time of freedom had arrived, a quick look in the mirror and a swift wipe of the nose and I'm ready to go. Walking out to the bar I now want the full effect of my freedom and ordered a tequila, the two together was that buzz that every person found too good to stop. After a few beers I was starting to feel more free and the mask of entertainment goes on. Standing at the bar telling stories about myself and making everyone else laugh. I don't know why but it made me happy seeing others happy and I found something that I was good at. Then I decide to have a little look around and out of the corner of my eye I catch a beautiful girl standing with a mate at the bar. I couldn't believe my eyes, it was only my first love, you know the girl from the back of the bus! Looking as stunning as ever she smiled at me, I melted, I was absolutely sniffed out my head and didn't want her seeing me like that so I said 'how ya doing? Give me a minute' then I slipped off to the toilet. I washed my face with cold water to try and bring me down a bit, sorted my hair out and made my way back out to the bar. She smiled at me and we started speaking like nothing had happened and I had that same feeling, that I wanted to be with her but I couldn't risk anyone finding out my secret. I played it cool as a cucumber and wearing my mask, I would talk to her for a while, then go crack on with the boys, and doing what we do best and that was getting messy. She stayed in the pub for a while and then left, probably due to me acting like I didn't care when deep down I did. At this point I was dating a girl who came in the pub, we got on really well and within four weeks we were behind the pub totally pissed up having sex on a regular basis. By now I was totally becoming out of control, taking more and more cocaine, blocking out my demons and becoming more of an arsehole as time went on.

Me and the girl ended up going to Tenerife for two weeks but argued most days due to my drink and drug problem. Of an evening I would make my way into the town center and score myself some cocaine at two o'clock in the morning off some random bloke. Sad as it seems, for me it was all I knew and was the only thing that made me block out my problems and feel normal. On our journey home we would hardly speak to each other, it was all down to me and my insecurities. Yet again I would start to push her away, she was getting way too close for my liking.

One night in October 1997, at her parents' place, I would simply start an argument just so I can get out and have a beer. We were constantly arguing and the relationship wasn't going anywhere, I was totally wrong but at the time I just didn't see the pain I was causing her and couldn't deal with it all anymore. I left her house and jumped into my car which I just financed for £6.000.00, with at least two pints of beer in me already I drove off like a looney thinking I was someone special when really I was being a class a prick that could have killed someone.

Finally back in Welling I go meet my dealer, pick up my cocaine and make my way to The Falconwood Club which is another place I would go too to get messy. I walked straight through the front door into the toilet and had a quick line then walked into the bar. My cousin was in there with her best mate who I had never met as I didn't go to family parties as I was always too out of it.

She looked lovely and had a face like a china doll, we made eye contact with each other and both smiled. We clicked straight away and was talking to each other for a little while and then I would join a few mates in the club and we would have a game of pool. My cousin would then join us with her mate where we would spend the rest of the night socialising and drinking. At the end of the night we all said our goodbyes and everyone would go their separate ways.

I now know that after chatting to me that night my cousins mate turned to my cousin and said 'I'm gonna have his baby', bit strong after seeing each other for the first time that evening but she must of fell for my charm, well, the mask at least! We would meet up on a few more occasions at family parties and in the club, then we would start to meet up with each other without anyone knowing which kind of made things pretty exciting if I'm honest. My only problem was I was still drinking a lot and still getting through at least 6 grams of coke a week. Also, maintaining a job and now having to maintain the mask around somebody that I really started to like. I contemplated knocking the cocaine on the head as this is exactly how I lost the last girl I was with but if I carried on the way I was going I would lose this girl and that was something I couldn't let happen. Then someone would know that I wasn't right and I couldn't let that happen. If the truth be known, I didn't stop, I just cut down on the amount I was consuming as I couldn't deal with my brain without it. Also I didn't want to lose this girl as things had only just begun and it felt good plus, I was doing what your average bloke was doing and that was getting into a relationship. I was doing the norm and what a perfect way to hide my secret by creating what everyone else had, so that's what I did.

Now seeing each other on a regular basis and still not many people knowing, we decide to make it official. I wouldn't say I was 'in love' with her as she was more of a good friend at first, always listening and never judging. Could I tell her my secret? She seems to get me, I don't know how as I didn't get myself at the best of times but she just did.

My feelings for her were growing and I found myself with her more and more but still managing to socialise with my mates and still fit in a cheeky little session every now and then, in moderation of course. Well if you believe that, you'll believe anything as there was no such thing as moderation on these nights. These were brain break nights and I would take full advantage of them, it's what was getting me through a week and keeping my demons at bay. After being with each other for a while we were in a full blown relationship. All of my mum's side of the family had met her and given her the ok so I decided we would go over and meet my dad's side of the family in East London. There were two people's opinions that always meant everything to me and that was my nans (dads mum) and my aunts (his sister), these two ladies were very special to me and made my childhood so much easier. My new girlfriend would meet my Nan and my aunt and they both loved her as she was a people person and had no problem maintaining a conversation. They also saw that I looked happy and if I was happy then so were they. It was becoming easier to maintain a mask and a smile now as I was getting used to it, I would still struggle with my demons on a daily basis but found myself becoming stronger. Well that's what I thought, not realising my life was good because of the self-medicating I was doing and blocking things out rather than dealing with them. I had two people who I trusted more than anything but I still couldn't bring myself to tell them my secret as what could be done now? Nothing in my eyes, it was 15 years ago now and no one would remember or believe me. Still, nothing was going to stop me being in a relationship with a girl who understood me and if I'm honest, loved me. Another thing that was good about my new life is that I was keeping things on the down-low and edging away from all the pubs and messy sessions. I was finding myself spending more and more time with my girlfriend.

My girlfriend and my best girl mate got on really well which meant I had two people that really meant a lot to me and they got on like a house on fire which was a bonus. As long as they didn't want to know anything about my past.

So, things were on the up for me and I was starting to take control of my life even though I was dealing with my past most days. I suppose I was becoming stronger and sort of taking ownership of what happened to me. After all, if I would have listened to my mum that day, nothing would have ever happened to me so I knew it was my own fault.

Then those thoughts would go away for a while as the news of my Nan (dads mum) having breast cancer hit the family. I was devastated and couldn't believe that the nicest lady on the planet was to be given such a terrible illness. My Nan was Old School and she took it on the chin like a true warrior.

Now at the start of the Millennium, I am 22 years old and what a perfect time to announce that my girlfriend is pregnant. Things were on the up, just like I hoped and I could now focus on someone else as I was going to be dad. I couldn't have been happier and neither could my girlfriend. Even to the point where I asked my girlfriend to marry me at a family party, I could have done it in a bit more of a romantic way rather than hiding the ring in her mash at dinner as she nearly choked on the ring. That's just the crazy sort of mad things I would do. We went to see my Nan as she was ill and we told her the good news, she was over the moon and so happy to see me happy, that's all she ever wanted for me.

During this time I was living with my girlfriend at my mums as we were waiting for a flat to come up with the council. They gave us temporary accommodation which we didn't stay in as it was a complete shit hole and we couldn't do anything to it as it was only temporary. So it was easier to stay at my mums until a flat came up for us to live in. Then, just like that, with everything on the up things start to decline just as quick as they started. The day was now here for my girlfriend and me to go for our 12 week scan. She was so happy and she couldn't wait to get to the appointment to see our little bubba. We would sit in the waiting room talking about our future and how once we had a flat, our little family would be complete. Her name gets called and we walk into the little room, my girlfriend laid on the bed and pulled her top up over her belly with her nervous little face. The nurse entered the room and turned on the equipment and started to scan my girlfriend's stomach, then there was a pause, then another pause, then another pause, it was never ending. I look into my girlfriends eyes and see the tears running down her cheek. 'Where's my babies heart beat? Where's my babies heart beat?' The nurse looked at my girlfriend and then my girlfriend started to cry saying 'there is no heartbeat is there?' My eyes start to fill up but I need to remain strong as I can't imagine what pain my girlfriend was in but I felt like everything was taken again just like that. I walked over to my girlfriend, put my arms around her and just remained as strong as I could. After all, there wasn't going to be a baby as our little bundle of joy had died. With devastation in our eyes I looked at her and said 'I Love ya, let's get you home. You need to be at home and relax'. We then was informed that we had to go and then come back for our beautiful baby to be removed, my girlfriend was in a bad way and all I could do is comfort her as no one ever plans on how to deal with the loss of a child. Two weeks have passed and my girlfriend has had the operation and been through a very traumatic time but, like she did most of the time, she was also good at putting on a mask and getting on with things. I promised her we would have a child and we would be rewarded after losing our first child but that didn't help her as she just wanted the child we lost. I was just trying to make her feel better but I'm not sure if what I said was right at the time. My girlfriend went back to work and after a few weeks was acting like nothing had happened. I knew that was her way of dealing with it and she was keeping her mind occupied. I would go back to work at BT and everything would start to get back on track, it wouldn't be long before my girlfriend would say 'I want to try for another baby' then we would argue. It's not that I didn't want to, it's just that her body had been through so much and needed to heal but she didn't see it that way, she wanted another baby and nothing was going to stop that. I wanted a family unit to as I needed to focus my mind on something. I was struggling inside with my demons and having nightmares most nights as I wasn't self-medicating as much with alcohol and cocaine. I still I maintained the mask and stayed strong for my girlfriend.

Into March and I get a call from my Mum saying my nan was being put into a hospice and it wasn't looking good, she said I should go and visit her to pretty much say my goodbyes. What was going on? I was struggling already with my own shit, I had just lost a baby and now I'm going to lose my Nan. I would go visit the hospice with my family but at first I didn't want to go in as I wanted to remember my Nan with her brown curly hair, her rosy red cheeks and her glasses that she always wore. Then my mum explained this is your last chance to say goodbye son, it will be hard but it's not about you, your Nan would want to see you. I walked into a room holding back the tears and asked where my Nan was. A lady pointed to a bed and this little old lady looked nothing like my Nan, she looked so ill but like she was ready to go if that makes sense. I was there two minutes as I couldn't face it. As I walked out the room I turned right, fell to my knees and cried my heart out. I have felt the worst pain in my life as a child and this was just as bad. My Poor Nan. What had she ever done wrong in life? Nothing, nothing at all. A few days went by and then the family would get the news they never wanted to hear, my loving, caring, beautiful Nan had passed away. I was devastated and just couldn't believe what I was hearing, then I made the biggest mistake, I remembered that when I was in pain and struggling and couldn't face things I turned to alcohol and cocaine. So that's exactly what I did. I didn't think of my girlfriend and what she was going through and also what the rest of my family were going through. I just couldn't take any more pain as I was already dealing with my demons on a daily basis. It was all too much for me.

After my dear nans funeral in East London, my family and I made our way home and I was in a mess, struggling to deal with everything all at once. As we came down Shooters Hill I asked my mum to pull into the BP garage to get some fags, then once finished in the garage I said was going for a beer in The Anchor and Hope pub which was next door. When I got to the bar I ordered myself a beer and then went outside to meet my dealer as I had already texted him whilst in the BP garage. He looked at me and smiled, I said to him 'just give me the fucking gear, I ain't in the mood today mate'. He said 'sort yourself out mate', my reply was 'I would if ya stop replying to my texts ya prick' and I walked off.

STEVIE - BEHIND THE MASK

Now back in the pub, I make my way to the toilet and go straight in for the kill and sniffed the whole gram of cocaine from the two lines I'd cut. Within five seconds, everything had gone, my feelings, my emotions and I was ready to start my brain break. I ended up getting in a right state that day and had no cares or feelings at all regarding my family and friends around me. Selfish? Yes, maybe but no one else was dealing with my head so if I'm honest, at the time, I couldn't give a shit what anyone thought.

A couple of months later and after creating issues with my girlfriend we are starting to work things out, not that she had done anything wrong as it was always me that had the issues, not her. We decided to book a holiday to Tenerife and had booked to stay in the Hotel Bitacora, which is the same place that my family and I stayed when I was a kid. It was a well needed holiday as we had a lot going on recently and just needed a break from reality.

We spent two weeks there and had a great time as I managed to keep my alcohol consumption down which was a 'win-win' for everyone. We would spend most days around the pool, swimming, relaxing and just having a well needed break from England, we had a lovely time. I was dealing with my demons while we were away, I would be up and down like a yo-yo many times throughout the week but after experiencing it for so long I was getting used to it. Well so I thought or was it down to the self-medicating?

We got back to England and after being back at my mums for a couple of weeks, and that time had come again when my girlfriend would tell me that she was pregnant again. I was happy as a pig in shit but my girlfriend was a bit distressed as she had lost a baby and she had the thought in her mind is that she may lose another.

I told her that I was there for her but no matter what anyone did, she wouldn't accept anything until the new baby was born. I can understand as a man, what it is like to lose a child but for a woman that had carried that child, I could never imagine how that felt. She was so over the top and paranoid during the pregnancy but that was understandable considering what she had been through. Then that day would come, the day I think I was dreading, so god only knows how she must have been feeling. It was the three month scan. We arrived at Queen Mary's Hospital in Sidcup and we both couldn't wait to get into the room and check for a heartbeat. The nurse came in and told us both to relax and she then carried out her examination. We both looked at the screen and there it was, a beautiful little baby moving around with a very strong heartbeat. The tears in my girlfriend's eyes were priceless as they were tears of joy and not sadness. One healthy baby on the way and things were on the up again, surely they weren't about to get even better were they? Well yes, they were as at the start of 2001, my girlfriend and I got our first home which was a one bedroom flat in Lee Green that we were given by the council and it was just round the corner from her parents' house. This was a blessing for my girlfriend being near to her mum, especially now we had a little bubba on the way. I'm not sure if it was a blessing for me as her parents weren't exactly my biggest fans but I couldn't blame them, it's not like I gave them many reasons to like me if I'm honest. Maybe that would all change as it was now my time to prove them wrong by decorating our new flat with my dad. I spent a few thousand pounds on getting the flat in top notch condition for my new bubba and girlfriend but it would take more than that to win her parents over. They wanted someone who was going to look after their daughter and really that's how it should have been but I struggled sometimes putting that into action.

After a few months, the flat was all finished and my girlfriend was a month away from giving birth to our baby. We were settling into our flat nicely and was eating take-away most nights as my girlfriend craved curry. I suppose you could say we were happy and cosy awaiting our new baby and by this time, we knew we were having a baby girl. We would spend the night in bed thinking of names for our baby girl and for some random reason I asked my girlfriend what month our baby girl would be born in. I must have been out of it at the time! She replied 'May' and straight away I said 'why don't we call her Maisie?' She looked at me and smiled. Yes, I had said the right thing to my pregnant partner. Is that even possible? Well it is now. She said 'Maisie, yes I like it'. Well, for once I was right, I couldn't believe it, no laughing, no piss taking, she actually liked something I thought of, and I'm on a roll.

It's now 15th May 2001 and the day is finally here and my girlfriend went into labour. I was coked up again like the wrong'un I was becoming. I got all the bags and accessories together, got in the car and we made our way to Queen Mary's Hospital. Once we arrived there we were taken into a room and then I had a reality check, thinking to myself 'I'm just about to have a baby and be a dad and I'm in the labour room sniffed out my head!' What sort of man does that at one of the most special times of his life? Then my girlfriend starts to feel the pain of contractions but I'm sitting there now addicted to the gas and air machine, cracking jokes and laughing. I remember her calling me a 'fucking idiot' as I was acting like a kid.

Then, what I thought was going to be a romantic moment as she grabbed my hand, something that she never did, I quickly realised was far from romantic as she was squeezing my hand so tight trying to cause me as much pain as possible. I saw the look in her eye, that look that said 'You did this to me ya bastard' squeezing my hand tighter and tighter. She then relaxed and it was my time to escape and I asked the nurse if I could stand at the other end and watch my baby come into this world. Her reply was 'yes, of course you can, you're brave'. I walked around to the other end and look down, I start to see the baby's head, and it was the most amazing thing I have ever seen in my life. Shouting out to my girlfriend 'she's coming babe, keep going, keep going'. Then just like that, my baby girl comes into this world. I just had the most amazing experience of my life and I couldn't believe this little bundle of joy was fifty percent me. Finally I had done and got something right in my life. The nurse would then ask if I would like to cut the cord, my reply was 'I would love to'. So I grabbed the scissors like I know exactly what I was doing and I cut the cord but I only got halfway through which caused the blood to build up then like a complete plum I release the scissors and blood shot all over me, just like a fountain. Only I could fuck that up!

The nurse then put my little girl in a blanket and gave her to me, she was so beautiful, and I couldn't take my eyes off her. Her little hand wrapped around my finger straight away, she was a strong little thing, straight away we connected and I looked at her and said 'no one will hurt you darling, daddy loves you and I will always be here for you'. For once, I experienced real love and that was my baby girl. My baby girl was here and weighed 8lb 2oz and was born at 12:16 on the 16th of May 2001, a very special day in my life.

The next day people would visit to come and see the new addition to the family, I had no doubt in my mind that my best girl mate would be there to meet Maisie. She fell in love with her straight away, I looked at her partner and said 'you'll be next mate', he looked at me and said 'yeah mate, one day'. Mum and dad would come in the recovery room and see their first grandchild, my dad is a very hard man but he melted, straight away my baby girl had grandad wrapped around her little finger, I wouldn't have minded but she hadn't even spoken yet. He was hooked just like everyone else that visited, my mum wouldn't leave her alone either but I could see that my girlfriend just wanted to rest as she had done all the hard work. Once everyone had gone my girlfriend would go to sleep and I would just sit in the chair looking at this beautiful child that I created. I would talk to her knowing she couldn't understand but I didn't care I just wanted her to know how much I love her and no one would ever hurt her.

STEVIE - BEHIND THE MASK

Now back at our new home with our little bundle of joy, I find myself not wanting to block things out as I had my baby girl to keep me occupied. It's far from easy trying to bring up a child but I was going to give it a good go, nothing was for me anymore, it was all about my daughter. My girlfriend struggled big time with breast feeding and after a couple of days she decided to stop but if you want my opinion, it was the best thing for everyone as she couldn't sleep and we started arguing. I could have been a lot more supportive to her if I'm honest as she was doing most of it on her own but with time I started to pick things up which even surprised my girlfriend. Even to the point of saying to her every now and then, this dad thing is a piece of piss, she wouldn't even reply but just showed me her middle finger. As you can see she loved me dearly. We hit Bluewater and the credit card would come out lively, with me finding any excuse to spend, spend, spend. At the time Baby GAP was the place to be and that's where most of the credit card money went. My daughter got a whole new wardrobe and three hundred quid later my girlfriend had had enough of GAP and decided to make her way to some other overpriced shop and spent sixty quid on a newborn baby grow, I didn't get that if I'm honest as she would grow out of it in two weeks! I think my girlfriend was just making me pay for putting her through labour, oh yeah and for being a shithead most days.

My baby girl is growing fast and I start to notice than when I talk to her, she is trying to talk back to me, she was so addictive and I just wanted to be with her all the time, it was just the best experience. Like I said before, starting a family is not easy, especially for me and my partner as we were at such a young age, plus I was dealing with my own head on a daily basis and maintaining the mask, if not for myself, then for the person I loved most in this world and that's my daughter. The pressures were slowly building for both of us, even though we were a family unit. My girlfriend took everything one hundred percent seriously but I didn't, in fact, I was being a complete prick and finding myself pushing the people closest to me away again. Why? I couldn't tell you at the time, all I know is every now and then my personality would just change and the anger I would feel would be so strong. I would never hurt my girlfriend or my daughter, it was more anger towards myself, like a self-punishment. We would start to argue more and more, then I would become stubborn and just go out. Yeah, you guessed it, straight to the pub. She in return, would go over to her mums for the day. Her mum didn't like me as I wasn't really standing up to the plate like I should have been. Her mum had every right, I thought the world owed me a favour and I was contributing financially but not practically and emotionally like I should have been.

Then my daughter's first birthday would arrive. At this point I was struggling with my demons more than ever as I had seen the brothers a couple of times. It was at the point where I wanted to know who raped me that day as my secret was eating away at me bit by bit. I now had a child which made me think 'how could anyone hurt a child in that way?' I was trying so hard to maintain some sort of stability in the relationship and make things work but things were getting worse and worse, even arguing whilst the baby was in the room. This is all down to me not dealing with own issues and trying to bury them all the time.

Then the day would come that I would probably regret for the rest of my life. We were arguing and my girlfriend had my daughter in her arms, sleeping and me 'Mr. Insecure' decided to start shouting and arguing. My girlfriend ignored me, which is exactly what she should have done as I was being a complete arsehole, sniffed up to the eye balls again, with that, I put my hand through the balcony door window. Glass went everywhere. I could have seriously hurt anyone in that room with my explosive behavior. My hand opened up and blood was going everywhere. I then looked at my girlfriend and she looked at me as if to say 'I can't do this anymore'. She took my daughter to her mums and took me to the hospital as I needed ten stitches in my hand. If I were her I would have told me to walk after the trouble I had just brought on my new family. After that situation arising there is no way my daughter can grow up seeing this and just like that I had lost my new family that was keeping me going. Then that thought enters my mind, you fuck up everyone and everything around you, always pushing people away, always lashing out and it can't go on. If I stay away from the people I love and care about, everything will be ok. As there was no way I was telling anyone about my secret and was even willing to lose my own little family over it. People may think 'why? Why put yourself through this torture?' But, at the time it wasn't as easy as that and if I'm honest, that's why it was easier to block things out. So that's what I did. I blocked my secret out and I blocked out everything else in my life that was going wrong. I took the easy way out, after all, if in doubt block it out.

CHAPTER 5
GIVEN SO MUCH BUT LET IT ALL GO

AGE: 23 - 30 years old
YEAR: 2002-2007

Why should I apologise for the monster I have become? No one said sorry to me for making me this way. As you can tell, I am starting to notice that slowly but surely I am not only dealing with my childhood trauma, I am now dealing with addiction but I didn't care as I was happy, as far as I was concerned. After all, I had just lost the most important thing in my life, my little family but that thought hadn't even entered my mind as all I could think about was how I had hurt everyone around me and I am better off being on my own. Basically, I took the easy way out.

Now I am facing the humiliation of having to move back to my parents, this is when my addiction of alcohol and drugs would go up to the next level. The only problem was that I had already gone up a few levels regarding the drug ladder but my drug addiction was becoming out of control as it was taking over my everyday life.

From what I was told, my partner and my baby girl went to her mum's caravan for a long period of time. This made me think she was moving on with her life and I was to do the same. She was happy without me and if I'm honest, I would have got as far away from me as well if I was her, for her safety and for my daughters safety. I was totally out of control. I had no thought for anyone else's feelings but my own and the reason for this was that I was self-

124

medicating and blocking out life in general. I was starting to become the monster I never thought I was capable of being. Due to my drug and alcohol abuse increasing I found myself taking more and more time off work, not coping with my situation at all. I had already lost my family and now at the age of twenty five I was struggling to hold on to the job I had always wanted. My personality changing slowly but surely. My temper increasing the more and more I block things out but still I would continue to punish myself as my self-medicating was now becoming a full blown addiction. When I mean addiction, I'm talking ordering my cocaine on a Saturday morning at about eleven thirty just so I had it in my pocket before I had even gone to the pub. That way, I would start to feel that if I didn't have it before I left the house, I would feel naked! It was my mask for everything, my mind, my body and my soul. I felt normal whenever this substance was in my body. My body needed it and so did my brain as that would be the only time I felt that I was functioning properly.

Then one day I receive a letter in the post from my employer, explaining how I had to attend a meeting with higher management. I knew what was coming and that I was going to lose my job, but by then I had already hit the 'fuck it' button and my life was pretty much fucked and I only cared about one thing and that was to block out any pain in my life. The day before the meeting I finished work a little early as I knew what was coming so I thought 'don't give them any more of your time' but really I was just finding an excuse to go out and block out the real world and get into my world. I ended up meeting with a good mate of mine that was always there for me. He could have a fight and didn't exactly have the best start in his life, bit like myself if I'm honest. His outlook on life was the same as mine 'if in doubt block it out'. We spent the whole afternoon in the pub and into the evening as well, drinking and sniffing, sniffing and drinking, the night would then continue on as me and my mate were invited to a mate's house in Plumstead just near the common. I was in a bad way and had totally forgotten about my meeting in about five hours' time. Then things started to get out of hand and me and my mate end up on Plumstead Common, both with a Beretta gun in each hand firing blanks with real loud gunshots at each other thinking we was in the army rolling over the common. God knows what the people living around the common were thinking. It wasn't something I would do often and if I'm honest, it was just a strong bit of coke, that took me to a place away from reality and that's just how I liked it. 'Ring, Ring...' my phone alarm goes off and I opened my eyes. I didn't have a clue where I was. I shit myself as I remembered I needed to be in a meeting in an hour. I opened the front door to the house I had stayed in and lucky for me, my work van was only a five minute walk away. I practically ran to my van and once inside I felt a bit more at ease about making my meeting. Before I start up my van I had a quick look in the wing mirror and I couldn't believe what I saw. All I can say is it was lucky that I looked in that wing mirror or things would have got a lot worse at the meeting. My mate had decided to write the C-word across my forehead in red lipstick in massive capital letters. Not only had I been running along the street in my work uniform, out of my face but I also had that word written across my forehead. With that, I opened a bottle of water in my side door and washed my face while driving to my meeting with higher management. Finally I was starting to sober up. I popped a couple of mints in my mouth and sprayed on some deodorant to make myself feel fresh so I could go and face the music.

I was in the office for ten minutes and I couldn't tell you what was said, I was barely with it. All I know is that I heard the words 'your employment with us is being terminated with immediate effect'. Was I gutted? In all honesty I should have been but I wasn't. All I wanted to do was get out of there. Another engineer dropped me home and even waited while I went in and took my uniform off so he could take it back with him. Just like that another important thing I had lost in my life. First, my little family and now my career! The two things in life that makes a man feel like a man. I then had to go through the process of telling my mum and dad that I had now lost my job and not just any job, a job with prospects, a job with a pension, the list goes on. My dad acted like he didn't care but I knew he did and my mum was gutted but was still there for me. She had seen that I had lost my little family and was losing things as the weeks went on. They had no clue of my alcohol and drug abuse as I was good at hiding it, just like I was good at living behind a mask and hiding my childhood trauma. After all, the longer you do something the better you get at it and the mask was something that I was now a master at.

STEVIE - BEHIND THE MASK

Now at 26 years old and with no family and no job I find myself slowly but surely getting lower and lower. This wasn't all down to my secret but was the alcohol and cocaine starting to take its toll on my mind and my body. I was better off staying behind the mask because with the mask alone, I was a nice person putting on a smile and everything was ok, but now hiding behind the mask and on alcohol and cocaine things would now go from bad to worse.

I would find myself waking up on Boxing Day morning and this day would be the day that I would be using the second of my nine lives. A day I couldn't forget and yet again I would bring pain to my family and friends, well what friends I had left. After a day of drinking and a few arguments on the phone to my ex-girlfriend asking to see my daughter, I find myself blocking out more, sniffing cocaine and drinking a lot more than what I normally would. My mobile phone rings and my ex-girlfriend is on the other end ranting and raving about my behaviour, she tried explaining that if I sort myself out I can see my daughter but I wasn't having any of it as, at the time, I thought the world owed me a favour. I wasn't letting anyone control or tell me what to do, that happened once as a kid and it wasn't happening again. She was trying to help me but my head was all over the place and I was starting to have enough of everything. Maintaining my secret was getting to me, even though I was now under the influence of cocaine. The drug that was blocking everything out was now not doing its job as my brain was becoming more immune to it as I had been taking it for 8 years and it wasn't blocking out like it used too.

We continue arguing on the phone then I tell her to 'fuck off' and hung up. I was keeping myself to myself and then some bloke in the pub turns round and says, 'no wonder you don't see your daughter mate'. I look at him and my reply was, 'what did you just say you little prick? Then, like a brave man he said the same thing again but before he had finished I had flipped, I grabbed an ashtray and smacked him in the side of the head with it. Then I jumped on top of him and started to punch him in the face, there was blood all over my hands and two people ran over and dragged me off of him. They were telling me to 'calm down' and 'this ain't you Stevie, you're a nice bloke. What's wrong mate?' 'Fuck the lot of ya' was my reply. Yes, I am a nice guy, until some prick starts talking about my daughter. I don't care if he was right. If he'd have said anything else I would have been fine but this random bloke wants to talk about my daughter! No man talks about my daughter but me and that's just how I saw it at the time. I'd had enough and in this moment I planned my first suicide attempt but the crazy thing was that I was actually going to go through with it. I called up someone and ordered six ecstasy tablets and met him up by Shoulder Mutton Green, before that I had walked into the off licence and bought a half bottle of vodka. I made my way to the middle of the green where it is pitch black and sit down going over my life trying to find some sort of reason for wanting to live but nothing, not a single thing. I look at my phone and it's 1:00am and there isn't anyone is around, now it's time. I put my hand in my pocket, pulling out a rizla and I roll myself a joint. I smoked it as quickly as possible and then I wrapped all six ecstasy tablets in a rizla and put them in my mouth, washing them down with the whole half bottle of vodka. Finally, no more dealing with the thoughts of my childhood. Finally, I could be at peace and I was praying that I was successful and wouldn't wake up.

Well surely taking six E's in one hit would do the job. After all, I already had about two grams of cocaine in me and at least twelve pints of beer. Well the job would have been done if a lady hadn't decided to walk her dog across the middle of the green at two in the morning. She found me on the floor, foaming at the mouth with a start-stop pulse. From what I have been told the lady called an ambulance and because of this she saved my life but at the time that's not what I wanted. They got me in the ambulance and was putting drips, etc. in me and I was in a really bad way. I don't remember much in the ambulance but once I was at the hospital I would start to realise my surroundings and would break down into tears. Why am I here? Why didn't I die? Which one of you arseholes saved me? You have got no right, it's my life and I decide what to do with it!

Within a few hours of being in the hospital, I would find myself being sectioned for attempting to take my own life. I was admitted to Oxlea's and was now a full member of the 'nut house', I had lost the plot and was under twenty-four hour watch for my own safety. My room had a fake mirror so I couldn't cut or hurt myself and all phone chargers were kept in a locked cupboard to stop me hanging myself. I was at rock bottom. I really didn't see the point of being here as I was so damaged as a child, I knew I was different and for that reason I didn't want to be here and deal with my secret anymore. The hospital gave me every chance to tell them about my secret but all I could think was 'what would people think? Would they even believe me?' I blamed everything on the alcohol and drug abuse as it was the easiest thing to say rather than deal with my secret and let the whole world know what I had been through.

After ten days of being in a prison, I would find myself a lot happier and being off the cocaine and alcohol was giving me a clear head, well that's what I thought at the time anyway. But really I was still a junkie as I was now being controlled by legal drugs from the chemist, I was on daily medication in the hospital. That is the real reason that I was happy, I was dosed up with drugs to suppress my brain and numb my emotions as they didn't know what was wrong with me. Everything was slowing down where I was so knocked out from the strong medication. Yet again, I was being controlled by people I didn't know which was something I struggled to deal with. I would start arguments and accuse them of poisoning me, when really I was paranoid and was on a 'come down' from all the drugs and alcohol I was so used to consuming over the last 8 years.

Then one day I was called into the office where I would have a conversation about how I was feeling. I wasn't honest with them and lied and said 'I'm feeling fine' as I was locked away and felt that I was being controlled. I just wanted to get out of there but that wasn't happening. After all, I had no idea of how serious the recent events was as I was too out of it to realise. Then one day my mum and dad would come to visit me and it was dinner time in the hospital. I had sausage, mash and beans and the reason I'm telling you this is that I thought I would play a little joke on my mum and dad. I asked the people at reception to let them in and while they walked down the corridor, I looked at my plate, grabbed a big lump of mash and put it on my head, followed by two sausages which I pushed into the mash making me look like a proper crazy person. My mum looked at me and nearly started crying. She looked at my dad and said 'look at him? He ain't better, he has gone mad!' With that, I wiped it off my head, smiled at my mum and said 'got ya'. Her reply was 'you bastard, I thought you had proper lost it'. Then she smiled and gave me a cuddle as she saw a bit her old son coming back, she looked so happy bless her. You would think that smile would be enough to make anyone change but not for me as I was dealing with my secret and my poor mum and dad didn't have a clue. Before leaving, my mum would say to me 'someone wants to come and visit you', I asked who she was referring to, and then she said a name I thought I would never hear again. She mentioned my first loves name. I looked at my mum and my eyes filled up, mum said she had been asking after me and asking how I was. I was so happy as she knew me more than anyone, she didn't know my secret but she just got me.

Then after a good six years the day comes that my first love would come visit me. I had lost her once and I never wanted that to happen so I wasn't going to let it happen again. She must love me as she had come to a hospital to see me which couldn't have been easy for her as it wasn't your everyday hospital, in fact, it was a very unpredictable and scary place. She walked into the visiting room and she looked stunning. She hadn't changed one bit, she still had them features, looking like 'Baby' from Dirty Dancing. Blond curly hair, beautiful soft skin and lovely white teeth. Pristine condition as always but something was different, she didn't look happy but was trying to hide it. We talked like we had never split up and she mentioned that when I am better and out of there we could meet up. Finally, things were coming together and I spent the next week concentrating on getting better. The thought entered my mind to tell them in the hospital about my secret but now my first love was back on the scene, I couldn't risk losing her for a second time. I knew if anyone could get me through, it would be her. All I wanted was to go home so I could get my life back on track and hopefully get back together with my first love. I didn't let her know how much I wanted to get back with her as I was still maintaining my mask and not letting my emotions or feelings known to the outside world. Then they decide I am well enough, in their eyes, to go home and start to rebuild my life. I was happy to leave but that place pretty much saved my life and managed to give me some hope in moving forward, so I was a little sad to leave if I'm honest. I was given my medication and was free to leave. I was admitted in December 2003 and was released in January 2004 and it felt like I had been in there ages. I walked out the door and got my first breath of fresh air and I felt good but also nervous about coming back out into society. The sun was shining, the air was fresh and I suppose for the first time, since my suicide attempt, I was glad that the lady walking her dog had found me.

I would meet up with my first love a couple of times, then she would ask me round for dinner at hers. She lived in Charlton so we went to a little pub near there where we would have a few drinks but for some reason I was drinking slowly and taking in my surroundings as I knew how easy it would be for me to get right back into the situation. I made a promise to myself in hospital that I would try and maintain some sort of stability as I couldn't go in hospital again as I didn't want anyone knowing about my secret. We would laugh and joke with each other, talking about old times and how we used to spend ages talking on the house phone. Then we walked back to her place and she cooked me dinner and we got more comfortable. We both sat on the sofa talking while drinking a glass of wine each. She looked beautiful, as always, I remember thinking 'how can I be in a Mental Health Hospital bed four days ago and now I could end up sleeping in my first loves bed?' For once in my life I didn't feel lonely as even though she didn't know my secret she just seemed to understand me. She was in love and so was I but we both didn't show it at first. I ended up staying the night at her place and we had a lovely time. She made me feel complete and made my situation so much easier to deal with in my head as she was the one who knew me best. I felt I could be the real me a bit as she took me for what I was, a little crazy but my heart was in the right place when needed. I was a lucky boy! In the morning she even cooked us a fry up, then dropped me home as she had to get back for her kids. She was a good Mum as until she could trust me to be in her and her kid's life, she wouldn't introduce me to them. That just made me like her even more as she was a loving caring mum, just like my mum.

My mum and she got on so well, but that was never in doubt as they were both good mums that loved their children and had so much in common. I would start to go to family parties more often as I now have a good one on my arm and as the saying goes 'behind every good man is a good woman'. Things were the best they had been in ages and we were happy doing the things that happy couples do, going to social gatherings, parties and other places where there were many people drinking. I would start to slowly drink more as I struggled to be in busy places with people I didn't know but at the time my girlfriend looked so happy and I wasn't going to let my situation mess up the rest of her life as it had already destroyed most of mine.

After a while my girlfriends ex would start to cause a bit of trouble for me as he wanted no other man in his kids life apart from him. I totally get it as I would feel the same with my daughter but he had his demons as well so at first I would ignore the situation. He was confusing his own kids and I was just starting to get on with them but their dad is their dad so no matter who is in the wrong they will always choose their dad and so they should. In turn, my partner and I would argue through no fault of my own and already her ex was coming between us. I should have ignored it but I had the thought in my head of being controlled by her ex just because he didn't want us to be together. I wasn't putting up with it and her poor kids were now confused again, already there was so much drama in the situation. In turn, my girlfriend would go a bit cold as her focus was her kids and I totally got that. Things were up and down like a yo-yo, all because her ex didn't want her but didn't want anyone else to have her. We would argue with each other as I didn't agree with the way her ex was acting, bearing in mind I had done the same thing with my ex and only saw my daughter when she was at my mums. Then I would do what I normally do when I couldn't deal with things and that's push people away and block out my problems rather than deal with them head on. I should have ignored the whole situation regarding her ex but he had got what he wanted and that was for us to be apart. Now, not knowing if we are together or not as many arguments have now been caused, it's time to do what I do best and turn a molehill into a mountain in my brain. I wanted cocaine and I wanted alcohol as I didn't have to put up with all this shit in life. So, do what you need to do Stevie, just like that I switch and make my way to the pub on Shooters Hill that I would drink in when on a blocking out session.

I remember that if my account had no money in I could buy a drink and get £45.00 cash back and you could do that many times. I did it about eight times and was just short of £400.00. I stopped it after a while as I was fleecing the bank out of money. I was on self-destruct and now had £400.00 to help me on my journey. I walked out into the pub car park and made the call, 'three grams please mate' I said, he said 'give me ten minutes mate' and I said 'let's make it five minutes mate and 1 will take four grams'. He arrived in ten minutes and I still bought four maybe that was an excuse to buy another one as I knew he wouldn't be five minutes. As soon as they put it in my hand I felt complete again, I can't explain why I felt this way, I'm guessing that's addiction for you. I didn't care what it was, I was happy! My problems were gone and I took the easy way out again. As soon as I walked in the toilet, I would have no consideration for anyone or anything as I needed my fix and that's all that was on my mind. I sniffed a whole gram in two lines and made my way back to the bar ordering a double vodka and red bull. I was on the top shelf tonight and was totally on self-destruct.

I wasn't nasty to anyone. The only person I punished when in this situation was myself, going to the toilet every fifteen minutes, sniffing a line, then straight back to the bar for a double vodka and red bull. I would repeat this at least ten times.

It's then that I would just be free from all my problems and I could start to get a bit loud saying exactly what I wanted and how I felt about the world but I would never mention my secret, no matter how drunk I was. I would get into arguments with people as they would look at me like I'm shit, casting judgement without even knowing me, like they were something special because they could handle what life has thrown at them. Well I couldn't as I knew no different, I saw the world different from such a young age. I wasn't changing, unless someone could remove my secret from my mind, which no one could so I was just going to continue fighting through the tough days and self-

137

medicating until someone could tell me otherwise. At the end of that day I had consumed three grams of cocaine and 16 vodka redbulls. That may be hard for you to understand but I felt normal, I felt happy and most importantly, I felt free.

Me and my first love would be on and off like a light switch and things were so unstable in the relationship. After all, I was back on the cocaine and alcohol and it was all down to me again and my insecurities in life. She would try so hard to get to the route of my unstable behaviour, always asking why I have to get so bladdered all of the time and why lie to her about cocaine. 'Just talk to me' she would say, 'I will help you through things'. Yet again, someone gave me the opportunity to open up and deal with my secret so I could start to live my life rather than just be an existence, but I was having none of it. How would they understand? How could they help? Would they believe me? I would just say to her 'you will never understand' and I would walk out of the room, putting on a brave face and totally ignoring the fact that yet another person was giving me the opportunity to talk but it wasn't as easy as that. I would think of the ripple effect it would cause my family, more hurt for my parents and most importantly the effect it would have on my daughter as I was already a shit Dad and that would have already impacted her.

I will forever feel the pain of how I treated my daughter but at the time I didn't love myself so how could I love anyone else. Plus, my addiction started to control my life more than ever and my feelings and emotions were becoming more numb as time went by.

STEVIE - BEHIND THE MASK

Now into July 2005, yet again, my girlfriend and I have split up for about the fourth time and yet again, I take full ownership and it was my fault. I was still drinking and sniffing but I am realising my life is going nowhere and I make the decision to give myself something to focus on and decide I will start 'the knowledge' once I get myself a bike so I could become a London Black Taxi Driver, just like my dad and hopefully make him proud for once.

My mum and dad helped me finance the bike, it was brand new and I could now get about rather than walking everywhere. After a week or so, the company that sold me the bike said I need to pop into the garage so they could do a general check to see how the bike was going. I said 'no problem' and I would pop my bike in the morning. I got up in the morning and went out and started my bike, got myself ready and made my way to Swanley where I bought the bike from. While driving down the road it becomes more open and it was a sunny day. I thought I was nuts on a moped and was only wearing shorts, t-shirt and crash helmet. In front of me is a rocker type person with what I could only describe as half a car and half a bike welded together, more of a cruising bike, nothing too fast.

Then I noticed the car/bike was indicating over to the left, so, as I was taught on my bike lessons I indicate to edge out to go round her doing 40mph. As I go around her, she full locks to the right to do a U-turn, she hits me and I divert and am thrown fifteen feet in the air. I land, scraping my body across the floor wearing only shorts and t-shirt. I landed thirty feet from the impact and was cut and scratched down one side from shoulder to toe. In shock, I jump up and collapse straight away and correct me if I'm wrong but I've just used life number three of nine. An ambulance was there within minutes and I was strapped to a board, which is something I didn't deal with to well as felt it like I was being strapped down and tied up. Once at the hospital I was taken in and checked over, I couldn't believe that apart from some deep cuts and grazes down one side of my body, I hadn't broken a bone or damaged any organs. Mind you, the pain from my skin scraping along the road was stinging like mad and as usual I was loaded up with medication to kill the pain. I would spend the night in the hospital and then the next day I could go home, limping on crutches as I had a bit of a bruised leg which had tightened up over the night. My bike was a week old and was a complete write off. I was in a complete state and I was back to square one again. All I wanted was to try and make something of myself and I end up in an accident through no fault of my own. Yes, you guessed it, back on the cocaine and alcohol. Taking the easy way out again.

By this time I was having no contact with my ex as I was in no fit state to maintain a relationship as I could hardly maintain myself mentally. As far as my physical appearance would go, I didn't look like your average junky. I would always look smart and take pride in my appearance as it was part of the mask and keeping my secret deep within. By now, I had pushed all my mates I had grown up with away as well, due to my drug and alcohol abuse and crazy behaviour. I was now on my own little journey doing what I needed to do and if I'm honest, I wasn't happy but anything was better than having a clear head and dealing with my problems. My alcohol and drug abuse was increasing rapidly, to the point where there were some nights I would have parts of it that I don't even remember! There was this one night, I was on a complete mission for total block out, but on this night I would take things to another level! The only reason I know what happened was due to people that were in this place at this time and they told me and also I received a text from someone.

It was a miserable day in 2006 and I'm 28 years old. I find myself in a pub in Welling with three other people, I wouldn't say they were good friends but more like acquaintances and had the same two things in common with me, alcohol and cocaine. After a messy session in the pub and last orders were just called I'm now wanting to carry on through the night and start planning where the afters are going to be. Then one of the blokes I was with says 'let's go brass house'. Before you know it, we are outside the pub and decide to go to the brass house. For anyone that has never heard of a brass house it's basically a brothel. Plus, it was somewhere you could have a late drink as well so I was more than up for that, so off to the brass house we went.

Once outside, one of the blokes would push the buzzer and the mistress would answer asking what we wanted. One of the blokes would say his name to her and she would let us have access. We walked up a dark flight of stairs expecting everything to remain dark. We would then come to a door, once through the door there was a few sofas and a lady sitting on a chair looking as kinky as you like. Did she look sexy? Maybe, but I didn't give a shit what she looked like as I had just had a line of cocaine and now needed beer. A few of the blokes would go off into rooms with ladies and do what they needed to do and I would sit in the main lobby with the madam and drink fosters at £2.00 a can. Not only were they cleaning up with 'money for sex' but they were doubling their money on every single can of beer they was selling. There would be a few other blokes in there and everyone was doing their own thing but I noticed this one bloke was sniffing something out of a bottle. Me, willing to do anything to block out my secret out, asked him what it was, his reply was 'poppers, try it mate'. Normally I wouldn't entertain it as I didn't trust people but when I was 'out of my face' that all went out the window as I was numb and my feelings were nowhere to be seen. I then take the bottle from the bloke and put the bottle under my nose and sniff, taking in the fumes from the liquid in the bottle and inhaling them through my nose. Then, I heard a voice say 'count down from five'. So I do. Five, Four, Three, Two, One and have some of that! I went to another level. My head went fuzzy, all of a sudden everything was happy. I felt like I was dreaming, then thirty seconds later I'm back and the buzz had worn off. The problem I had was that it didn't last long, which means I wanted more. The other people are all having a regular sniff of this bottle and for some reason I just come out with 'can you drink that stuff to get a longer buzz?' his reply was 'you're off your head mate!' He then passed me it in a way as if to say 'you wouldn't mate', well that's what I thought he was thinking. I take it from him, put the bottle to my lips and do what I usually do and take things one step too far. Swigging from the bottle I feel some liquid enter my mouth and then I swallow. This time there was no five count down as just like that, everything is total block out. What I mean by this is, I was alive but I don't remember what happened and don't remember anything else after that point.

The next thing I open my eyes and can hear my mobile phone ringing. I sit up and gather my thoughts, look around and I'm in my own bed. Happy Days, I must of had an early night or did I? I look at my phone and I have four missed calls from a number and a text from a random number. I open the message and it says 'alright Stevie, can you bring that £80.00 to me from last night and I will see you soon'. I reply 'who is it?' She says 'the brass house you were in last night', she then gives me the address and I'm thinking it's the blokes I was with in pub, winding me up. I get out of bed and walk into the bathroom, turn around and there are black footprints on the bathroom floor so I look at the bottom of my feet and they are black on the bottom. I jump straight into the shower and sort myself out and get ready. Before I leave the house, I look for my Gucci loafers and can't think where I had put them so put on a pair of trainers and made my way to brass house. I press the buzzer and the madam asks who it is and buzzes me in. Once upstairs I walk through the door and there are two security people and the madam. I notice that my Gucci loafers were on the side and they were all smiling and laughing at me. She asked me for the money and gave me my loafers back. I said 'what the fuck happened last night?' her reply was 'the best night in here for ages!' then I said 'why?' She then explained what had happened last night and I didn't believe a single word of it until I had spoken to the other two blokes who I went in there with the night before. I drank some poppers and apparently was really funny and doing crazy things, but the craziest had to be what I am about to tell you.

I normally just go in there for a late drink but after drinking the poppers I started demanding a lady for free but in a funny, joking way, then the madam said £80.00 Stevie and you can. I said I had no money and took off my new Gucci loafers which cost £260.00 and slammed them on the desk saying that should cover it. Then I had a prostitute which is something I had never done before but to make it even worse, once I had finished, I took a beer out the fridge opened it and said 'see ya later everyone' and walked out. I had walked all the way to Welling which was a good 2 miles barefooted hence the dirty feet, just so I could sleep with a lady, not sure if it was to feel like a man or because I was so out of my head. As you can now start to tell, the more and more I kept my secret in, the more damage I was doing to myself, self-medicating day after day would take its toll on anyone but my self-medicating was no longer my medicine but my addiction.

I would start to blame society for what I had become. I would blame family for what I had become. In fact, I was blaming everyone apart from myself for what I had become. My secret was not my fault but not dealing with it and blocking it out with alcohol and drugs was my fault. At the time I wasn't taking ownership of my problems or the decisions I had made in life as I just couldn't face them, I didn't know how to. I would notice, as a kid, my moods would change from one day to the next and I was never really maintaining any stability. Now on the alcohol and cocaine I would find my moods changing not only daily but hourly, totally blocking out reality.

Yet again, I was doing what I need to do and I couldn't care who was suffering or who was hurting. I simply didn't give a fuck about anyone. My own family, I would treat terribly and what friends I had left, I would push away. I was content being on my own as that way, I wouldn't have to explain myself to anyone and go about doing what I want, when I want, like the selfish arsehole I was. All due to my thoughts and feelings being clouded by alcohol and drugs. It's because of my selfish attitude and disregard for anyone else's feelings that I would now use the fourth of my nine lives. Another trauma happened that changed my outlook on life forever.

It was Friday 4th August 2006. I wasn't going out as much because I wasn't liking the block outs I was having so I was avoiding meeting up with any Tom, Dick and Harry, just to get on it. So, it's Friday morning and I feel like I need to get out of the house as my mind was processing so many thoughts because I was fixating on my secret again and I was realising that this was keeping me stuck in the past. I end up going food shopping with my mum and dad. They could see my life slipping away and had already seen me lose everything slowly but surely, they weren't giving up on me just yet though as they didn't know why they were losing their son, slowly but surely. Once up Bexleyheath, in the open, I would start to have a chat with my mum and dad and doing what I should be. Then, it took one thing and one thing only for me to forget everyone around me and do what I wanted to do again. After all, no one else was living the nightmare in my head was they? One of my mates, who I had grown up with and had a few messy sessions with, was in the pub with his a couple of his mates. I was having a chat with him about something then just turned around to my mum and dad and said 'you go, I'll have a couple of beers and I will be home soon'. My dad looked at me as if to say 'that didn't take long' and even said as he walked out, 'see ya tomorrow' he was shaking his head but at the time I didn't care, I was about to have another brain break. It started off well but as some of you know, sometimes you go out, but as Micky Flanagan says on this day we went 'Out Out!' The beers were flowing and me and my mate had met up with a few others and the alcohol and cocaine started to flow. Straight away, I would be on form, having a laugh with people, cracking jokes, maintaining the mask and doing what I do best, pretending my life and world is the best it's ever been.

As the night progresses, we end up going back to one of my mates flats in Slade Green. We go through the whole night, getting on the cocaine, drinking alcohol like it was water, smoking joints like cigarettes and taking ecstasy tablets like smarties. A good night out? Just a bit, but it wasn't stopping there, well, my mate was and he was trying his hardest to get me to go with him as he knew I had hit the 'fuck it' button. After a while of trying to get me to get a cab with him, he gave up and went home which is exactly what he should of done and so should I but I wasn't stopping anytime soon and neither was one of the other blokes. When my mate left, the other bloke took me under his wing and kept an eye on me. He was a lovely bloke and made me feel very welcome when I was out with him and I was ok with him as he was a bit of a face around Slade Green. He then received a call to say there was a garden party at someone's house where there would be food and alcohol, not that I was eating but the alcohol was enough for me to go. I had now been on a 24hr session and it was about midday and I was still sniffing and blocking things out and I was becoming out of control, but my mates mate was still there keeping an eye on me. There was a paddling pool that was about two feet deep and was full of water so the kids could play in the pool as it was a very hot day, one minute it was empty and the next minute it was full. The kids were all around six to ten years old and were all laughing and having fun. I would start to think 'why couldn't I have been happy like them kids? Why has my life like turned out like this? It's that bastard in the woods fault! With that, the kids all get out of the paddling pool to eat and the pool is empty. Just like that, I thought 'I can't deal with life anymore'. I ran, jumped into the air with my head in a diving position and enter the two foot paddling pool at full impact. I intended to kill myself. Whether I ended up with brain damage or died, either way, I won't have to deal with my thoughts anymore. My head impacted the bottom of the paddling pool and the force of my body weight impacted my neck. I was face down in the pool and must off knocked myself out for a bit. I then jumped up with all my neck and head feeling like jelly and my head falling back and I couldn't hold it up. I laid on the floor

147

holding my head either side shouting my mates mate name out. He came over and said 'you ok?' I said 'I can't feel my legs and I can't move my neck, I need an ambulance'. He went and called an ambulance straight away and was by my side until the ambulance arrived. I can honestly say that if it wasn't for him that day I certainly wouldn't be here as he calmed me down and stopped me from getting up or moving. Before I know it, I'm numb all over but I can feel shooting pains up my spine, the ambulance needed to get me on a board and it was the most painful thing I have ever experienced. They took me to the ambulance as slow as they could but the pain was too much and I remembered that I kept passing out. The next thing, I'm in a machine in the hospital strapped up and having no feeling from the neck down. I felt trapped and starting crying. I was trying to move and shouting out 'get me out this fucking machine' then the next thing I know, I was being sedated and was put to sleep. They would spend the next hour studying my neck to see what damage was done. I then woke up and was told to stay still and that I was being transferred to Stanmore Hospital but because I was in a critical way, I would have to be airlifted by helicopter from Darenth Valley Hospital. I didn't know what was going on, all I knew was I dove in that pool with intentions of causing damage to myself and I had got my wish. I had paid a very big price as I had broken my neck! I remember being escorted out to the helicopter as I could hear it but I couldn't see it as I was strapped to a board with a neck brace on. I was so scared but if you do the crime, you do the time! Trying to take my life was the crime and living with a broken neck would be the time. I lived and I didn't want to. I couldn't even think of a decent way to kill myself. I even failed at that. I was then injected with morphine and everything went dark, the next thing I know I'm in an Intensive Care Unit at Stanmore Hospital with a load of wires and machines hooked up to me. I felt so trapped, just like I did that day in the woods and yet again I would start to cry and cause drama within the hospital where I was just sedated again.

At this point, while I was dealing with my shit, my mum would get a phone call from the hospital saying I was in hospital and before they could tell her why my dad shouted out in the background 'fuck him, leave him there'. It might have sounded harsh but I had already caused them so much pain and hurt and was showing no signs of changing and being the man he wanted me to be. Then the lady had explained that it was very serious and my mum and dad would make their way to Stanmore Hospital where they would be informed of what had happened to me.

I remember my mum walking in to the room and seeing me holding back the tears as she had just been told that I might not walk again. I was still feeling numb and if I'm honest, I felt like a football and that was it. The football being my head as I couldn't feel much else. I was so trapped and was now dealing with a clear head and my problems but I couldn't move, it was absolute hell. As if I hadn't been through enough already! But, that's what happens when it comes to keeping secrets and letting it eat away at you, blocking out with alcohol and drugs. I didn't know at the time that my mum had been told such sad news and I just lay there waiting for a decision to be made, then the specialist doctors came up and told me I would be operated on. They would cut me open on the back of my neck where they would put metal plates, nuts and bolts in my neck during a four hour operation. Then they would stitch me up afterwards, leaving a naughty scar right down the center of my neck.

Life was at an all-time low and I wasn't really fussed about whether I was alive or dead. All I was just an existence. Please let me die. Please. But no, him up there wasn't going to take me yet. He still had plenty in store for me, that's for sure. Then, a while after the operation my eyes open and I jump up out of bed like nothing had never happened. Pulling wires out of me and having feeling all over my body but my neck was very sore. The doctor looked at me as if to say 'how's this possible? You broke your neck in a serious way yet you're standing there right in front of us'. They lowered me into bed where I was sedated again as I needed to keep still as I had just had a major operation. Yet again, I was alive and I was going to be ok. That was life number four out the way, 'what you got in store for me next?' I would be admitted to my bed for a good week and had a morphine drip in me as the pain was so bad, sometimes I would just pass out. I would also be feeling sorry for myself, asking my mum and dad why no one was visiting me but I actually had lots of visitors, I just couldn't remember as I was so sedated.

I did hit my head hard that day so I probably still had concussion from trying to take my life. What a pathetic way to try and take your life. Why didn't I take another overdose? That would have been easier and would have caused less pain for myself and others around me.

In the bed opposite me was a really nice bloke, he was in the army and was fit and healthy. He was on a fun day out spending time with his family and decided to put on a big soft sumo suit so he could entertain his children by running into another person who was wearing one. It was all safe and many other people were doing the same thing but he fell funny and had broken the third vertebrae in his neck which was less of an injury than I had. The difference being, this bloke could not feel anything from the neck down and would maybe get the feeling back in his arms but never like they used to be. I would struggle to deal with his situation as he was doing nothing wrong. All he was doing was being a good dad and spending time with his family. He didn't drink or take drugs, he was fit and he was in the army. Then there was me who had broken the second and third vertebrae in my neck and I was going to make a full recovery. Yet, I was a coke head druggy that spent more time drinking than anything else. I was a shit dad, a shit son, I did nothing with the family and I'm fine. That wasn't sitting well with me as it should have been the other way around. He was contributing to society and his family, whereas I was a menace to society and giving absolute zero to my family. Plus, I meant to cause myself damage and he didn't. What was I doing? Apart from being the most selfish, self-absorbed person on the planet.

The thing that made me feel even worse is that I would lie to family and friends about what really happened regarding me breaking my neck that day. I told them that on that day, a baby was swimming in the pool and had gone under the water, so I leaned in to get her and slipped. Trying to be a hero rather than a selfish druggy arsehole. I'm so so sorry to all my family and friends that I lied to but at the time I couldn't tell anyone my secret from my childhood and I would do anything to stop it coming out. I have taken ownership of my situation now and am no longer afraid to speak the truth as I'm no longer hiding a secret or hiding behind a mask of alcohol, drugs and fakeness.

After a lot of time in hospital, finally the day would come that I would be able to go home and try to rebuild my life yet again after using the fourth of my nine lives. The specialist doctor explained that my recovery would be a marathon and not a sprint and my injury wouldn't heal by next week. He also stated that I must wear a plastic and foam collar around my neck and take my time in anything I do. Another thing I was struggling to process, as I was a hyperactive person and had spent the last ten years out in pubs, getting messy and spending very little time in doors, now I had to stay at home. I had so much going on in my head as I had to stay in bed, it would take me ages to get up the stairs and if I'm honest, it was so painful. I would hardly sleep at all which wasn't the worst thing as whenever I had a clear head and did sleep, I would have nightmares and it was always the same one about that day in the woods. My moods would be terrible, talking to people like shit and like they owed me a favour. The reason for this is that I was no longer getting my fix of alcohol and cocaine, which would show how reliant I was on alcohol and drugs as they blocked out my childhood and let's face it, I was now an addict. The more time went on, the more frustrated I would become as I was stuck in my bedroom. I could hardly move and was dealing with all my problems which were now on the front of my mind due to getting a clearer head. Then, I would lie about my sleeping pattern saying I was getting no sleep because I was in pain all the time. I know this was wrong but at the time I needed something to block out the thoughts and feelings. I couldn't go anywhere and was stuck in a room most of the day. I managed to get someone to get some cannabis for me which was helping with the pain but now at least I was getting a brain break from all the thoughts in my head and was starting to have a more relaxed outlook on things as my brain was now numb from the medication and cannabis I was taking. After all, there is no way I could deal with my head as now I was limited to where I could go and what I could do, so it was easier to just hide away from society and smoke cannabis. Just like every other drug, you become used to it and need more but the problem I had was that I was now relying on a drug to block out my problems but I had no income to be able to pay for it as no one was going to employ someone with a broken neck. As time went on I would find myself becoming more of a hermit. I was more than capable of going out but I was avoiding society as much as possible as I knew how easy it was to get back into an addiction that was ruling my life and had already taken so much from me.

I couldn't take any more staying in as my mind needed to be active while recovering from a broken neck. I decided to start walking up the green to the shops on a daily basis, it would take me a lot longer than normal but anything was better than dealing with my thoughts and emotions in a square room most of the day. As my physical health increased then so would my mind set and I would start to take the bus to Bexleyheath and start socialising more and getting out in the real world, rather than living in the dream world like I had been living. I would not have the patience and would notice my personality going up and down like a whores drawers. It was like I had two personalities and I had suffered like this since my trauma. I didn't pay much notice to it before but now I was off the cocaine and alcohol my mind was clearer and I was seeing the real me and I didn't like it. I could not seem to maintain any stability regarding my mind set and it's something that I just could not control. The longer I kept my secret in, the more I was destroying myself. I was fighting the demons in my head every day, trying to fix myself which was impossible as I wasn't willing to take ownership and until I did, the pain will keep on coming. Yet again, I was building up for yet another failure as I wasn't accepting help from anyone as I wasn't willing to open up to just yet. I wanted to so much but how could I? Then, yet again, my brain starts to tick, no one will believe you, everyone will think your gay, but on the other hand, things can't be worse than what they already was. There were so many people out there for me who would have helped me whenever I needed it, but that still wasn't enough as I see the world in a totally different way and because I had held things in for so long, I felt that I just didn't fit in and was totally different to everyone else. Not realising that I was gradually talking myself into thinking that going out, drinking alcohol and taking drugs was ok, because no one would accept such a damaged person into their life. I actually believed this and before long my mind had beaten me yet again and I would go into self-destruct mode, even though I was recovering from breaking my neck and wearing a neck brace. I would then use this to my advantage as I needed money and having a neck collar on was the best way to take the heat off me in tricky situations. What I was about to do was scummy but, at the time, that thought didn't enter my mind. I needed a brain break and I would do whatever I could to make it happen. I would start to visit Bexleyheath Broadway most mornings. Just like I was going to work and had a proper job but my job was different and made me money to get my alcohol and cocaine. I was so desperate so you've gotta do what you've gotta do.

Once in the shopping center, I would become a sneaky little rat and start to steal things out of shops. All the stuff that I knew people in pubs would buy. Mainly aftershaves, perfumes, razors, and general cleaning stuff for men and women. They were easier to steal plus I was getting money for it all as that's what people wanted. I would then make my way to a few pubs on the way back to Welling and by the time I got back to Welling it was two in the afternoon and I would have seventy or eighty pound in my pocket. I walked straight in the pub and would order myself a double vodka and red bull and then make a phone call and order some cocaine, then I would walk straight in the toilet and sniff a whole gram in two lines. Just like that I was back in the mix and my head felt numb and I felt free. Not free as in no problems but free as in blocking out my secret and putting it to the back of mind but that was the worst thing I could have done. When I thought I couldn't get any worse I found another way of making a bit of money and it was at the destruction of others. It's not how my parents brought me up but I wasn't me anymore, I was just an arsehole thinking the world owed me a favour.

I realised I was drinking in a pub with many men who were all on cocaine and sometimes they struggled to get some. I suppose in a sense, I became a drug dealer as I would pay £30.00 a gram and would start selling it in the pub for £40.00, making a ten pound note each time I got it for someone. Before you know it, I was making money in the nastiest way and clearly didn't care who I was hurting and whose families I was destroying. It wasn't me, it was the monster I had become. I saw no way of getting back to reality as I already knew myself that I was given so much, but let it all go.

CHAPTER 6
LIVE OR DIE BRING IT ON

AGE: 30 - 36 years old
YEAR: 2007-2013

I had finally lost everything and what I was hanging on to that was good was slowly slipping away. I was feeling very low every day and trying to find a reason to live. I had friends but was now on my own little mission as I had truly given up on ever becoming someone but I was happy at the time to carry on being a no one.

The more I lost, the more I thought about that day in the woods. I was thinking about finding out who it was that destroyed my childhood and the rest of my life so I could kill the bastard and get justice without anyone knowing my secret and with one less pedophile on the streets. I would go through this process in my head most days, planning on how I'm going to kill him when I find him. The way I looked at it was, take one life and save hundreds as these bastards never stop at one.

That's why they are called predators, always looking for their next victim, just waiting to destroy another life. The more and more I would fixate on my secret the more I would want to block it out. Plus, I was now an addict and was now battling with another problem, creating issues that I didn't need to. All I needed to do was speak out. It seemed so easy but at that time but it wasn't. I didn't want this eating away at me for the rest of my life but on the other hand, I was so scared of what everyone else would

157

think rather than thinking of myself. Yet again, I would take the easy, happy way out and before you know it, I was back in the mix. Out most days and blocking out my problems rather than deal with them but that's all I knew and if it ain't broke then don't fix it!

Now, at 30 years old, I had been living a lie for 23 years and it wasn't getting any easier. My mum and dad now knew I had an issue with drink and drugs and we would argue most times when I walked through the door of a night. So, rather than go home, I would find myself staying out to avoid an argument, thinking I was clever. This just made my mum and dad more angry and I would get double bubble from them whenever I did walk through the door, it could be one day later sometimes it was as many as three days later. I was treating their house like a hotel and had no respect for the rules my mum and dad had put in place. It was hard enough living at home at 30 but it was only me that would be able to do anything about the situation. Why would I? I was content and happy to block out my childhood and I didn't care what others thought as they wasn't me, living a nightmare 24/7.

Call it self-punishment, call it existing, call it what you want, but at the time, it's all I knew and I wasn't changing or telling my secret to anyone anytime soon. The paranoia and psycho stage was at an all-time high. This was due to the amount of alcohol and cocaine I was taking but, as crazy as it sounds, it was worth dealing with those stages as it was nowhere near as bad as dealing with a clear head and dealing with all of my problems. By this time, I was moving from pub to pub so no one would know how much of a problem I actually had. I would have a couple here and a couple there, it would look normal to everyone else. Well, that's what I thought anyway, not realising that I was losing everything in my life. Even to the point that all my close friends walked away, which didn't bother me in the slightest as I was in no man's land and didn't really care what others thought. As, if you don't care about your own feelings and don't love yourself, how can you do the same to anyone else when you know no different and have always pushed people away? I would spend time in the pub on Shooters Hill where there was a mixture of blokes my age all getting smashed and having to live life with a clouded mind as that's what they liked. They would all work and would not let the alcohol and drugs get to them and all maintained jobs. For me it was different, not because I didn't want to work but I was in no fit state to. Who would want to employ a down an out like me? If I'm honest, work was the last thing on my mind and so were my family and my daughter. You may ask why, but at the time I wasn't myself and it's something I regret and also something I will have to take to the grave with me. I am truly sorry for the people I hurt but I was on my journey and that's all I cared about. The only time I could maintain some sort of stability was when I was fucked. Sad, but true as that is what addiction does to you. It takes you away from reality slowly but surely and some people get through it and some don't. I was the one who didn't. I suppose you could say, it was like going over to the dark side and once you were there it was very rare to ever come back.

STEVIE - BEHIND THE MASK

Sometimes I loved it because society had done me no favours, so why should I give any favours to society.

Everyone knew me as a clown that was always out of his head, making people laugh, laughing with me but sometimes at me. Either way, I didn't care as I was just happy that no one knew my secret.

I so wanted to be normal and do what everyone else around me were doing, settling down, and having a family, going to work. Now the addiction was too strong and it took priority over everything in my life and it was all based around pubs, alcohol and drugs. No one or anything else in my mind mattered but me being on another level to make myself feel like every other human being. Faking relationships so I looked normal, faking liking various different ladies to feel normal and spending money I didn't have to feel normal. You name it, I tried it and nothing could beat alcohol and cocaine together. I felt unstoppable as my emotions and feelings in life didn't exist as my brain was numb from the world.

Still pissing it up and sniffing most days I now find myself becoming more used to alcohol and cocaine which in turn made me think even more about my life but, as per usual, it was easier to go up another level than to try and stop and deal with my life. Then with that would come more pain as what I was already putting in my system was causing damage but I would always take it one step too far and would now be using number five of my nine lives. Going through yet another trauma, all down to my alcohol and drug abuse. This would end up being one of the scariest moments for me, yes you heard it right, I was about to become scared and start to realise just how low my life was getting and to make things worse my poor sister would be there.

It was a Saturday and I had already been out most of the day drinking and sniffing in a few pubs with different people. I was already hammered and had more than enough to get me through the next two days but as you know with addiction, no amount is ever enough.

Someone suggested going up to a bar in Bexleyheath and my sister was going to come out with me as she needed to get out as she was arguing with her boyfriend and just needed a night out having fun. We got up to Bexleyheath and I was in a complete state, if I was a bouncer I wouldn't have let me in but, money is money and they had no problem letting me in as long as that till was full of cash they couldn't give a fuck. I was going in the toilet a lot more than I should have been but I was on one and thought everything was going to be ok. I found myself on the dance floor, dancing and fully charged from the line I had just had in the toilet. Then, out of the blue, just like that, I get a shooting pain in the right side of my head and I bend down as the pain is off the chart! My left arm started to get shooting pains up it and then started to go numb. The pain then travels through my body to my chest and it was excruciating, I felt like someone was standing on my chest! I hit the floor like a sack of shit. I was in so much pain and I couldn't breathe. My sister is screaming 'Help!!! My brother can't breathe!' I could hear her crying and shouting 'please help him, please!' and then everything went dark and I must have passed out from the pain. Then I opened my eyes and I was still struggling to breathe, I heard an ambulance in the background and was thinking 'this is it, I'm fucked. Finally him upstairs is not going to punish me anymore and is taking me where I can be happy and to see my Nan and Grandad's.' Then a voice says 'Stevie, can you hear me? This is the paramedic', that's all I remembered. I couldn't tell you who came to the hospital with me as the next thing I remember I woke up in hospital with a load of wires in me again and loads of patches over my body, thinking 'fuck you god! How many more times are you gonna bring me back? Ain't I been through enough?' I was happy to go at the time if I'm honest as I really had had enough of dealing with my head. I wanted to die as I believed I was going heaven as I never intentionally hurt anyone and only ever punished myself. My sister would come up and see me with my mum and dad then I would get the full extent of what had happened. The ambulance came and I was struggling to breathe as my throat had swollen up and I couldn't breathe as my nose was totally blocked up with cocaine. So the ambulance medic put two long prongs up my nose then banged it to clear my airways, then I started to breathe again as I had no pulse at the time. I also had a mild heart attack and was lucky to be alive, again! My parents were in a complete state and just kept saying 'Why are you doing this to yourself?' yet again, giving me the opportunity to speak up. But, just like every other time I would make up some bullshit excuse and pull through one way or another. It was at this point when I started to realise that I couldn't go on like this much longer and something needed to change. The pain I was putting my family through was wrong on so many levels plus, I had just used life number five of nine. The doctors came in and had a chat with me, explaining how bad the situation was and how lucky I was to still be alive. My reply to that was 'you think I'm lucky do ya? You don't know me.' His reply was 'well, I think you're very lucky to be alive', my reply was 'what do you fucking know? Why didn't you let me die?' Then I was prescribed another lot of meds for my heart and was told to take things slowly, my reply was 'Yeah, alright mate! You don't know fuck all. Thanks for nothing'. I don't know why they even bothered helping me as I treated them all like shit. I was blaming them for my insecurities and drug and alcohol abuse, when really I should've owned it and then everyone would have been there to support me. Stevie knows everything, even though I had just used another of my nine lives, I still thought I knew what was best for me. Really, the alcohol and drugs had now taken over and they knew what was best for me. After another stay in hospital I was ready to go home and couldn't wait as I hated being in hospitals. I had spent so much time in them already, this would only bring me down to another low level, reminding me of all the other times I had been in hospital. Yet again, I was holding on to the past but really I had never ever let go of it as I still wouldn't deal with my secret. I even threw the heart medication I had been prescribed away as soon as I got home. Now I was confined to the house and I was told to relax and get better. Relax? Me? No chance! I have never ever felt relaxed in my life, I have always been on edge since I was a child. I would spend a few weeks at home driving myself mad and needed to get out of the house and occupy my mind with something so I ended up going out with one of my cousins for the evening doing door to door sales. It was working fine as it was keeping me out of the pubs and giving me something else to focus on rather than my demons. It was becoming a routine thing in my life and we would even go to the gym in the daytime and then meet up with a few mates that had a furniture shop in welling. I was maintaining stability in my life and was heading down the right track regarding moving forward, you could say I was taking ownership and trying to move forward with my life rather than keep going backwards. Was I really happy though? No, I wasn't. As I would yet again have a clear head and I would start to think about the two things that I thought made me happier, alcohol and cocaine. Stupid I know but it's all I knew and as far as I was concerned it had never let me down and was the only thing that made me feel normal. I couldn't have been further from the truth as what I was actually doing was giving in to my addiction and looking for an easy way out yet again.

Then that day would come again, you've probably guessed, Stevie is on self-destruct again! I was outside the furniture shop talking to one of my mates, who sort of took me under his wing, he could see I was struggling but he knew my heart was in the right place and that I just needed a bit of guidance. This is one of a handful of people that are the reason I am here today and able to share my story. Anyway, back to the story. So, I was having a chat with my mate outside his shop and he was saying how well I was doing out working. Then I took a walk to the newsagents to get some fags, I look up and walking towards me I saw one of the brothers that was there that day in the woods. I stared at him and he nodded at me saying 'alright?' I froze and wanted to say something but my mate was only a few doors away and I didn't want to make a scene as he didn't have a clue about my secret. I wanted to ask him if he remembered that day as it was now starting to play on my mind more than ever but I couldn't so I just looked at him and said 'alright', that was it. Inside I was fuming as that was my chance to get the ball rolling as cracks were starting to show. I went to the shop and then went back to my mate. He said to me 'you ok? I would reply with 'yeah mate, I'm fine' then he added 'are you sure?' then I replied 'yeah mate'. My cousin pulled up and said 'ready for work mate?' I said 'yeah mate, let's get going' and I got in his car like nothing had happened, when really inside I'm fuming and my brain starts to go and the thoughts of 'I can't deal with this' is running through my brain. I then say to my cousin 'stop the car!' he says 'you wanna go pub don't ya?' I say 'just stop the car mate' and he pulls over asking if I'm ok. Yet again, I start pushing everyone away as I can't control myself and I'm not willing to talk to anyone as I just wasn't ready. So, all I could do was go back to punishing and destroying myself as it was so much easier than talking to someone, well that's what I thought at the time.

My cousin pulls away and I happen to be bang outside the pub that I went in every now and then, somewhere not too many people knew me and I could just go and get on self-destruct. I walked to the bar and ordered a double vodka and redbull knowing full well I was told by the doctors not to drink whilst recovering from my last trauma. I downed it, then ordered another and walked into the garden with my phone to my ear and ordered a couple of grams of cocaine. That was it, back on it, just like that and just as easy as that. The addiction was good for me at the start as it did what it needed to do but like anything, after a while, your body gets used to it and then it starts to take control of your mind, your body and your soul. I was drinking like there was no tomorrow, trying to block out my feelings and put myself back on cloud nine as that's when I felt happy and normal, well that's what I thought but really all I was doing was feeding the addiction and causing myself more pain and upset deep within. Before I knew it, I was in a place of freedom but looked at things a lot different. I would end up talking to two girls and they seemed like friendly girls. Then there was a discussion between some blokes next to the girls, I heard the word rape and totally flipped, going crazy as the girls needed to be protected and then everything went dark and that's all I remember again. Then I wake up and am outside the pub with two girls sitting next to me, I'm ok but my ankle is killing me. I ended up in a fight with a few blokes and was clearly out of my face and was hit from behind. My ankle was swollen big time and from what I was told, a bloke was stamping on my ankle. An ambulance was called as I could hardly walk. Once in the hospital my ankle was x-rayed and I would need an operation so they could put pins in my ankle. Yet again, I walk out my front door and with six hours I'm back in hospital again. It was only four weeks ago that I was admitted to hospital with heart problems. The true signs are showing of how much I was on self-destruct and just how much I really wanted to die. The only thing that was holding me was my daughter. I had already let her down in her childhood and now she was close to not having a dad. Selfish? Very, but at the time I didn't love myself so how could I love anyone else? The only thing I loved was alcohol and cocaine and if you were living the lie and the life I was living, maybe you would have done the same to make it all go away. I ended up having four pins put in my ankle but my ankle was so swollen the doctors were worried as the blood in my leg was not flowing like it should, which means the muscle dies in your leg and you could end up losing your leg. Another trauma riddled with pain and I really was struggling at this point. I was now starting to realise that if I carry on like this, I will end up in the ground which wasn't a problem for me but for my daughter, I just couldn't let it happen!

Once again, drips in my arms and medication to take so I can feel normal, whatever that is. The problem now was that I had a lot of time on my hands again and more time to think about where my life is going. I decided that once my leg was better I would start the knowledge for a second time so I could be a London cabbie, just like my Dad. I knew this would take up a lot of my time studying and would keep my brain occupied but I was determined to make something of myself. I had nothing to lose by doing it and everything to lose by not doing it.

After a few months of being indoors waiting for my leg to get better, I am now walking about with a Beckham boot on which allowed me to move around a bit more rather than sitting indoors all day thinking about my problems. Just before my 32nd birthday I ended up getting a new moped with the knowledge board on the front and was ready to start the knowledge again. I did my first four runs up London and did them wearing my Beckham boot as I wanted to get started as soon as possible to keep my brain occupied. As soon as I finished them I felt a sense of achievement and I wasn't thinking about anything but the roads I had just driven down. Would this be something I was finally good at and could focus on? Only time would tell.

In eight weeks I had completed the first eighty knowledge runs involving fifteen hundred roads and managed to maintain them all in my head, without any mistakes. My mum would call over them with me and I would say all the routes back and she was amazed saying 'you ain't made one mistake! Keep going my boy'. The more I was getting into the knowledge, the more active my brain would start to become. I would find myself getting into a routine of going out and completing sixteen knowledge runs a week and was on track regarding completing them. Like anything, after a while I would find myself settling into studying and maintaining some form of stability, even to the point of doing my knowledge runs, popping in the pub on Shooters Hill for a pint of beer then home to study my map of London on my bedroom wall. I was still dealing with the demons in my head but I was able to put it to the back of mind as passing the knowledge was my only focus. Becoming a London Cabbie would make me look like your everyday man, out looking for work and trying to make something of himself. Rather than being a complete 'down and out' who is hiding a secret that had already destroyed most of his life.

As time went on studying the knowledge, I find my brain is becoming more trained and is opening up more. Now that I was putting my brain to good use, rather than suppressing myself and blocking out with drink and drugs. For the knowledge this was ideal, but for my secret, it really wasn't doing me any favours. The more I studied, the more the memories and feelings were starting to come back as I was now living life without drinking or self-medicating. Slowly but surely the thoughts of my childhood would be at the front of my brain rather than at the back. Then slowly, the nightmares would start to come back most nights but the thing was, the nightmares were all the same and it was a repeat of what happened that day to me in the woods. All I was trying to do is move on with my life. To try and make something of myself and start living life in the present and stop living life in the past. It wasn't as easy as that, as I have been living in the past ever since it had happened. That's the result when you keep secrets like mine from your childhood. They eat away at you and you remain stuck in a time you so wish you could forget. You can't forget as you're living it every day and always will, until you open up and share your secret. How could I share when there are so many questions unanswered? It all seemed too much to deal with so one night, I woke up crying like the little boy I felt like and ran into the bathroom. Then bending over the toilet, I put my fingers down my throat and made myself sick. I had never done this before and just when I thought things couldn't get any worse they did! Whenever I would eat from that day on, the chances are, within seconds, I would find a toilet and go in and throw up all I had just eaten. The feeling I would get is that I'm empty and all the bad thoughts and feelings in my head had come out of my body and are now down the toilet where they belong. I would also start to lose weight and would find myself becoming more conscious about how perfect I needed to look on the outside as I was so damaged on the inside. I suppose it was the only thing I could control in my life. Everything else, I had lost and I couldn't control anything, not even the thoughts and memories of what that sick bastard had done to me. Finally, the cracks of my secret were starting to show and the weaker I was starting to become. I had been fighting for so long to keep this secret but I was at the point of wanting to talk to someone about my situation. The difficulty was finding someone I really trusted to talk to without them saying anything to anyone else. After thinking about it for a few days, I decided to keep it in and try to move on with my life, again! I really wasn't sure about talking to anyone as what will people think? Would my life be any better? At that point in my life the answer was no. There was only one thing I could do and that's block it out and start drinking alcohol again but as you know, once the alcohol starts to flow then so does the cocaine and before I knew it, I was back on the booze and sniff. I didn't want to but as an addict, it was easier as I could feed my addiction plus, I could also block out all my problems and troubles rather than deal with them.

Now I find myself going out less on the bike studying and more time back in the pub and doing what I thought was best for me at that time and if I'm honest, I loved it. My mind was clear and I was happy. I just couldn't face my problems and I took the easy way out which is what I always did as its all I knew at the time. All through my life I have suffered with maintaining some sort of stability, even as a child, I would never be the same person for more than a couple of days at a time. One minute I was happy and the next I felt low without any explanation. It was like I was someone else but with alcohol and drugs I felt it was controlling all of that as my mind was empty and so were my feelings. I was happy to stay in a low mood and just carry on doing what I was doing, rather than being 'up and down like a whores drawers' it was so draining, it was like I had two personalities and there were two of me.

Yet again, the 'fuck it' button had been hit and I was on self-destruct. It wasn't a case of wanting to be but a case of having to be as any other way would involve me having to deal with my problems and still, after all the damage I caused myself and my family, I couldn't see the light. All I could see was darkness and destruction, very sad but so very true. The cocaine was doing what it needed to do but at times it would start to have the reverse effect. I was becoming more and more fixated with my situation and was wanting to know who the arsehole was that had destroyed my life and I needed to find out sooner rather than later. Why should I live a life of misery? I haven't done anything wrong. He needs to be punished and that's that. I was now at the stage where I was becoming more obsessed with my secret and wanting answers. I had to think about this carefully as I needed to find out who did this to me, without family and friends knowing as he needed to feel the pain I have felt, ever since that day in the woods. The problem was the cocaine that used to block out my problems was now making me more obsessed due to me not thinking with a clear head, increasing my anger levels and sending my anxiety off the chart. What the cocaine was doing was completely changing my mindset. The reason for this is that when on cocaine, your brain is on a positive high and that is all well and good but your brain can only take so much, then you have to hit a low and this is known as a 'come down'. I had so many come downs over the years that now my negative thoughts were increasing and I was thinking darker and deeper than ever. Not giving myself time to have a clear head and think like a normal person. Suicidal thoughts were at an all-time high again and I was losing my mind and thinking 'what's the point in being here'. My moods were so up and down and I couldn't face dealing with so many personalities in a week. I wanted to die, it was all too much for me and I didn't want to deal with my problems anymore.

After another messy night on the cocaine and alcohol, I'm in my box room at my mum and dads and I can't deal with the thoughts in my head. Plus the mix of too much coke and alcohol was bringing me lower than I needed to be, all I wanted to do was go to sleep and never wake up. So I decided in an instant, that's what I was going to do. At the time I was taking two different types of medication for my Mental Health and they were very strong and not to be taken like smarties but, that's exactly what I did. While pissed and sniffed out of my head I took about fifteen of the strong tablets and washed them down with half a litre of vodka. I was now using life number six of nine as I had taken so many tablets, then everything went dark. The next thing I know, my eyes are open. Then I realise, I can't even overdose properly but what I took was more than enough to do the job! The problem now is that I can't move and I start to feel trapped, so I roll out of bed onto the floor and try to get up but I can't. I was permanently dizzy and it wasn't going anytime soon, I crawled to the bathroom where I was sick. This wasn't your average sick, this was a mixture of bile, phlegm and clots of blood. I felt like I was choking and my throat and stomach was burning. My Mum and Dad had gone out as we had an argument the night before and they just didn't have any time for me as I was so out of control. I crawled back to my bed and just laid there with the room spinning and while all this was happening I would start to get shooting pains in my chest. Then I thought 'I should ring an ambulance and get some help' but then I thought 'no fuck it, if I die, I die!' Then everything went blank again. The next thing I know someone is pulling me and my eyes open, it's my dad. I slept through the whole day and night, it was now the day after I had taken an overdose. I remember my dad saying 'You need to get up and sort your life out mate. You can't be taking overdoses like that, you have a daughter to think about and a family that love you'.

STEVIE - BEHIND THE MASK

My 34th birthday had been and gone, I was at an all-time low and was starting to have enough of the way my life was going. I needed to occupy my mind and try and maintain some sort of stability in my life as I was just a complete 'down and out' without anything to my name and nothing to show for my life. So instead of getting ready and going out on the piss, I had a shower, got ready and made my way up to Bexleyheath Job Centre. I felt so scummy going in there as it made me feel worse, being wrapped around a load of 'down and outs' that didn't want to work and at the time, that was me. A complete down and out with no future at all, sniffing coke and staring into the bottom of a pint glass. Now in the job center I begin to flick through the jobs, hoping that there was something for me. I wanted to work, even though I was dealing with my demons and my secret. I just wanted to be and feel like your average man, working and making something of myself but my secret would always hold me back and stop me from moving forward. I would keep fighting for a normal life but no one was ever going to know about my secret. Whilst looking for a new job I come across a job vacancy for a big energy company. The job was to install electric meters and payment meters which was right up my alley as I had already worked for British Telecom and had a good electrical background regarding employment. So I printed off the job number and details and made my way back home as yet again, another great chance had come up to work for a company with prospects, a pension and everything else I needed to feel like someone. Once I got home, I emailed my CV and all my details over to a forwarding address and from then on it was a waiting game. Then, just before Christmas 2011, I received a letter from the energy company regarding an interview. I was over the moon in one sense but nervous as hell on the other. I turned up to the interview all suited up and I remember the lady in the job Centre saying I need to make eye contact with the person interviewing me as that would benefit me in the long run. I can't tell you how happy I was when I walked into the room to be interviewed. It was only a lady interviewing me! I personally felt more at ease and comfortable around ladies, due to my situation. This was all in my favour and the interview went very well. The lady who interviewed me made me feel very at ease and I felt like I connected with her in so many ways. What made it even better was that she was the manager of the team that I would be working with at the company. This made me feel even happier as I wasn't going to be taking orders from a male manager. So, if I got the job, I would be happy to take orders from a lady, no problem. Then the interview came to an end and I was told by the lady that they would let me know the outcome in due course. I then thanked them for their time and made my way home. Once I was at home my parents would ask me how everything went and I was smiling so my Mum said 'I take it it went well son' and my reply was 'yes', then she would smile and say 'that's my boy'. Then, just a few days before Christmas Eve I received a phone call from a lady at the company. I was so nervous as I was hoping that this would be the time for me to get my life back on track and hopefully the start moving forward in my life. She then informed me that I had got the job. I couldn't believe it, I was so happy that I was making my way back up, from the lowest point I could be. Now I had something to hold on to and keep me going, I felt over the moon and couldn't wait to tell people. Even though I still had problems and secrets to deal with, I would maintain the mask. This was a little easier if I'm honest as I was now about to get back out in the big bad world and try to make something of myself and keep my problems and secret at bay. That Christmas I would be buzzing from happiness and not drugs. All I wanted to do was tell my family and my friends about my new job, trying to make myself look and act like I was back in the mix, doing normal things with normal people. I would meet up with family and friends over Christmas and managed to keep my alcohol and drug abuse on the low. I now had a new job to think about and wanted to be a bit 'with it' when starting my job in the New Year. I was a little concerned about working in my new job but I put things to the back of my mind and carried on as that's what I needed to do and I couldn't let my secret destroy yet another good thing in my life. After all, I had already lost so much and wasn't going to let my demons destroy any more of my life. The main thing that concerned me was that I was already struggling to maintain some stability in my life, due to my moods being so up and down and dealing with more than one personality. This had been going on throughout my life. Always dealing with more than one personality, it was hard at times but I couldn't say anything to anyone as they would think that I am crazy, which in turn could lead to someone finding out my secret.

STEVIE - BEHIND THE MASK

Now at the start of January and the day has finally come that I would start my new job with my new company. To say I was nervous and anxious was an understatement after all, anything new involving mixing with society was hard to deal with, hence why I would use alcohol and cocaine to keep my feelings and emotions at bay. I made my way to the office I was based at, not having a clue what to expect as I had been out of work for a while and had been living a totally different lifestyle. What I'm trying to say is that I had been away from reality for a very long time and was also dealing with the mask as this was my fresh start, yet again. I wanted it more than anything. Finally, I could be somebody and not feel like a nobody. My new boss made me feel at ease on my first day, explaining everything I needed to know about the job and she would make sure I understood everything before moving on to the next part. We clicked straight away and got on really well. After the first day I felt like I had known her for years already, which made things so much easier for me, especially knowing my first point of call was a female.

With my first day coming to an end my new boss and I would go out for a cigarette and talk about how my first day was. We were joking and laughing and my first day went a lot better than I thought it would. Once home, I would get through the front door and get straight into the shower as I hated feeling dirty and there was no better feeling for me than being clean and tidy. At the time I didn't know exactly why I felt the need to stay so clean but it was in my routine and had been ever since that day in the woods.

STEVIE - BEHIND THE MASK

After a week or two with my new company, I had completed the training that I needed to do before going out and working. I would then go out with people each day, trying to help get their outstanding debt sorted by installing prepaid electric meters. I wasn't happy doing this as I think you are either built for a job like that or you're not and I certainly wasn't. I didn't want to give people that struggled even more grief as I knew exactly what that felt like. It needed to be done as everyone has to start somewhere and this was at the bottom of the company. It was down to me to get to the top as if I proved myself, I could get to where I needed to be which was installing electric meters, like for like, rather than putting pressure on people to pay their bills.

After a month of working, pay day was finally here and all of a sudden I've got money that I have earned and it felt really good. To contribute and doing what's expected in society but if you've ever been an addict that's a bad thing as money helps to feed that addiction. So now, I had to be very careful and not let things get to me as I had already had so many fresh starts and wasn't up for trying again. I would go out drinking and keep my consumption of alcohol at a normal pace. I was enjoying the moment and everything was finally going how it should be, I even started to have a few nights without the cocaine. If I'm honest, I didn't enjoy it but it was something I could deal with as I had will-power on my side but the problem with will power is it doesn't last forever, especially if you're an addict.

STEVIE - BEHIND THE MASK

I was settling into my new job and I found myself really getting on with my manager. She seemed to understand me and not judge me as she had no clue about my alcohol and cocaine addiction. I don't know why but it's like she knew I struggled every now and then without me telling her anything. I don't know how though as I really didn't give much away and I was an absolute genius at maintaining the mask when around others, especially people I didn't really know. If I was going to trust anyone and tell them about my problems it would be her as she was not a family member and was just an outsider looking in. It was at this time the cracks would start to show in my own mind and I would find myself wanting to find out who it was that destroyed my life that day in the woods. I wanted to forget about it but it wasn't as simple as that. Now, I was wanting justice as I didn't want to lose yet another good job as I hadn't dealt with my Demons and I thought to myself until I face them, I will always lose jobs. After all, I really had an opportunity to move on with my life and progress within the company so I wanted to get this sorted, it had gone on far too long. Then, just like that, one night I would end up having a few beers and some cocaine on a work night. Why? I couldn't tell you, well I'm lying actually. Of course I can tell you. It's that poxy word again addiction, addiction, addiction! Just like always, once I started, I wasn't stopping as all my Demons would disappear. But, as I mentioned earlier, after many years of cocaine abuse and boozing, I would start to get the opposite effect and find myself wanting revenge and justice. Just so I could get closure and move on with my life. So when I got in that night, I would hit a downer and would have to get up for work in the morning. I was on my phone and just like that I thought 'I'll go onto a social media network and inbox the two brothers that were there that day in the woods and ask them some questions'. I had had enough of hiding and not dealing with things.

I inboxed the younger brother first and all I wrote was 'do you remember us going over the field as kids and building a camp?' I must have waited ten minutes then my phone pings and I have a message. It's from the younger brother whose reply was one word only and when I saw that word I instantly started to cry. Tears of sadness but also tears of happiness as that word was 'yes'. My chest tightened and I didn't know whether to laugh or cry. Straight away, I messaged him back 'Do you remember a red chair in the camp?' My heart was beating at a hundred miles per hour. In my mind, I am thinking 'say yes you bastard, say yes, please'. Five minutes go by and no reply. I have to get up for work in the morning and there is no way I'm sleeping until he replies. Then my phone pings, the answer to everything is depending on the answer to this question. Seems crazy but I was so scared to open the message up as this is the most open I had ever been about what had happened, please let the answer be yes. I open the message and the answer was yes. I went from walking up and down my bedroom to falling on my knees and crying as I had just been giving confirmation that someone else remembers that day in the woods. Finally I could get justice and find out who this bastard was and even though it was good news that I received. It would have a sad and dark effect, all in due course. I didn't reply and left it at that as I still needed the older brother to remember. I wasn't silly as I knew if he remembered that's two witnesses and that bastard would finally get what was coming to him!

I went to work the next day and for the first time in a long time I didn't feel that I was hiding behind the mask as much. I knew that in good time my day of justice would finally come and felt relieved that I already had one brother that remembered that day. I remember my boss would say 'what you on today? Why are you so happy?' my reply would be 'just loving my new job boss, just loving my new job', little did she know. I would wish the time away at work so the day could finish and I could get home and message the older brother as I'm on a roll, surely he remembers he's older. Why wouldn't he? This is it the start of getting my life sorted, I can do this. That evening I would send a message to the older brother, the message I sent said 'do you remember us being over the field that day and building a camp?' within minutes I got a reply saying 'yes mate'. With that I asked him if he remembers the red armchair. This time he didn't reply as quick which made me think he doesn't remember, how can he not? Then my phone pings and I get a reply saying 'it was a long time ago mate'. I didn't ask how long ago it was, I asked if he remembered the chair. Straight away, I'm thinking 'it ain't a case if he can't remember but a case of he don't want to remember'. But why? Had something happened to him? I didn't get any other replies and I was absolutely gutted. How would I get closure now? One person wasn't enough. I needed both to remember so that bastard could suffer like

STEVIE - BEHIND THE MASK

I have since I was a kid. I took the next day off of work saying I didn't feel well and I had the shits. Luckily my boss was ok with it. I was good at making excuses for work as I was a professional bull shitter and had been for many years, hiding behind a mask telling people what they want to hear.

I was 35 years of age and just when I thought everything was on the up, I let that bastard get to me! I started to take time off work to drink alcohol and take cocaine. This was all because the other brother couldn't or didn't want to remember and I couldn't talk about my demons as I didn't have enough proof. Seems like an excuse, maybe it was, maybe it wasn't but at the time I needed to block everything out. The only way to do that was self-medicating, not even thinking about how it was having the reverse effect and the more obsessed I was becoming with my childhood trauma. I was sort of seeing my first love again, on and off as per usual because of my insecurities and me not talking to someone who actually loved me and wanted to help. I pushed her away again, just like I did to everyone else that got close to me. That night she had had enough and told me to leave her flat. I popped in a pub in Old Dover Road and had a couple of beers and started to feel sorry for myself. Blaming everyone for my secret when really I should have been blaming myself. Then just like that, I walked back towards her flat and crossed the bridge which went over the A2 motorway and it was now I would use life six of nine. I looked around to make sure no one was looking then I climbed up over the bridge railings and got on the other side with a 40 foot drop in front of me and cars driving past at high speeds. I was crying and shouting out 'why me? Why me? Look what you've done to me you bastard'. Then I hear someone, an American voice says 'don't do it mate, it ain't worth it'. 'What do you know mate?' I reply 'Now fuck off and leave me alone, you don't know me'. Then like a complete arsehole playing with death, I turn around and am holding onto the rails now, facing the American guy, changing hands alternately, letting go with one hand and then grabbing with another, totally playing with death and not having a clue what I was doing. Then he grabbed me from the other side of the bridge and wrapped his arms around me so I couldn't jump, he then pulled me over the railings and wrestled me to the floor. I was screaming and fighting for him to let me go, I know he was helping but I now had an older man on top of me which freaked me out even more. After a while I calmed down and he got my mobile phone and rang my mum. I remember him saying 'sorry to bother you mam but I'm with your son and I have just stopped him from throwing himself off the A2 Bridge. You need to get here mam as your son is not in a good way, he needs help'. My poor mum had already gone through enough with me without any answers, now she received a phone call saying her son tried to throw himself off a bridge. I remember my mum pulling up and crying. Then she would cuddle me, put me in the car and took me home. While driving home, she said 'why are you doing this? What's wrong? Talk to me' but, without the other brother remembering, I was telling no one. The next morning we went to the doctors and before I knew it I was being sectioned again and was back in the Mental Health Hospital. My life was going backwards again rather than forwards and the cracks were showing even more. How much longer can I hide behind the mask before it cracked for good? I arrived there in the afternoon and was seen by a psychologist and a doctor. They asked me what had changed for me to be back in hospital again and I remember saying 'nothing's changed, absolutely nothing and that's the problem'. Then I would say 'you don't know me, you think I'm crazy, you ain't got a clue'. 'Tell us then Stevie so we can understand' and just like that I blamed the alcohol and cocaine as that's what I was known for. What's the point in telling them my secret when I didn't have backing from the other brother? It would be pointless to, unless I had enough to get that bastard locked up for destroying my life and get the justice I deserve. Before letting me go to my room they asked for my belt and my phone charger so I couldn't hang myself. They didn't give a fuck about me all they was doing were covering their own backs. My mum rang my boss at work and she was very supportive about the whole situation. I was lucky to still have a job and an understanding boss regarding my Mental Health.

To say my time in hospital was good would be a lie as every time I went into hospital the worse I would get. I was still struggling to maintain some sort of stability in my life and I knew I wasn't progressing but still had to fight as that's all I knew. I ended up getting into a few fights in hospital as any talk of rape, child abuse or mental abuse would cause me to just explode and put the world to rights, exposing what these sick people do to their poor victims, nearly slipping up about my secret. Even more cracks were starting to show in the mask as anger would now take over as the tears wouldn't help me anymore. I wanted revenge and I wasn't going to stop until I got it. My time in hospital would drag like you wouldn't believe, thinking about my secret 24/7 as I could no longer self-medicate with alcohol and drugs as they didn't sell it in the hospital. That was the worst thing for me as it wasn't just for blocking out but simply to feed the addiction as without it, in my eyes, I wasn't a nice person. That's when all my anger would come out as holding this secret in just made me angrier and angrier the longer I held it in.

My time in Oxlea's Mental Health ward was coming to an end and after another three week stay in hospital I was released under the care of my mum. No matter what happened, she was always there and would protect her baby boy even though I was an adult. She knew I was no angel but also realised that I wasn't right and suffered with mental health which she couldn't understand. That's because she gave me such a good life and I suppose she blamed herself for me being the way I was. After all, she didn't have a clue what had happened and the longer she didn't, the better. No mum wants to hear that this had happened to their child, it would destroy her and without being sure of justice, I couldn't put her through that until I had enough evidence. So, not only was I now dealing with my secret but now I was dealing with trying to keep my job. I was slowly losing everything again and was not sure I could come back from losing yet another job. The main thing on my mind now was, my daughter. She always was but now, after a second admission in hospital, it was time I would realise what a shit dad I really was. I was there up until she was 1 years old and down to my secret and insecurities, that was another good thing that I had fucked up. I would see her on a weekend but even though I loved her dearly, the addiction won and it devastates me to say that but at the time I didn't know how to deal with my demons so I just blocked them out.

This poor child just wanted her daddy and he wasn't there. Choosing alcohol and drugs over their child? What sort of person does that? Well, I will tell you who does that, a man that loves their child dearly but pushes them away as he can't get too close to anyone because he is keeping the biggest secret ever and can't risk that secret coming out as they don't know what society would think or say. I can't turn back time and if I could, I would. Do you know why? Because I would have turned left that day as a child and not right. Then it would never have happened and I could have been the person I was meant to be. A fun loving dad that gives his child everything rather than fuck all. It was at this point that yet again I would use will power and come off of alcohol and cocaine. This was far from easy to do in my eyes as that was my self-medication which had helped me get through the last eighteen years, but I needed to be there for my daughter. I had tried umpteen times before but I wouldn't give up trying to be a good dad. After all, my dad was the best dad so why shouldn't my daughter have the same.

Four weeks go by and I have been off alcohol and cocaine for twenty eight days. People would say that's a good thing but at the time it was far from a good thing as now I had my secret at the forefront of my mind, dealing with all the emotions and nightmares with a clear head. For me it was devastating, I can honestly say I was having the same nightmare every night and it was a replay of everything he did to me in the woods that day. Call it an excuse to get back on alcohol and drugs, call it what you want but that's how it was. I was also an addict and I'm sure that would contribute to how I was feeling. No one else could understand unless they had been abused of how a person would do anything to block out the flashbacks and nightmares and if it took alcohol and cocaine to do it then so be it, if you were suffering in silence like me then maybe you would do the same. Then I would decide, before things got out of hand, that I would go back to work to keep my mind occupied and take up all the free time I had, it was the only way to stop me getting back out in the pubs and destroying my life more than it had been already. My manager welcomed me back with open arms as she had been talking to my mum as I was in no fit state after my second visit to Oxlea's. She explained to me that she understands that I struggle sometimes in the job I was doing and that I would spend some time in the office doing office duties and assisting her. It felt so good to know that I would be in the office as I was struggling to knock on people's doors and help settle their bills, it just wasn't a job I was happy with. Now feeling much happier that I am back to work and will be in the office for the next few months as my trust was at an all-time low and I was not really maintaining any sort of stability, the office was the best place for me. Plus, I would get to spend time with the person I actually started to trust and that was my manager. I don't know what it was, she just seemed to get me and understand me even though she had no clue what had happened to me. The way she treated me was that she knew something was up and just couldn't put her finger on it. Over the next few months I would open up to her more but still keeping my secret at bay. She would do whatever she could to make me feel at ease and she was starting to become someone I could trust. I knew she would do me no wrong and that was a lovely feeling to have as I didn't trust many and the ones I did, you could only count on one hand. In the office she would teach me many office skills and went above and beyond until I fully understood them. She would also take me out on visits to check people's work and we would meet up with other engineers and have lunch together. I would feel a bit on edge as the cafes could get busy but now with my new mate, my manager, everything was a bit easier as I knew she would always be there for me. I so wanted to tell her, since I had known her. If I was going to tell anyone it would be her, the reason for this is I felt she wouldn't judge me or tell anyone else and she was now not just my manager but my friend and a good one at that.

As you now know my will power was becoming weaker. I was an addict, for one and was also not willing to talk up until I had gotten enough evidence. So, that night I would be at home and decided to inbox the older brother that was in the woods that day when we were kids. All I messaged him was 'do you remember the man taking us from your house to the woods that day and a red armchair?' I waited an hour and got no reply. Why didn't he reply? Is it because he felt guilty that day? Because if he did, he didn't have to, it wasn't his fault. It was that dirty bastards fault and that's all there is to it. Three days later and it's a Friday, I had not received a reply from the brother and I was getting angrier as I knew that if someone witnessed what happened to me that day, they would never forget what had happened. In my eyes, that was just a cop out and ignorant as he knew he could give me justice. I wasn't asking for him to talk about himself, I want to talk about me and what he witnessed, it's not a lot to ask to help someone feel freedom. With that, I decided to hit the 'fuck it' button and go to my local pub and go block out some feelings and emotions. As I walk straight into the pub who is standing at the bar? Only the younger brother. He nodded at me and carried on like nothing had happened. I wanted to smack him in the face and say sort your brother out and tell me who raped and abused me that day, but I couldn't. So, I ordered a few shots, downed them, gave the younger brother a dirty look, walked out of the pub and lit a cigarette. Then I made a phone call and asked for three grams. You got it, self-destruct again and getting angrier and angrier by the minute. I got my three grams of coke, went to the shop and bought a small bottle of vodka and made my way to the fields. I cut down the alley where I picked up a bag I had put there ages ago and in that bag was a rope. I'd been planning this for a while. I couldn't get justice so fuck it I will go block everything out with alcohol, cocaine, and prescription drugs and then I am going to hang myself. The drugs were no longer blocking out and were only making me worse but that's how I needed to feel if I was going to hang myself and I needed something to push me over the edge.

I sat where he abused me and sniffed all the cocaine and drank the alcohol followed by prescription drugs. Then I took the rope out the bag, tied a noose in it and started to make my way up the tree. I remember crying and shouting out in the woods 'this is your fault, you evil cunt, you've made me do this! Why did you do this? Why did you destroy my life when I was 6? You evil, evil bastard'. I was crying and had had enough.

I thought if I hang myself where it happened then everyone will find out what he had done and maybe I could get justice that way. I was at the final stage of live or die, bring it on. I was about to use life seven of nine.

CHAPTER 7
FIGHTING FOR JUSTICE

AGE: 36 - 38 Years old
YEAR: 2013-2016

I climbed halfway up the tree with the intention of overdosing on alcohol, cocaine and prescription drugs then I was going to hang myself. This time I would make sure I wasn't coming back. If I couldn't overdose properly, I would suffocate myself by hanging myself and I was intending to do the job properly but before I got to the top of the tree everything went dark. The next thing I know, I open my eyes and its pitch black in the woods and it was night time. I had fallen from the tree under the influence of three grams of cocaine, alcohol and prescription drugs. I had hit the floor and my head was throbbing but before I came round, I remember my eyes closing again and everything going blank. I then opened my eyes again and the sun is shining in my eyes. I'm lying on the floor in the middle of the woods, I must have been there from the afternoon the day before and it was now the morning of the next day. I remember thinking to myself 'what happened there?' I looked to my left where there was a rope with a noose in it. It then all started coming back to me and all I could think was 'how did I survive another overdose? It wasn't exactly a small one. Then I remembered what I was going to do. Now that I had a clearer head I started crying, thinking of how wrong that could have gone if I had made it up that tree without falling and what could have happened. I would say I spent some time laying on the floor in the woods looking up at the sky, thinking how many times have I tried to move forward while holding in this secret. The truth of it was that until I disclosed my secret to someone I would never be able to move on. I then sat up and reached into my pocket and took out my phone, looking at the screen I saw five missed calls from my mum. I then listen to the voicemail and it's my daughter, she was 12 years old at the time, the message said 'hello daddy, I'm seeing you at nannies today and I have been waiting for you at nans since last night, I love you daddy'. Then I started to cry again and realised the hurt and pain I was putting my daughter through, she had done nothing wrong. I was making her feel different and in pain just like I was as a child. It was all wrong but at the time it didn't seem that bad as the alcohol and cocaine were numbing my feelings and emotions. I got off the floor and sorted myself out. I then walked from the woods up into the fields and into the bottom of my estate. Once through the front door my mask went on and I walked into the kitchen like nothing had happened. I had a bump on the back of my head and my eyes look like two piss holes in the snow. I heard my daughter say 'nanny, it's daddy'. My daughter came running up to me and put her arms around me and squeezed me as hard as she could. This child loved me so much. I couldn't understand why as I had done nothing to help her turn out the way she had. That was all down to my mum and my daughters mum but still she loved me like I was the best dad in the world. While my daughter was cuddling me I would get an evil look from my mum as if to say 'where have you been? She has been waiting for you all night!' Really my mum would want to rip my head off but she wouldn't start an argument in front of my daughter as her number one priority was my daughter, whereas mine was alcohol and cocaine. My daughter would stop cuddling me and I would go upstairs and get into the shower where I would cry as quietly as possible. For some reason and for the first time in 12 years, since my daughter was born, I started to feel guilty for not being there for her and letting my mum and my daughters mum bring my daughter up on their own. I got out of the shower and made my way downstairs where I apologised to my mum, like I did most days, she just looked at me and said 'it ain't me you need to apologise to, it's that beautiful, brave little girl in the living room that needs to hear it'. Even though I was an arsehole my mum would still try and help me and my daughter build a relationship but I was too out of it to realise what she was trying to do. The weekend finally came to an end and my daughter would go home to her mum. No doubt I would get a phone call saying what a shit dad I was but I didn't need to hear that as I already knew I was a shit dad.

Monday morning is finally here I can keep my mind occupied with a fresh week at work as I was in the office and keeping busy. I had been doing some office duties for my manager when she called me to have a break and we went out for a cigarette. While out there, I received some good news. I would be going over to metering and installing electric meters which is the job I always wanted to do as it would keep my mind occupied 8 hours of a 24 hour day. I was over the moon and the only reason this was happening was because of my manager. She knew I was struggling with the other job I was doing. It was a good point in my life as I felt I was finally getting back to how I was when I was at BT. I would yet again be given another chance to make something of myself and move forward from the shit existence of a life I was leading. Before I knew it, I would attend and pass some training courses and would be starting my first day in metering. I was given a new van with all new tools and everything I needed to do my daily job installing electric meters. Finally, things were on the up again, I wasn't giving up just yet and was happy as I could keep my secret at bay. I was doing something that I enjoyed and I could block out all my demons while doing this.

Three months into 2014 and I was now into my daily routine at work. I found myself maintaining some sort of stability and learning what I could while working with electricity as I was looking to move on to gas after. Once I got into the gas side of the business there would be a lot of overtime which would mean more hours to occupy my mind and to also keep me out of pubs. I also started to interact with the customers and found my daily routine was becoming easier and easier and was taking up most of my day. My confidence was gaining traction and I would start to move away from the dark side and started to see the light a bit. Don't get me wrong, as you can now tell, I was no angel and still managed to have my brain break a few times a week with alcohol and cocaine. That was only when I had too much free time to think and when I didn't have much planned.

Then, one day while on a social network site, I noticed someone I knew needed a bit of help doing his driveway. I already knew him from when I was bang on it in pubs, he would always come up and say hello even though I was in a bad way. I suppose he felt sorry for me at times. I commented on his post saying I would give him a hand if he wanted, he replied 'nice one mate, a bit of food and a few beers in it for ya'. I thought to myself that will do nicely, a few beers, not in a pub and a bit of grub, that will do me. He only lived around the corner from me so I took a walk to his house but on the way I had to pass the two brothers house, which were there in the woods that day. Looking at the floor I passed their house only to look up and see one of the brothers outside the house. It was the older brother, he said 'hello' but I just nodded and walked past him as I couldn't deal with all this shit again. Staying focused on helping an old friend, I finally got to his house and he welcomed me. This was unusual as when I was out normally people didn't want to be wrapped around me as I was an addict and when I was pissed I was a complete pain in the arse. He offered me a beer and explained what he needed help with, we were cracking on and catching up with each other about my silly antics in pubs a few years back. He said I looked well, little did he know and we would crack on digging up his drive with a kango drill. I met his wife and kids and they all made me feel so welcome in their house and I had the best day in a long time as I wasn't being judged for the person I was and was accepted into their house with open arms. I can honestly say that meeting my new mate and his wife allowed me to finally deal with my demons and are another of the few reasons that I sit here today writing but I will explain that more as I get further into my story. Anyway, I felt at ease being around him and I couldn't tell you why but he sort of got me, even though he hardly knew me and that day would be the start of a very special friendship.

Now I find myself spending more time out of pubs and more time working and going to the gym in my mate's garage. Plus, I noticed how much time he spent with his children which in turn would encourage me to spend even more time with my daughter. After all, I had missed out on so much of my baby girl's life due to my addiction and pushing the people closest to me away. My mate and I would spend more time socializing and meeting up with a few lads every now and then, everything was going just how it should be. Then one day near the end of June, while out working, I hear the word 'pedophile' said on the radio. I pull over in my van and turn the radio up. I then I hear the name 'Jimmy Saville', thinking 'what the fuck is going on here?' It turns out that Jimmy Saville, who died recently, was discovered to be the biggest pedophile on the planet. Not only was he the biggest pedophile but also into necrophilia with children, it was sickening to hear. I couldn't believe what I was hearing and started to break down, crying. When I was a kid, I always watched him on TV, plus I was a victim of such a cruel act as well. Then my mind went back to my childhood and I remember writing a letter to Jimmy Saville on a programmer called Jim'll Fix It, I remember saying I want to be on TV when I am older. I then remember going into the kitchen and asking my mum for a stamp so I could send my letter in, her reply 'I have used my last one and don't have any more'. That day my mum did me the biggest favour as I didn't get to send my letter to that dirty sick bastard!

Getting back to the story. I was in my van and I was in a bad way as my feelings and emotions were all over the place. I couldn't believe what I was hearing and turned the radio off. After ten minutes of getting into a complete state I managed to sort myself out and made my way to the office. I make my way to the toilet and wash my face as my eyes looked like two piss holes in the snow where I had been crying. My boss looked at me and asked if I was ok as she knew I struggled every now and then, I told her I was fine and I was free to go. On the way home I bought a load of chocolate and crisps and made my way home. I couldn't control what that sick bastard had done but there was one thing I could, I had control for the last six years of it and that was my bulimia. I went straight upstairs and went into my bedroom where I ate all the crisps and chocolate, then drank a pint of water so it would be easier to purge, then I put my fingers down my throat and brought up the rest. I had been doing this for six years now and found that it was the only way to release my emotions as I couldn't really tell anyone what was going on in my head. I would spit the rest of what was in my mouth in the toilet once I had finished and five times out of ten I would spit blood up but

I didn't see that as a problem at the time. How else could I release all the pain I was feeling?

It was the only way I ever dealt with anything to do with my secret and that sick bastard Jimmy Saville didn't do me any favours. Now I was dealing with all the demons in my head and before I knew it, I was making a phone call and ordered some cocaine. After all, if in doubt, block it out! Maybe you're thinking 'why do that?' but at the time it's all I knew and no one could tell me any different plus being an addict didn't help. Now was my opportunity to speak up as the Jimmy Saville thing was all over the news but still I battled with my head thinking 'how can I bring this out now? It was thirty years ago'. Then I was battling with the other side thinking 'until you do, you won't ever get over it and get better'.

After much thinking it was easier to keep it in and carry on being a slave to this piece of shit that had destroyed my life as a child and still was destroying me.

Now realising that my demons were in the forefront of my mind every day, I find myself taking on call outs at work which would stop me from drinking and taking cocaine a few nights a week. Plus, I would take meter inspections which were to be completed on a Saturday day time which would keep me out the pub on a Friday night. Since helping my mate with his drive I would spend more time with him, meeting up around his garage in his back garden and I started getting into something a bit healthier and a way that I could release my anger. We bought a multi-gym and was working out a good three times a week and I even found myself eating healthy, trying to better myself, even though

STEVIE - BEHIND THE MASK

I was struggling with my head. It made me feel good going to the gym, I could concentrate on the outside of my body as I knew the inside was already damaged. Plus, if people see me looking good on the outside they wouldn't have a clue what was happening on the inside and that is exactly what I wanted. My weekly routine would still continue, going to the gym with my mate as it was a good way of releasing all my anger and keeping my secret at bay. I would also try to occupy my mind at work by doing callouts and keeping myself busy there but what I was starting to do was burn myself out as I was gradually getting back to my bad habits, alcohol and cocaine. It was just me trying to look as normal as possible and do what every man should be doing and that's trying to better their self. I was starting to struggle after a while and over the next six months I would start to take more time off of work. I was trying so hard to keep my job as with a job, I was someone but without a job I was a no one. Then things would unfortunately get worse for me as the Jimmy Saville case was getting bigger and more people were coming forward. I was becoming obsessed with it as I would start to hear the stories of other people that had experienced what I had been through. Really I should have ignored it but I couldn't as I realised there were people out there feeling exactly how I was feeling. I was now aware that if I could bring myself round to telling someone then maybe, just maybe, I could get my justice. But how? Who? Where? When?

Halfway through September 2015 I was becoming out of control and I was struggling yet again to maintain any sort of stability at work. I had already had two bad van crashes and I was struggling to keep up with my work. I wouldn't mind but the work wasn't even hard as my new manager had a good understanding of Mental Health and he was very supportive regarding this, yes he was a man. I kept my mask on while at work but even he could start to see the cracks in my work. He would ask me most days if I was alright and my reply would be 'yes' but by now, I would be turning up to work half cut from the night before where I had no sleep and needed the release. I was dealing with nightmares on a daily basis and would bang out a gram of cocaine and a few beers at least three days a week, just to get me through a five day working week. Yet again, blocking out my demons rather than facing them, causing more pain and self-punishment to myself, I was simply on self-destruct. I had already debated many times taking my own life, which wouldn't have been a problem being that I was working with electricity six days a week and was working on the main feed coming into the building. I remember one day when I was struggling, I left the fuse plugged in on purpose and was going to grab the live and neutral cables and just end it but a customer came in the room and said 'what are you doing?' my reply was that I am doing a test when really I was about to electrocute myself. By now I was struggling to keep things in and really wanted to tell people so I could try and get my life back on track. Then the day came that I thought would never happen. The day I would speak out for the first time, a day I thought would never come. It didn't happen the way I wanted it to but it was a case of having to on that day and there was no going back, well not for me anyway. I had just finished work and wasn't in the best mood anyway as I had already had a shit night's sleep the night before, dealing with the nightmares in my head that were getting worse as time went on. It was in the forefront of my mind and the anger in me was off the chart. Once home, I went into the toilet knocked up a line of cocaine that I had picked up on the way home and couldn't wait for my brain break to begin. The problem I had was that I had far from a clear mind and it just made me feel worse as it didn't have the effect it used to have, I was so immune to it now as I was an addict. My mate that lived around the corner, who I helped do his drive, called me and said 'do you fancy a few beers and a gym workout?' My instant reply was 'yes', any excuse for a few beers and a bit of company with someone who understood me for some reason and took me for what I was, all because I helped him do his driveway. He didn't know what I was up to regarding the cocaine, well he probably did as he wasn't silly but he never said anything to me about it so as far as I was concerned we were all good. I polished off the rest of the cocaine and made my way round to his house, looking like I didn't have a care in the world. I knocked at his door and he welcomed me with open arms asking me how I was as soon as I walked through the door. We cracked open a couple of beers and started to do a gym workout. By this time I was buzzing off my nut but kept it well hidden, I was giving myself the much needed brain break that I always craved. After about an hour in his garage, doing a work out, he said 'shit, got to go and get the kids from school. Do you fancy coming with me? I said 'yes mate, no worries, let's go' and with that we left to go and get his kids from there school disco. We pulled up near the school and was waiting for the kids to come out. Then my mate turned on the radio and just like that I hear the name Jimmy Saville on the radio again. My mind starts to go into overdrive and then I say three words to my mate, 'dirty, horrible cunt' his reply was 'yeah, tell me about it'. He pauses and says 'I feel sorry for the people he has abused and the sad thing is, some of them will end up abusing other kids too'. I looked at him and said 'what did you fucking just say to me?' he said 'sorry mate but on stats it's proven that some turn out to do that to others'. I said 'stats you cunt, you know where them stats come from?' he went 'no I don't. Calm down mate', I said 'I fucking won't calm down when you say something sick like that to me mate'. I then carry on exploding explaining why those stats are bollocks. I go on to say to him that the stats are based on the dirty bastards standing in court, bang to rights and they know they are going down for a long time. So they look at the judge and say they were abused them self so they get less time in prison. I then went on to say that anyone that has been put through that pain would never inflict it on someone else, it just ain't right when you've lived that pain yourself. He then pulls the handbrake up on his car and said 'Stevie mate, what's wrong? Has something happened to you mate? You can talk to me' I look at him and the things that were going through my mind, 'now tell him Stevie this is your chance'. Then I look him in the eyes and say 'I need to tell ya something, I can't deal with this anymore mate this is killing me inside'. I then sat there for ten minutes telling him everything that had happened to me but not too 'in depth' that I pushed him away. He looked at me and I see his eyes fill up as he himself has kids, one of them being the same age as me when I was abused, he could only imagine what trauma I had been through. He was so in shock but what made it special was he said 'I'm here for ya mate and we can get through this don't worry'. I made him promise not to tell a single person as I needed to deal with this in my own time and in my own way. We got back to his house and there was an atmosphere in the air, not a bad one but more of a sad one, he was in shock, there is no denying that but he was always strong faced and there wasn't much that would phase him, but this certainly had. I then decided to call it a night and felt somewhat relieved that I had finally let my secret out the bag but for now, one person knowing was more than enough for me to deal with. I didn't sleep much that night as I felt such a weight had been lifted from my shoulders and I didn't want that feeling to stop. I turned up at work fresh and ready and was determined to get through this, especially now that my mate knew what I had been through as a child. I had a spring in my step and a gleam in my eye as the weight was now lifted off my shoulders and I would carry out my daily duties at work and was getting myself back on track, yet again. I would take overtime at work and try to keep myself busy for the next four weeks as I would need money as Christmas was just around the corner. I didn't get much time to think and that's what I needed, being that I was closer to letting my secret out to my family and friends. I was happy but also scared at the same time as it's not the sort of thing you just bring up in conversation.

Halfway through October I find myself struggling again at work as I burnt myself out at work the month before. My boss had sent me out to do gas meter checks as he could now see me struggling and more cracks in my work showing. I would drive down the coast just to get away and try and do some gas checks on meters in people's houses that were hard to access. It was good for me as I was under no pressure and spent most of the day driving keeping myself occupied. Then on the way down to the coast I end up pulling over in the hard shoulder and have shooting pains in my chest, probably the years of making myself sick had finally done damage. It turns out I had my first heavy panic attack and a break down. It was all because I couldn't deal with my situation, I started crying at the steering wheel and called my old female boss who I got on so well with, saying to her 'I can't do this no more I really can't'. She told me to calm down and she would come and get me straight away. Finally, I had cracked and wanted to tell the world how much I was suffering and that I needed help. She pulled up in her van and I said 'I'm so sorry' but she didn't care, she just wanted to know that I was ok and cuddled me. I broke down like a little six year old boy 'please help me, please help me'. Her eyes filled up but she remained professional and said 'don't worry, we will get you sorted'. We then made our way back to the office and had a chat with my bosses and we all came to the conclusion that I needed to take time out from work and deal with my problems as they had now been brought into work. I was devastated but at the same time, soon everyone would know and I could hopefully move on with my life, get the help I needed and start being the real Stevie. My old boss, bless her, put me in her van and said let's get you home to mum and dad and get this all out in the open, everything is going to be ok. I said 'no it ain't, it really ain't' and on the way to my mum and dads I told her everything, she was trying to keep me calm and make sure I was okay. Once at my mums I was in tears at the front door. How could I tell them? It would destroy them but I needed to do it as I could no longer face and deal with this situation on my own. I remember being in the same position when I was 6 years old knocking on my mums door and wiping my tears away and now thirty odd years later I'm knocking on their door to give them the worst news ever. The door opens and my old boss and I walked into the kitchen and then she said to my mum and dad 'I think you both need to sit down'. My mum can't wait and said 'what's wrong? Is it your job Stevie?' My reply was 'no mum' as tears filled my eyes, then my mum looked at my old boss and says what's going on I couldn't speak I just didn't know how to tell them.

Then just like that, I said 'mum I'm sorry but when I was six just after we got back from Marbella in 1984 I was raped and abused by a man over the fields and there were two boys that was there with me'. She looked at me as I had a tendency to have a bit of a joke, I looked her in the eyes and said 'no mum, this is for real. This bastard is why I am the way I am'. My dad was in complete shock and so was my mum, I broke down. Finally, after all these years,

STEVIE - BEHIND THE MASK

I had told my mum and dad, which is something that I never thought I would do. Then it must have hit home as my mum started crying, my old boss was supportive as I'm not sure I could have told my mum and dad without her being there. She made it so much easier and helped me and my mum come to terms with things and calmed the situation down. Now, as a family we needed to stick together and get justice so I could start to move on with my life for the first time since that day in the woods, when I was a little boy.

I spent the next two weeks at home with my mum and dad talking through what I had been through and why it had taken so long to tell them. Up until two weeks ago, I don't think I would have been able to answer that question but now I could and it was the start of me getting my closure. I explained to them how when I was 6 years old, this terrible thing happened to me and I had thought at the time, it was all part of growing up and everyone had to go through it. I then explained how when I became old enough to realise what he did was wrong that I had to hide it as I would worry about what people would think. Would they think I'm gay? Not that being gay would have been a terrible thing but that's just how that pedophile had made me feel. Would people talk to me? All that stuff would go through my mind. I then explained to them how I trusted no one and pushed everyone away that got close to me. Also, how if someone is being nice to me then something bad is going to happen or they are out to get me. By this time my poor Mum would be crying but she needed to hear it then hopefully she could have an understanding why I was the way I was. She would cuddle me many times and thinking about it now, she probably felt guilty that she couldn't protect her baby boy. There was only one person to blame for what happened to me that day and that was all down to me. If I would have listened to my mum that day and did a left and met my cousins instead of thinking I knew it all and did a right into no man's land it would never have happened. It's something I have regretted ever since that day and if I could go back now, believe me I would but I can't and it's me that will have to live with that till the day I die.

Some days were ok and some were bad but when the bad days happened they were extremely bad. I would become that 6 year old boy again, crying and having sleepless nights, all down to now having a clearer head and fixating on my demons as I was so determined to get justice one way, or another. The nightmares were coming every other night, the exact same nightmare, a repeat of what happened that day in the woods. Not only was I living it on a daily basis but I was now dealing with it while sleeping. When can I get a break from this? I've told people now so why are things not getting any better? One evening, I walked into the bathroom, fell to my knees and started crying but in a very distressed way. I just couldn't cope anymore and also my mind was playing tricks on me, trying to divert me back to the brain break of alcohol and cocaine. My mum walked into the bathroom as she must have heard me crying and just sat on the bathroom floor next to me and cuddled me as hard as she could, just to let me know she was there. This is this most amazing lady I know as her heart had been broken due to the news that I had told her, yet here she is with no regard for her own feelings but putting her heart and soul into mine. After a few minutes I hear my dad coming up the stairs, he then comes into the bathroom and sees me and mum sitting on the floor and I'm crying. He then does the most bizarre thing that I have ever seen, he looked at me with no expression or emotion in his face whatsoever turned around and walked out of the bathroom. I then felt even worse as all I wanted him to do was cuddle me, show me some sort of emotion, tell me everything will be alright and he is here for me but nothing, nothing at all. My mum would then put her hands either side of my face, then looked into my eyes and said 'you need to go to the police and tell them everything, they will get the bastard'. I then broke down even more as knew that I would have to sit in a room feeling like I had done something wrong, being made to feel even more dirty and scummy with cameras facing down on me and telling a complete stranger everything that bastard had done to me. This was just the beginning of my fight for freedom but I knew my mum was by my side and I knew in my mind things were going to get worse. If I wanted to feel free and be the real Stevie then this was my only option. Before going downstairs, my mum explained to me that my dad cares but he just struggles to show any emotions, she then said 'trust me, I've known and been with him since I was twelve, he loves me dearly and he certainly loves you my boy'.

I woke up the next morning and we're now into November and I decide today is the day that I am going to go to the police and report that bastard. I wanted to try and get some sort of closure so I could move on with my life and take off the mask that I had been living behind for the last thirty years.

My Mum, bless her, took me to Bexleyheath Police Station. Once outside, my anxiety would start to kick in and I said 'I can't do this', then my mum put her arm around me and we walked into the station together. Once at the counter I said 'can I speak to somebody to report a crime please?' The officer said 'what crime is it you want to report?' My reply was 'rape and abuse to a child'. He looked at me in shock and said 'please bear with me a minute and we can go into that room over there' pointing to where it was. My mum sat outside and I walked into the room where I sat directly opposite the police officer, I looked at him, my eyes filled with tears and I started to cry. He was a lovely bloke but I was struggling as it was a male officer, who was older than me and I didn't trust him one bit but I needed to tell him everything. He looked distressed while I was telling him what happened, all I kept saying to him was 'please get him, please! He has taken so much from me and I have lost so much, I just want justice'. He looked at me and said 'I'm going to book you an appointment at Lewisham Police Station where you can attend an interview with a specialist team that deal with historical child abuse' I then cried again but they were tears of relief as I knew I was getting closer to finding out who did this to me and I could finally be free. Once finished in the police station I walked outside and a big weight had been lifted from my shoulders but I wasn't getting too excited as this was only the start and I already lived with the guilt for the amount of other children's lives he may have destroyed by me not speaking up sooner. I wasn't just doing this for me now, I was doing it for all the other kids as well. I don't care what anyone says, if he had done it twice to me in a short space of time, he had done it again, so giving up wasn't an option in my eyes. Once home, I would think more and more about what I had lost and also what had been taken from me. This was a good thing for me as it made me more determined to get justice and find out once and for all who the sick bastard was that thought it was ok to rape and abuse a little 6 year old boy, twice! Then send him on his way like nothing had happened. Angry was an understatement as to how I was now feeling but I needed to keep calm as the following day would be the day that I would be able to tell the right people exactly what happened that day and the start of my justice could begin.

I would like to say that I had the best night's sleep that night but that wasn't happening as how could I even contemplate sleeping with all the thoughts I had running through my mind. The morning finally arrived and today would be the day I could tell the historical child abuse team what had happened to me. You would think being a 38 year old man, I would be able to deal with this situation but believe me, I see the world very different to the way others see it. I struggled throughout my life with my emotions and maintaining some sort of stability. Well today was no different as I struggled to trust anyone and would now be sharing what happened to me in-depth. I tried to remain calm on the way to the police station with my mum as I knew if I started shouting they wouldn't even entertain me.

STEVIE - BEHIND THE MASK

I must have felt every single emotion on the way to the police station just to get it out of my system before I got there. Outside the police station I would look at my mum who was there throughout this whole process, she would smile and say 'you can do this. Once it's done, it's done'. We walked through the doors together and having my mum by my side made things that little bit easier. After all, when you aren't well, who do you want? Your mum.

Now I'm sitting in reception waiting for my name to be called, then I hear my name 'Stevie'. Then it hit me, I was like a bag of nerves and for some reason the tears then start to run down my face. 'Don't worry Stevie, we are here to help you', but that meant nothing to me as I didn't know these people and why should I trust what they say? I then walk into a room where there are two ladies, thank fuck for that as I really didn't want to be dealing with two males as the whole thing would have gone a totally different way. They informed me that there were cameras in the room and that I would be doing a video statement first and then we would take a break that would be followed by a written statement. I was far from happy about being filmed as I found it weird if I'm honest. Why film me? I ain't done anything wrong. That bastard should be in this room being filmed so the world could see what he had done to me. Then, before the Interview began I said 'why am I being filmed? I ain't done anything wrong, it should be that bastard sitting here, not me'. The lady replied in a nice voice and said 'we need to gather all the evidence first before we visit the person who carried out the crime'. I then asked 'why two types of interview?', but before they could answer I said 'what ya think I am lying? Her reply was 'no Stevie, but people do make things like this up sometimes'. Then I start to cry and raise my voice, 'why would anyone put themselves in so much pain if they didn't have to? Are you for real?' she said 'yes, as we have had many cases where people have lied'. I couldn't believe what I was hearing. Who in their right mind would put themselves through this if they didn't have to? In turn, I became more angry thinking 'there are arseholes out there making this shit up when I'm living it for real on a daily basis' The interview had only just started and already I didn't want to be there but I knew I had to carry on so I could get my justice and get that bastard put away where he couldn't hurt any more kids. The first interview was filmed and I tried my best to give them a clear picture of what happened to me but I had to break a couple of times as I just broke down, especially when telling them what he had done to me. You would think over the years you would become stronger, living it day in, day out. You don't, it gets worse but slowly and before you know it it's eating away at you and you don't even know what day it is. After what seemed like forever, the police lady said 'that's the video statement done, now we will have a break and then we can start the written statement'. She did ask if it was too much and said that I could come back another day and do a written statement, but my reply straight away was 'no, I will finish it today'. The longer I left it the longer he would be out there hurting other kids and I couldn't have that on my mind anymore, after all I had done nothing wrong. Well that's a lie as I had done the worst thing wrong and that was that I did a right instead of left that day. How can something so small like that change the way my life went for the next 30 years.

Once the break had finished it would be time to start the written statement, they had most of the information from when I had first come out with it to the policeman at Bexleyheath Police Station. They had an idea about what had happened after completing the video statement but I suppose they wanted to see if I was lying and see if both matched up. Once finished, the first thing I say is 'you will watch that video and you will read that written statement and there won't be one word different. You know why? Because I'm telling the truth'. I was getting angry at the wrong people really as the ones I should have been having a go at is the fake fucking liars that think it's ok to make shit up and mess it up for the real victims. I then ask them what would happen next and they said they would interview the two brothers and hopefully they will tell the truth. The only problem I had was that I didn't know who it was in the brother's house that day. I knew what he looked like but I didn't know his name, but they did. I needed to make sure they did tell the truth as it was only them two people in the whole world that could give me my justice and there was no way I was not getting it, one way or another.

Back at my mum and dads I spent the next few days keeping myself occupied but I couldn't help thinking 'what are the brothers going to say?' I had already spoke to both of them over social media and they both remembered going over the field that day and they remember the red chair. I was worrying for no reason as if they remembered that stuff then they would remember everything else. My dad was happier, seeing me out of pubs and not taking alcohol and cocaine to block out my problems and deal with them head on. I don't think he realised that when I was under the influence of alcohol and cocaine, I actually felt normal. He wasn't me, dealing with what I was having to deal with. Even after talking to the police and telling my Mum and dad what happened, I still would stick up for the two substances. Not realising that over time it was now an addiction and no longer a way to block things out, it was now part of me. It wouldn't be long before I would get angry for no reason at all, what I was doing is finding a reason to go out and use alcohol and cocaine. Very sad, but very true and then one day in the middle of November I got my way. After a few weeks of maintaining some sort of stability, I end up in a pub, in a toilet, with two grams of cocaine and some money in my pocket. This was no longer to block out as that didn't work, this was clearly because over time I had become addicted and it was just as regular as putting sugar on your cornflakes. Yes, I was taking it with the intention of blocking out but by now it would do the opposite and I would become more fixated and angrier. All I had to do was wait for the police, but no, I couldn't do that and that just goes to show you what addiction really is. It's something you can't be without, without it you feel naked and without it you feel like there is no point to life. I'm not going to lie that first line is amazing and the problem with that is the next time you do it you are simply chasing that first line but I'm here to tell you that you will never get that feeling again as once the body gets used to something and you can't find that buzz, that's when your addicted. Everything was going so well and now this poxy addiction was stopping me from moving forward. For the first time in my life I realised that it was alcohol and cocaine that was stopping me from moving forward and being the real me.

So that Friday night I walked into Queen Elizabeth Hospital and said 'if you don't help me, I will kill him and then I will kill myself'. It was the only way to keep me from taking cocaine and alcohol and actually killing that bastard! That evening, I was sectioned again under the mental health act. Most of you may be thinking 'why not just wait for the police to go get him?' It wasn't as easy as that. All the anger, all the emotions and all the feelings were hitting me every day. I couldn't deal with it and I just wanted all of the memories and thoughts to go away, I just wanted to be me and I just wanted to be free. I suppose there was some good that came out of me being sectioned in Oxlea's this time, maybe now I could tell the psychologist and other health professional what had happened to me. Every other time I was sectioned I blamed it on the alcohol and cocaine as I wasn't willing to talk about my demons. Now I was willing to talk as I wanted to get better and be clear of mind altering substances once and for all. They would monitor me throughout my stay noticing that my moods were always up and down and never stable. I would talk to the doctors about my situation a few times to give them an understanding of how I was feeling, so I could be diagnosed with something. I knew that I was different from others by the way I reacted to things and how I saw the world differently to everyone else. Plus, I couldn't maintain any sort of stability in my life and that was something I had always struggled with, which is why I always pushed men, women, family and friends away. I couldn't let them see me up and down it was so degrading knowing I was different and so tiring hiding behind a mask for many years. Many times I would ask for a diagnosis and they said I was diagnosed back in 2013 with Emotional Unstable Personality Traits but since me telling them what had happened to me they had now a diagnosis of Borderline Personality Disorder due to childhood trauma. Finally an answer to why I was different, my moods were always up and down ever since that day in the woods and for years I wondered why I was the way I was. I was upset at first but then to have an answer as to why I was this way gave me some sort of closure as I felt better knowing that this was brought on due to what that sick bastard did to me that day and that it wasn't my fault. I was ill for so many years.

I had a few episodes in Oxlea's throwing chairs and causing drama but I put that down to struggling with my demons. Plus, my body was craving alcohol and cocaine as, let's face it, no matter what way I looked at it, I was still an addict even though I had demons it was my choice to take the drugs and nobody else's. I was on a high enough medication to suppress a horse and that was clearly to stop me doing anything stupid like take my own life in their care. I couldn't tell you what day it was and I would spend a lot of time in my room thinking more and more about the bastard who destroyed my childhood and my life. The way I was thinking was far from normal as I wanted to hurt this arsehole and I wanted to mentally torture him, just like he had to me for the last 30 years. I needed a gun as to me a gun would solve all my problems. The way I saw it, I could take a life to save hundreds from living a life like I did. Could I be the one that goes against the justice system and stop him from ever hurting another child again? So, I would spend many hours planning how I could take care of this bastard once and for all, prison wasn't a bad enough place for that sicko, the only place good enough for him was six feet under in a box and never to return. All I had to do was wait for the police to interview the brothers and then I would know who he was and then I could strike. Now I was the predator and he was my victim, it was time for the tables to turn. It may be sooner, it may be later but I knew my day would come and that was good enough for me for now. After three weeks locked up in Oxlea's, my day of being released was finally here. I was only allowed to go home as my Mum and Dad were willing to take care of me while dealing with my demons. The moment I walked out of the door and felt freedom I would smile at my Mum but she knew the smile was because I was medicated up to the eyeballs with tablets, it's like I was there but nobody was home. As soon as I got out, my mate who I told my secret to, visited me straight away. The first thing he did was give me a cuddle and that wasn't like him as he was a bit of a tough one, as I said before, not much phased him. I didn't really care how he was as a person as he was there when no one else was. As far as I'm concerned, that's a friend for life. His eyes did start to fill up with tears as when he was there my daughter turned up. She cuddled me and then she started crying, bless her, she was just happy her dad was out of the hospital and back at home. Once I had dealt with the visitors I would take myself off to my bedroom where I could process everything. It was then that I realised that I needed to get through this and be the Dad I should have been at the start, rather than halfway through her life. My daughter was amazing and I was so lucky to have her and her mum had done a fantastic job bringing her up and that's something I will always be thankful to her for. Not that I have any rights at all to say anything, as I wasn't exactly dad of the year.

Now, half-way through December and Christmas is just around the corner, it was that time when all the family meet up with each other celebrating another year. I wasn't looking forward to celebrating it if I'm honest but it wasn't all about me, so I just did what I did best and put on the mask as it was easier than sitting there with a miserable face spoiling everyone else's Christmas. After all, my family were just happy I was no longer in hospital and they could spend time with me, so the least I could do was put the mask back on for a bit and get this year out of the way and hope for a better year in 2016. I managed to get through Christmas and do what I needed to do in regards to seeing family members and having some sort of fun and socialising when I really didn't want to be there. I stayed in on my own on New Year's Eve as I didn't feel like I had anything to celebrate, even though I was starting my journey to freedom, it just didn't feel right.

STEVIE - BEHIND THE MASK

Now into January 2016 and I am trying to focus on moving forward with my life. I had started at a drug addiction rehabilitation group where I would meet up with other people in the same situation that I was. Some were worse than me and some weren't but either way we were all addicts in some way or another and wanted to be free from all mind altering substances. It was one of the toughest things to do, being free from the substance that helped me get through the last twenty years. Plus, the same thing that helped me forget my demons which, if I'm honest, was the worst thing I could have done. Now without cocaine I would feel very insecure as it was all new to me, living with a clear mind and I hated it, but if I wanted to be free of my demons and move on with my life then this just needed to be done. I wasn't the best person to be around as my moods were up and down like a 'whores drawers'. I tried my best to stay away from everyone while dealing with this as I got myself into this situation and it was only me that could get myself out of it. I was now six weeks clean from alcohol and cocaine, I would find myself fixating more on who did that to me that day. I decided to message the younger brother who was there in the woods that day as I had enough of waiting for the police to pull their finger out and go nick the dirty bastard. I started the conversation by saying 'hello' and then got straight to the point of finding out who it was, within two minutes my phone pings and I have a reply. I was shitting myself thinking 'please remember, please'. I open my message and there it is, in black and white, the name of the sick bastard who raped and abused me. My instant reply was 'is that the bastard that took me, you and your older brother over the field that day? You need to be one hundred percent sure'. He replied straight away saying 'one hundred percent' and I knew he knew as he was in his kitchen in the house that day. I then left it at that and even more of a weight was lifted as I now knew who destroyed my childhood that day and found it very hard to keep in. I was so relieved that one brother remembered and could I see the light at the end of the tunnel regarding my closure. Now I wanted to find out where he lived but I had to be careful about how I did it as if the police knew I was talking to another witness there is no doubt I could of got in trouble and totally fucked up my case against for that piece of shit.

I would spend time at my drug group trying to block out my thoughts and emotions. I was serious about getting alcohol and cocaine out of my life, the only favour it did me was to block out my problems but not dealing with them at the time was the biggest mistake I could ever make as that's what had made me the addict I was today. If I could go back now and not sniff that first line I'm sure things would have been very different but at the time no one was there to advise me but I am advising anyone, don't do it! Don't try it and you will make things in your life so much easier for yourself, believe me, I know. Finally things are on the up and just when I thought things couldn't get any better they did. It turns out, someone I had grown up on the estate with found out what had happened to me and the same thing had happened to her when she was 12 years old. The first thing in my mind was 'yes, I've got you, ya bastard' it had to be the same man as surely there weren't two of these sick bastards living on the estate. In time, I find out who it is and my cousin set up a meet for us and the good thing was she had recently started up her own flower shop in Welling and was keeping her mind occupied as she still hadn't got justice herself. The moment I saw her and realised her house backs onto mine I thought 'surely this was it. It had to be the same dirty bastard that raped and abused me as a kid'. She looked at me and I looked at her and finally there were two people in the same room who totally understood what one another was going through. It was a lovely feeling if I'm honest, not that she had been through the same as me, of course but just that there was no more hiding behind the mask as she totally understood me and we talked for ages. Then we got to the point that, if I'm honest, I wanted to hear as soon as I walked through the door of the shop and that was 'did she know who abused her? She turned to me and said she knew exactly abused her and she had a witness and was awaiting a court date as she was waiting for the witness to come forward. Then out of the blue I just said 'what was his name?' she looked at me, paused and I'm thinking 'come on love, don't hang it out this is my moment', then she said his name and my heart sunk down to my bollocks and I was devastated as his name was totally different to mine. I put on a smile and said 'not to worry, my two witnesses will come forward just like yours will, I just know it'. Why wouldn't they? The best thing to come out of it was the start of a friendship and for the next few months I would pop to her shop after drug group and have a chat with someone who totally got me. It was the best therapy for both of us.

She was married but her husband was very understanding and knew it would help her. Also, having someone who knew what she was going through and how she was feeling and could help, was a good thing.

My drug group was a big safety net for me because thanks to the people at the group, the teachers and others like myself, I now find myself sitting on four months clean of alcohol and cocaine. I wanted that feeling of 'I had done well' but it wasn't my main concern. My main concern was getting my justice and without alcohol and cocaine to block out again I slowly feel myself slipping, not back into drugs and alcohol but into emotions of pure anger and was becoming concerned with the way I was thinking about what I wanted to do to that sick bastard. I knew things were getting out of hand when I spoke to a 'bit of a nasty person' asking him if he could get his hands on a gun with some ammo. He looked at me and laughed and said 'that ain't gonna help ya is it?' My reply to him was 'you don't know what help I need mate, I just asked if you could get me a gun so can ya?' and his reply was 'yes'. Now correct me if I'm wrong but that isn't normal thinking and I needed to get out of this mindset, before I put my dangerous thoughts into action. What could I do to block these thoughts and emotions out as I could no longer deal with the countless nightmares and thoughts on a daily basis. I couldn't go back to cocaine as it no longer did me any good and only made things ten times worse. So I decide to make another stupid mistake which I would regret just as much as everything else I did that was wrong. I start smoking cannabis again, I thought it was a good thing to do as it would stop me from drinking alcohol and cocaine, so surely it was a good thing? All I was really doing was replacing oneself medicating substance for another and that was the worst thing I could have done but at the time it was working for me, well so I thought anyway. Just like that, I made a phone call and within twenty minutes I had a bag of cannabis and before you know it, I'm rolling my first joint and was looking forward to the brain break ahead and hopefully a night free from the same poxy nightmare. I smoked the first joint and within minutes I'm stoned with not a care in the world and life seems ok. Not thinking, as per usual. I then realise I start phycology on Monday and that's the whole reason why I gave up alcohol and cocaine in the first place, to get better. Me thinking I know it all thought 'fuck it', I won't tell them and still do psychology and everything will be ok, no nightmares and getting therapy at the same time. What could go wrong? I smoked cannabis over the weekend and if I'm honest, I felt great but I was doing exactly the same as what I had been doing before and that was self-medicating and blocking out all my problems. I was just using a different buzz to get me through the day, it wasn't the brightest idea I had thought of but it would do for now. Monday morning arrives and I had no nerves at all as I was still pretty stoned from the night before. What made things even better is that I hadn't had any nightmares for two days so my new fix was doing its job, bring on psychology. This would be a 'piece of piss'. My lovely mum, bless her, took me to my first appointment and I was okay until I pulled into the carpark, then my brain starts to go. Now I have to tell another lot of people what I had been through and tell them exactly how I felt. But how could I? I was still stoned from the night before and the chance of my head being clear and ready for this was zero. Yet again, my addictions and self-medicating coming back to haunt me. Not realising all I was doing was punishing myself. I would keep on smoking and attending my psychology, letting things build up again and as anyone knows, when you keep things in and let them build up, it won't be long before you explode. That's exactly what I was building up to, yet again the drugs were making me see things differently. All I was doing was punishing myself more and more, blocking out my problems and still pretending that everything was ok. Then one day, while having a therapy session things took a change for the worse. The psychotic episodes and paranoia was becoming worse but at the time it was still better than dealing with the Demons and thoughts in my head. We were talking about my trauma and was at a point where I had to talk about what that sick bastard did to me that day. It was the hardest thing I had ever done as I had to explain the pain I felt which ended up in me crying and become angry. I could even see the pain and emotion in the therapists face as her eyes filled with tears. That session ended and unfortunately so was the rest of the six sessions as she clearly thought I wasn't ready yet but really I had let another drug change the way I was thinking and stopped myself from moving forward. Maybe it was the addiction I had, maybe I wasn't ready or just maybe even she couldn't deal with what was going on in my head. Now I had lost the only thing that would help me get better and yet again the opportunity was there to move forward and I had basically refused it. All due to my self-medicating and trying to block out my feelings, rather than face them head on. So, with no help and support, until they thought I was ready, I was now back to square one. This wasn't a problem in a sense as I was so used to letting myself down and punishing myself, it was just like every other day in my life. With no one to talk to and help me on my journey to recovery, I find myself spending more time with my friend who had also suffered like I had and totally understood me. I would always take a joint out with me which was a clear sign. I needed it to be in my pocket and if it wasn't, my anxiety would have been off the chart but that's addiction for you. If you do the crime, you do the time. My friend would say to me 'you ain't gonna get better without a clear head, I know you don't want to hear it but it's true and you know it'. Someone else now trying to help me, but why? What do they want in return? Then, just like that, I would start to push her away as I knew she was right but, until someone could stop the memories and thoughts in my head, as far as I was concerned, everyone else could fuck off. I did this all the time whenever I couldn't deal with people, I would push them away. It was easier than them seeing me get angry and fly off the handle as I just didn't want to take any advice and was slowly becoming very reclusive due to my paranoia and psychosis from smoking cannabis. I wasn't living in reality. I was clearly living on cloud nine as reality for me was a living hell! Living behind a mask and constantly pretending to be happy, even though I had told everyone and their family about my trauma! Maybe people thought it was a bit much but when you hold something like that in for so many years, then all of a sudden you can get it all out, you just do. I can guarantee you would do the same if you were me and I hope you never have to. If you have, you will totally understand where I am coming from.

Anyway, getting back to the story. My life was yet again feeling at an all-time low. I had now dealt with my trauma by telling anyone and everyone but still, my life was in limbo regarding getting justice. I wanted justice more than life itself. Then one day in June and coming totally out of the blue, my phone rings and the caller ID says 'Operation Sapphire' who were the two ladies dealing with my case. My stomach turned over and I hesitated answering the phone but I finally got the courage to answer. I then start to feel excited as they said they would like to come to my mum and dad's house and talk to me, straight away! I said 'you can come round now, it's no problem'. I got off the phone told my mum and she was well happy. I said 'mum, they have probably interviewed the boys and now I've got the bastard!' I then ran upstairs to have a shower, shouting out 'we're getting the peado, were getting the peado!' that's how happy I was. Once showered and ready, I made my way downstairs and sat in the living room looking out the window like a little boy waiting for his dad to come home. Then I saw the car with the two ladies in but there was a man with them in the back, all suited and booted. I started to think 'what the fucks going on here?' Then the doorbell rings and I ask my mum to let them in. The wait from the front door to the conservatory seemed like forever but finally I saw them and they both smiled at me, yes this is it! 'Would you like to sit down Stevie?' 'No, I'm fine thank you' I reply. 'What's with the big man with you today?' Then everything went quiet. I'm now thinking 'come on tell me for fuck sake, I've been waiting over thirty years for this moment!' Their faces then became serious and they start explaining how they interviewed the younger brother and he said he remembers the man who took us over the field that day. They said that he also told them that the man said 'who's going to be in the gay gang today?', then how he remembered me climbing down the tree and walking towards the man who was sitting in a chair with his pants and trousers down. Suddenly I feel happy as one brother remembers so the other brother must as he is older. 'Yes! I've got the bastard!' I think to myself. Then the faces of the ladies change. Just like that, my dream of freedom is shattered as they then explain that the older brother doesn't remember and without him remembering, I will not get my closure. They explained that with historical child abuse, you need two bits of evidence and as I didn't know his name my evidence meant jack shit! I fell to my knees, lowered my head and cried. Just like the little 6 year old boy I was that day, they started to say 'sorry, sorry…' I said 'are you having a fucking laugh?' Then I stand up and start to lose my temper, telling them again exactly what that bastard did to me. I continue by saying to them 'if I would have asked the brothers first who it was, then reported it and given his name would things be different? She said 'yes, as two people know the name which means it could go to court'. I then become more angry and say 'so you're telling me, because I have done things the legal way I won't get closure but if I did things the illegal way, I would?' and they said nothing. They knew he was guilty, yet that was it as far as they were concerned. I then became louder saying 'you've only brought that man in case I do something and don't feed me with ya bullshit that he ain't, I ain't fucking stupid'. Finally, I finish the conversation with 'he won't do anything to me, you know why? He won't even arrest a pedophile, so you ain't doing anything to me'. Then I walk out of the house saying 'if you don't deal with it, I fucking will as he has done it to me so he is still doing it now. Once a dirty peado, always a dirty peado'. Once I had calmed down, I made my way back to my mums house where she said 'don't do nothing stupid', 'don't worry mum, I won't' thinking to myself 'yeah right!' I jumped on my laptop and inboxed the younger brother straight away asking where the piece of shit lived. His reply was near a certain pub but wouldn't say much more than that. With that, I made my way to my cousin's house where I banged on her door, shouting her name out saying open the door. She opened the door and saw the anger in my eyes and before she could say anything I said 'where does he live (shouting out his name)? She said 'Stevie, I don't know, I really don't'. I knew this to be a lie as she lived next door to the two brothers and knew the family well. I also know that she was protecting me as my anger was on a whole new level and she wanted nothing to do with the family next door since she found out. Then I said 'you know who he is so you tell that cunt when I find out where he lives, I'm gonna cut his fucking throat, trust me on that one'. I didn't see her daughter was in the kitchen and she looked upset, I didn't see her as all I was focused on was getting my hands on that sick bastard and putting him 6 feet in the ground where he would never hurt another child again. By now I am fixated with justice and there was no going back from this point as I now had his name and from this point on I was the predator and he was the victim. From that day on, I would make a promise that I would get justice, one way or another. After all, the police had pretty much confirmed to me doing things the legal way doesn't work, so now I was doing things my way as relying on others is something you can always be let down with. I wasn't letting myself down regarding this as I had let myself down all my life by letting him live in my head rent free for over thirty years. Payback was coming, one way or another and the legal way didn't work so now it was time for the illegal way and that was down to me to deal with now, not others. I want to see him suffer, cry, break down and drive himself crazy, then he will see exactly what it feels like to destroy someone's life and make them feel like an existence just like he did to me, revenge is sweet. I couldn't believe it and I was certainly not accepting that the older brother couldn't remember, it wasn't sitting well with me. Then I start to think it's more of a case of he doesn't want to remember. I'm not asking him to discuss anything about his life or family but I want him to be honest and do the right thing by saying that he remembers who took us that day. After all, his younger brother remembered. Why shouldn't he? I couldn't get to him to talk to him as I didn't know where he lived and I knew he had kids himself and if I'm honest there was no way I would go to his house as I wouldn't want his children to feel uncomfortable and get upset. It's just not a bit of me and they hadn't done anything wrong. I just don't get how there are billions of people on the planet and there is only one person that can give me justice and he won't! It just doesn't seem fair does it? Gradually, over the next couple of days I continue to fixate on my justice and I am not coping. Since the police gave me such devastating news, I find myself making myself sick after every single meal, even healthy meals. I suppose it was the only thing in my life I could control and it wasn't the right way to deal with things but at the time I knew no different and thought that if I was sick, all the feelings, thoughts and memories would come out of me. It would also calm me down. My head wasn't in a good place as I was still sitting in limbo over thirty years later. I wouldn't have minded but I did everything the right way and after the ordeal of reliving it again by telling the police and getting absolutely nowhere, my only option now was to deal with things myself. I had lost everything and pushed away everyone that was close to me. I didn't have much to lose, but in my eyes, I had plenty to gain as I was now fighting for justice.

CHAPTER 8
OBSESSION AND SELF PUNISHMENT

AGE: 38 - 40 years old
YEAR: 2016-2018

Now into June 2016 and I am wanting answers as to why that sick bastard did what he did to me that day. I now know that he lives just off my estate and is near a pub which I drank in many times over the years. This sick bastard had lived within 300 meters of my house and had done ever since that day! I wanted answers and only he could give them to me, his time was coming. I myself was smoking more cannabis than ever as at that point I needed something to stop me thinking about all the bad things I wanted to do to him but on the other hand, my daughter would always be a reason I wouldn't. We now had the best relationship and was spending more time with each other with me trying to make up for all the early years of her life when I was, let's face it, a shit excuse of a dad. She kept me going and now had an understanding of my Mental Health and how I may see things a bit differently to everyone else. She was my rock, my world, my everything and I am so sorry for any pain I caused her. Finally, father and daughter together and me trying to be the best dad I could be.

One day in June I woke up after having no sleep and many nightmares as I was fixating even more about my demons. I just wanted them to go away but in my mind that wouldn't happen until this sick bastard is punished. After breakfast I start having a conversation with my mum in the kitchen and tell her I'm struggling with my demons and just need to block it out, followed by 'can you lend me twenty pounds please?' She said 'yeah, no problem, when ya tell me what it's for.' We had already made a pact, no more living a lie. Now I'm facing my demons and wanted to be honest only, no lying. My reply was 'for cannabis' she replied 'no, not for that shit' I replied 'I always pay ya back'. True signs of addiction kicking in, to the point where my poor mum had done nothing wrong and I start shouting! No way for a son to treat his mother, she hadn't done anything wrong. Storming off like a kid into the living room, I try to calm down but I am struggling with the thoughts in my head, thoughts of hurting him. I finally calm down after using breathing exercises I had been taught in therapy. Where I had been up all night with no sleep, I find myself falling to sleep. The next thing, I wake up crying where I must have had a nightmare and nothing was going to stop me from doing what I did next. I jumped up, put my trainers on, grabbed my car keys, wiped my eyes and made my way to my car. Once in my car I lean over, open my glove compartment and take out a gun. I then load the gun with bullets, I take a kitchen knife out my glove compartment and made my way to the pub where this sick bastard lived as I had had enough and was going in the pub to ask where this prick lived. I drove round to pub car park where I hand braked on to the forecourt full of anger, there was no going back now. I kicked the pub door open and stood there with my gun and knife. I said 'which one of you cunts is going to tell me where that pedophile (and said his name) lives?' People were scared and started saying 'we don't know mate'. I said 'does he drink here?' and they said 'yes', I replied 'tell me where he fucking lives then. If ya don't I will go to every door across that road and kick them all off there fucking hinges'. No reply. I then walk across the road and someone says 'that one there'. Finally, someone has done the right thing and had some sort of empathy as to what I was going through. I kick the wooden gate open, walk down the drive and take the patio doors out there frame and throw them on his front lawn. 'Get out here you dirty cunt! I've been waiting for this day for over 30 years! Get out here now nonse'. With that, the front door opened and now was my chance for justice and I wasn't fucking about. Time to release 30 years of anger in 5 minutes. I pointed the gun at his head and said 'you shouldn't do it anyway but it looks like you fucked the wrong kid don't it?' While he backs down the hallway, the tables have now turned and I was now the predator. Justice was sweet. Then, the prick had the front to start crying! Saying 'what have I done? What have I done?' 'What have you done? Let me give you a little clue, my name is Stevie and over 30 years ago you raped me and abused me twice in less than an hour, all to make you feel better. Remember now, you dirty cunt, well I'm here to make ME feel better!' He then says 'it wasn't me, I didn't do anything'. I said 'well that's a lie ain't it as there were two brothers and one was a witness and he has named and shamed you for lying. I'm gonna stab you in the leg and every time you lie I'll stab you again'. With that, I stabbed him in the leg and he started crying, 'that's nothing as to what I'll do if you don't tell the truth'. Then I stabbed him in the other leg, just because I could. I felt amazing, finally I was in control and that feeling was here to stay. Then he lies again so I stabbed him in the arm, while explaining to him that next time it will be in the neck. He was in pain and I loved it. I felt like Darth Vader, if you get my drift. My last words to him were 'did you rape me and abuse me when I was 6 years old you dirty fucking arsehole? Then the word I wanted to hear after all these years came out of his mouth 'yes'. With that, I took the gun out of my Jeans and pointed it at his stomach and pulled the trigger twice, he fell to his knees. I could have put one in his head but I wanted him to feel the pain I felt before he took his last breath. Then I said 'why? Why destroy my life? I was a 6 year old kid doing what I should be doing and that was, enjoying life'. No regret or sorry for what he had done, he was just gutted he got caught and with that I looked into his evil dirty eyes, pushed the gun in his mouth and pulled the trigger, blowing the back of this dirty bastards head off. I didn't care about the repercussions of my behaviour as I was now free and he could never touch another child, ever again. Then I hear that noise that no one wants to hear when you have just killed someone and that was police sirens. I make my way out the back door where I could get over the back fence. Still with the gun in my hand I make my way through loads of stinging nettles and finally came to the stone path where dead man's tree was and I made my way up through the garages on to my estate. Just as I was on the home straight and running free, out of nowhere a police officer jumps on me. My instant reaction was to pull the trigger and to my horror I shot the police officer in the neck. We were in a scuffle and he pulled me to the floor with him, blood everywhere and then everything went blank. I then opened my eyes and I'm looking above me expecting to still see the bloodied police officer on top of me. It was all white, where was I? Hospital/ Police cell? It dawned on me that I recognised the ceiling, then it hits me, it's my mum's living room ceiling and it was all a dream. Albeit the best dream I had ever had! Most people would have been relieved that they hadn't killed anyone. The dream felt so real and it felt so good and that's what sparked me to do what I did next. I started to put things into action as I wanted to feel like I did in that dream, I felt amazing and nothing was stopping me now.

I had planned to copy my dream as it felt so good but I didn't have a gun to hand otherwise I would have used it, believe me. Even though it was just a dream it felt so satisfying and needed to be done in real life as that feeling was immense and would become highly addictive. Finally, time to expose that dirty bastard and now the fun would begin. I grabbed my car keys, put my trainers on and made my way to the pub to ask about and find out where he lived. Just like in my dream I hand braked my car into the carpark of the pub to get everyone's attention, making sure I left the car a bit in the road as I wanted everyone to see where he lived and what he had done to me. I jumped out of my car absolutely fuming and kick the pub door open, then shout out 'where does that dirty cunt and (said his name) live?' People say 'over the road mate', I then say 'if ya don't tell me where he lives I'm gonna kick every door off its hinges until I find him'. I get no answer and make my way outside where cars and buses have stopped to see what's going on. Finally, I had my audience and I felt amazing but also felt unstoppable. I then walk up the first drive and walk towards the front door. 'Not that one mate, an old lady lives there'. 'Don't fuck me about and tell me where he lives then', then someone shouts out 'it's that door there' and points to it. I walk up the drive, bang on the patio doors and shout out in front of the whole pub and passersby, 'get out here you dirty cunt. I've been looking for you for over 30 years'. Then the front door opens and there stands the fat bald little cunt that had destroyed my life for over 30 years. I said 'get out here now you dirty peado. Come and tell everyone how you raped and abused me, come on ya clever cunt'. He replies 'what you on about?' I said 'you know what I'm on about you nonse cunt'. Then my anger went to another level as I looked into his eyes and instantly knew it was him. I will never forget them eyes looking down at me while he made me carry out sexual acts on him. I then pulled the patio door off its hinge and made my way for him at the front door but just like the slippery cunt he was he shut the door just in time, little fucking weasel. I then kick his door in shouting 'I'm the predator now you prick'. My opportunity had gone to get my hands around that dirty bastard's throat and strangle the prick to death. I also noticed that there was a disabled minibus directly opposite his house and my brain starts to tick causing me to break down in the street, telling anyone and everyone what he did to me. A lady tried to comfort me but I didn't want any sympathy. I just wanted justice and as far as I was concerned, it was only just the start. He didn't know when my next visit would be and that was a sign that I was now in control and I was just biding my time until my next strike. I was going to cause this prick mental torture, just so he would feel like I had for over 30 years. Hiding my true identity and hiding behind a mask. I made my way to my car and before getting in my car I turned round and pointed at his window, making a gun out of my fingers and doing a gun action just to let him know I was coming back, this was far from over. I went for a drive to calm myself down then made my way to my mum's. Once through the front door I gave her a cuddle, told her I loved her and acted like nothing had happened. I apologised for my outburst which I always regretted but I just couldn't help it as this anger had been in me for over 30 years and I didn't know how to deal with it at that time. I now know what car he had, I knew where he lived and the games could now begin, but I decided I wasn't waiting, I was going straight back round there for round two the next day. The next day arrived and I got into my car and drove to the pub car park again. What made me angrier was that he didn't even ring the police after all that trouble. Correct me if I'm wrong but if someone was shouting out that shit and threatening me at my front door, I would ring the police straight away and that was another clear sign this sick bastard was guilty, right? I noticed his car wasn't there so there was no point in creating a scene so I walked straight into the pub again, in more of an assertive and less aggressive mood. I asked to speak to the landlady who came out and before they could say anything I apologised for my actions and for the way I spoke to everyone the day before. She was in shock and gave me a cuddle saying she had no clue and had known him for ages. Then someone else in the pub added that he picked up disabled kids in his minibus who were aged between 6 and 12 years old and drove them to various places through a company. My anger was becoming worse and as I walked out and said 'if you let that dirty cunt in here again, I will kill him on your premises and that's a promise not a threat, make sure you tell him that from me please'. Yet again, as I pulled away I looked at the house pointing my hand like a gun, just in case he was in there. Again, letting him know I will be back.

What I needed at this point was for the older brother to come forward and give an account of what actually happened that day rather than claiming to not remember. That didn't look like it was happening anytime soon so I guess I would have to have my justice without him corroborating mine and his brothers accounts of what happened.

Late afternoon that day the house phone rang and it was the police asking for me. They said they had received a call from a neighbour of the dirty bastard saying someone had started shouting and threatening their neighbour. Another sign of guilt, that bastard didn't even call the police after all that, guilty that's what that is. Then they asked 'was it anything to do with you?' my answer was 'no but it's a shame you can't look for pedophile's as quick as you chase so called criminals'. They then informed me that if I was to do with it at all then I would end up getting arrested. I said 'well you ain't doing a great job of nicking a dirty peado so I don't think you'll catch whoever it was yesterday' then I laughed and put down the phone. How dare they call me making me look like a criminal! Who the fuck do they think they are? From that point on, my hatred for the police would go up a level. After all, they had forced all my trauma out of me, making me come forward and get things moving quickly, telling me everything would be ok. Then when they can't resolve a case quick enough they fuck you off and let you down. So yeah, I hated the police with a passion as they were stopping me from getting justice in my eyes. I was also paranoid as fuck, down to the amount of cannabis I was smoking just so I could get a decent night's sleep and avoid my problems. Yet again, putting myself through complete punishment and relying on mind altering substances just to get me through a day. I'm not sure if it was because I wasn't ready to face things or whether it was all down to my new addiction of cannabis, which I now loved more than cocaine and alcohol. The cannabis blocked out things to a whole new level but as I said before with addiction and doing things regularly, you become immune and that was the worst thing for someone like me who just wanted to be numb. Once you're immune, you want more and with that comes more expense then more paranoia and psychosis. I didn't care as I wanted all the memories and thoughts of that day to go away and it was a true sign that I wasn't ready to deal with things at this moment in time. This is why counselling had stopped and I had no one I could talk to about things. When I mean no one to talk to, I mean someone who didn't really know me or was a family member or friend as it wasn't the sort of conversation you could have with them as it would bring them down and is traumatic to hear about. I started to try and cover up my addictions by trying to look healthier and in a way going back to hiding behind a mask, but the mask I was now hiding behind was to cover up my addiction not my demons. I would start having sunbeds, making everyone think I was looking good on the outside in the hope they wouldn't know how damaged I was on the inside. I would end up meeting the lady who owned the sunbed shop and before you know it I was going to see her and have a sunbed every now and then. I would find myself gaining a new friend and she was a lady full of empathy and understanding and was someone who wanted to listen and help me if she could. This lady became a very important person in my life as I noticed in her shop, not only would she help and advise me, but also others who were struggling in life. She was lovely, inside and out and I found myself feeling better in myself every time I walked out of her shop. I never really believed in things like this before but she was my guardian angel, someone who didn't know me but was willing to try and help me get myself back on track, something she didn't have to do but clearly enjoyed doing. I would spend more time with my other friend at her flower shop as I feel that I could relate to her more than anyone due to our similar pasts. She was someone who understood everything about my demons. I would give her a hand, trying to keep myself occupied as I couldn't continue therapy as they thought I wasn't ready. Really I was but I was seeing things differently due to my cannabis addiction. We could talk for ages and knew what the other was going to say due to both having the same demons. It made me feel normal for a few hours a day as others that hadn't suffered like we had just wouldn't understand how we both felt and what we had to live with daily.

She so wanted her justice and one day while I was in the shop with her she received a phone call saying her perpetrator was going to court and her day of speaking out had finally arrived. She was so happy but at the same time I could see the fear in her eyes knowing she would have to face the person that took away her childhood and even her adulthood as the road to recovery is no quick fix. She would even shed a tear as it was something she had always wanted but now it was here the reality of what happened to her would hit home. I loved helping her out and I'm not trying to say I was a saint because in a way it would be for selfish reasons, as if I was dealing with someone else's problems, I wouldn't have to deal with or face mine. I was so happy for her but at the same time I was thinking 'where's my justice?' Why can't I stand in court and tell my story? Just because the justice system wanted to save money! Haven't I suffered enough for many years without my voice being heard? I didn't let her see my own disappointment and smiled, giving her a cuddle and saying 'don't worry mate, he will get guilty and you can get your life back'. I wasn't sure he would go down but I told her what she needed to hear as the fight for her justice was only just beginning. She was a strong independent woman on the outside but I'm not sure if that was the case on the inside but she was also good at hiding behind the mask, just like I was.

STEVIE - BEHIND THE MASK

Just over a week later I was struggling more with my situation as I had been fixating about it most days and nights, which was all down to the amount of weed I was smoking. I myself didn't see weed as a gateway drug as I personally felt that the reason I used drugs in the first instance stemmed from a lot further back to my childhood and what happened. From that day on, I knew I had changed and that I saw the world differently to everyone else which in turn made me feel like an outcast, not belonging to society. Making me feel like I was the one in the wrong all the time, just feeling different in general. I would like to say the drugs made me feel like that but the fact of the matter is, my life changed forever after that day in the woods. I accepted that it was my fault what happened to me that day, doing a right instead of a left. I will certainly not take the blame for the way my life turned out after that day that was all down to that sick bastard. I waited a week but was pissed off and this sick bastard needed a visit and a bit of mental torture. Why should I suffer while he lives the dream? The only problem was I needed to be hidden, that wasn't going to be easy and I wanted to do it sooner rather than later. If I'm honest, I wanted to go and do it there and then but I couldn't take the risk of getting caught. Then it hits me! Halloween is six weeks away, perfect! I'll get a mask, wear black and cause him some mental abuse back, the dirty bastard. I needed to get away from this arsehole as my feelings of anger towards him were becoming weird. The things I was thinking of doing to him were on a whole new level. Then, half-way through October I had something go my way for the first time in ages. I received a letter in the post saying I had been offered temporary accommodation in Dartford which was a bit a distance from Welling but maybe that's what I needed, a fresh start away from him and do what I could to try and move on with my life. I wasn't holding my breath as until justice was done I would never move on, otherwise I would be condoning what he did to me, accepting it was ok and it fucking wasn't. Then just like that, I now find myself leaving my mum and dads with eight black bin bags of stuff and I am leaving Welling, I was devastated as my whole life was in Welling. I knew many people, family and friends here and I was leaving it all behind. I had nothing and it felt like I was losing even more. I know it had to be done but now I was alone and I wasn't intending on talking to anyone in Dartford as my trust issues were off the chart since the police and one of the brothers let me down. Plus, the sick bastard had taken all my trust in the woods that day. I should have been happy having a fresh start but I didn't feel safe on my own at times. Yes, I was an adult but my Mental Health wouldn't allow it on some days and it's something I just couldn't help. Yet again, other things affecting me due to that sick bastards actions and it just shows the extent of the damage he had caused me. My dad helped me move as by this time I had pushed everyone away and was now living alone in Dartford. This place was not to be painted as it was temporary so I couldn't do anything to it. It was dark and dingy and this is where I spent the next couple of weeks, locking myself away and pushing society away in every way possible. I was now smoking a bag of cannabis a day, blocking out every thought and feeling about my childhood and all the other shit I had been through. My thoughts were now being controlled by addiction to cannabis and I was on a different planet.

Halloween finally arrived and this was going to be the night I gave this sick a bit of his own medicine and cause him a bit of mental abuse by playing some mind games. I had already bought myself a scream mask and purchased a black tracksuit which was in my bedroom stashed away. I made my way to my bedroom where I opened my drawer and took out a co2 powerful air pistol that looked like a real gun and had the look of a Beretta. You couldn't kill anyone with it but it could still cause damage. Yeah, it should have been a real gun but my world and my rock would stop that from happening and that was my daughter. As much as I wanted justice, my daughter still needed her dad and that would always be my priority. After all, I had let her down for so long and things were just getting good between us. Getting back to the story, I put the co2 air pistol down my trousers and put the mask in a rucksack. I then put on a blue coat, so I didn't look too obvious walking along in complete black clothes and lastly I added a blue cap. I left my prison and made my way to Welling, heading straight for that sickos place, stopping in nearby fields and stashing up my rucksack, coat and cap. Then I take out my scream mask and put it up my jumper and start running to look like I'm jogging until I'm nearer to his house. Once across the road from his place I put on the mask and take the co2 pistol out of my trousers, it was a metal finish with a silver shine so he could see it was a gun. I then load up my pistol, point it at his bedroom window and fire two shots at the window to get his attention and scare him. Just like he did to me that day, the tables are turning again. Once I saw him come to the window and pulled back the net curtains, I make my way to the center of the road with my mask on where I look up at him and tilt my head side to side, freaking him out completely, just like he did to me that day. Then to finish it all off and totally freak him out, I take the pistol out of my trousers again and pointed it at him so he could see it was a gun. I then fired the other six shots at his house. Finally, he could start to feel how scared I was that day and in time he would feel the pain that I did that day. With that, I ran off to the field, leaving the thought in his mind 'who just did that to me?' The same thought I had when sitting in the bath at aged 6 years old washing myself with bleach. It won't make much sense to anyone else why I did this but to me it made all the sense in the world. After all, revenge is sweet and he needed to feel my emotions and pain to know exactly how it felt. I managed to get back to my flat in Dartford without getting caught. I felt amazing and if I'm honest, I thought 'I could get used to this'. He was now thinking 'who was it?' and 'why me?' just how I wanted him to feel as that's how I felt that day.

I spent the next few months locked away in my flat and my daily routine consisted of smoking cannabis, eating food and then making myself sick at least four times a day as my bulimia had grabbed me in a big way. This was, no doubt, down to mind altering substances and insecurities. I didn't even watch television, just locked myself away thinking 'I was protecting myself but all I was really doing was punishing myself'. I didn't want to be here anymore, I wanted to die but my daughter popped into my head again and I would battle with my thoughts more than ever. I loved my daughter so much but I just couldn't deal with having no justice and wanted to go to sleep and not wake up one day that would have been lovely. I may have been clean of alcohol and cocaine for a while now but the cannabis was my new fix, doing what it needed to do but also playing tricks on my mind. The reason I was locked away was down to the paranoia and psychosis from cannabis, it was so intense but it was better than dealing with my demons. I spent New Year's Eve in my flat on my own as, what the fuck did I have to celebrate? I still held on to the thought of 'new year, new beginnings' and all that shit. I wasn't very optimistic if I'm honest as every year I had thought the same and it never changed, so why would it now? The only way it would change, would be if I got the justice I deserve. Until that happened, I would continue to punish myself and become a lone walker, that way my trust issues would be protected.

The start of 2017 was here and nothing much had really changed regarding my daily routine. As far as I was concerned, I was ok but really I was getting sucked deeper into depression as now my medication was no longer working due to mixing them with mind altering substances, that being cannabis. The more I stayed in, the more I would drive myself mad fixating more and more about my demons and what I had lost. I had given up. I had no more fight in me and just didn't see the point in life anymore. I had been fighting for over thirty years, hiding this secret.

STEVIE - BEHIND THE MASK

The only reason I came out with it was to feel better and so I could start enjoying my life but I didn't, I felt worse as I was still in limbo, just like everything else in my life. I had no one and it wasn't anyone else's fault but my own. It was me that needed to man up and deal with things with a clear head but that wasn't going to happen until I got back into the real world and was free from any mind altering substances. Was I ready to do that? No, I fucking wasn't, not unless they could give me medication that stopped my nightmares and until someone could, I would carry on using cannabis which was stopping all the nightmares. I was addicted to it now and it did so much for me, I loved it, another clear sign of how addictive this substance was. While out walking one morning, I would end up walking past a lady I had walked past a few times now and she lived a few doors away from me. As you know, I trusted no one but we said 'good morning' a few times to each other and now and again we would have a chat. It was a big thing for me having someone to talk to who wasn't family or a close friend, I didn't want to talk to anyone if I'm honest but I was so lonely, I had no choice and my head was in a totally different place. I was surprised she even entertained me as I was permanently stoned, maybe she felt sorry for me as I looked like I was there but nobody was home if that makes sense. As I got used to talking to her I found myself opening up to her even more, being able to release how I was feeling on a daily basis to someone which was a good thing as it would save me from having one big outburst and doing something stupid. We became good friends and she was a very empathetic person and understood how I was feeling which in the end made me tell her what had happened to me. I just wasn't coping with my demons which was all down to me not facing things with a clear head. Also, feeling sorry for myself, thinking the world owed me a favour because of what had happened to me that day in the woods. It was only a matter of time before I would do what I normally did and I found myself pushing her away. Just like I did to everyone else in my life growing up.

I came out with this to get better but was still holding out, hoping for the older brother to come forward and do the right thing. If he did, I could get the justice that I needed. For the time being, I wasn't letting things go and if it made me more ill then so be it. I was not having that in my mind knowing he was roaming free, just waiting for his next victim. So holding on to getting justice and him being locked up so he couldn't hurt others was my only way forward. I spent another few months punishing myself, creating more paranoia and psychosis. I was smoking a bag of cannabis a day, but it would all be worth it to see this sick bastard get what's coming to him. Into May and things were looking up again as I was offered my own flat in Belvedere, not too far from Welling but not too close at the same time. Win win situation if I'm honest. I felt good knowing I could now have a bit of security and try to start moving forward with my life rather than blaming and punishing myself every day. My new flat was lovely and was in a very secure estate. It was a big thing for me as I just wanted to be alone so I could try and move forward. This was the perfect opportunity for me as my new place would be local to all my counselling groups which I didn't really commit to due to not being able to cope with the train journeys.

My mum and dad were supportive as always and helped as much as they could to get me settled into my new place. Without these two, I can guarantee that I wouldn't be here today, they made things so much easier but still struggled to talk to me about my trauma. I always thought they were being tough but then came to realise that if that was my child, I'm not sure I could deal with or hear about it myself. The way I looked at it, when there is no one else around who is always there, my mum and dad. Things were different regarding my situation though as I could always tell them anything but this was so traumatic that many people couldn't deal with it. Me and my dad would do the painting inside the flat and I did everything else myself as it was an ideal time to occupy myself and stop me thinking about my problems. In a way, I was avoiding my problems thinking I was being clever when really, they were building up to explode yet again by not facing things head on. Once settled into my new flat I decided to give up the cannabis as I needed a clear mind with a second round of psychology coming up in July. That was only a month away at this point so it needed to be done and then I could face my demons head on with psychology once a week and try and get myself fixed as I was so damaged inside. All that was keeping me going in life was my brave, beautiful daughter and she was the only reason I thought that life was worth living. Plus, the only reason I gave up cocaine and alcohol was for my parents, which was the wrong thing to do, I should have been doing everything for myself. Once all moved into my flat I find myself going out more and starting to integrate with society again after locking myself away for eight months, at the time it's all I knew and was the only way I felt safe, which was all down to the paranoia from smoking cannabis. Then one day, while on a social networking site I notice a group saying 'predators beware'. Straight away I want to know what this is all about. I clicked on to the group and discovered another way of hopefully getting justice. On this site they set up fake accounts and try to catch out pedophiles. My stomach turns and I become a little excited as straight away I'm thinking 'they can catch the sick bastard that did what he did to me'. Straight away I write them a message in the hope of getting a reply and helping me to get my justice. I took my time as I wanted them to understand how much getting my justice meant to me. Once I finished the message, I sent it to them and about another six online predator catcher groups, hopefully I would get a reply and things could start to move forward. I would like to share the message I sent to all of them with whoever may be reading this book. Just to give you an understanding of what I was going through and the damage he had caused to my life.

Hi,

My name is Stevie.

STEVIE - BEHIND THE MASK

34 years ago, coming up to my 7th birthday I was raped and abused in the worst possible way in the fields at the back of my estate. The person who did this was a lot older and there were two witnesses. The younger witness remembers and the older witness (his brother) does not. I can't get my head around that.

I found out after 34 years who did this to me. The younger brother (the one who remembers) informed me of who it was and he lived 200 meters from my parents' house and still does. I have attempted suicide and have been sectioned many times as I just can't get my head around it all. What did I ever do wrong in life to deserve this?

I can't get justice as this is classed as historical abuse so they need two bits of evidence to prosecute. As I was unaware of his name until after I had reported it, mine was not classed as evidence! So, unless the older brother remembers, I will not get the justice I've always needed and wanted. I have spent the last two years trying and I am now at a dead end. Once I was told where he lived I confronted this piece of shit at his front door, I saw them eyes that I could never forget looking down on me as a 6 year old child, I'd finally found him. He shut the door and I exposed him to everyone outside his house before breaking down in the middle of the street.

STEVIE - BEHIND THE MASK

I have a personality disorder that was brought on from my childhood trauma, I trust no one and I just feel like an existence. My life has suffered for so long and I am trying with all my heart to move on and am attending many classes to try and get well. I have taken cocaine, other drugs and alcohol to block this out but no longer do those to block it out as it's so tiring with everything else I have to deal with on a daily basis.

Anyway, I wondered if you could catch this scumbag out as I feel that if I get closure my life can begin. I can try and have the life I feel I deserve as the last 34 years have been a mask of misery. How could anyone look at a child in that way and do that? I just can't get my head around it, anyone would know that's not a normal thing to want or do. He is on Facebook and has pictures of young girls bending over cars, it's absolutely disgusting that someone can get away with this.

Every Halloween I feel helpless as I know there are kids knocking on his door and there's nothing I can do to help them. Because I kept going to his house the Police finally paid attention and visited his work, where he had been driving groups of 6 to 12 year old disabled children around in a minibus. He's no longer doing that job as I made sure of that, them kids needed to be saved no one deserves to live the life I have lived after suffering such a violent trauma, its soul destroying.

Sorry to go so deep but I have kept this in for most of my life and I will fight for Justice until the day I die!

If you can help I would really appreciate it as I just want to be the FREE Stevie not just the TORTURED Stevie.

Yours,

Stevie

I wanted them to see how much help I needed so I left it at that and it was just a waiting game getting a reply. By now I was a week into not smoking weed and was already struggling with having a clear mind and gradually the thoughts of justice and revenge would creep to the forefront of my mind. It's probably where I had suppressed them for so long with cannabis, it's not like I was using it in moderation, and I was smoking a bag a day, every day. Addiction is a cruel thing as now I was feeling the withdrawal and it wasn't a nice process to go through. It was causing me to have nightmares and feel the full force of the emotions I had been holding in. I would use my daughter as a way of getting through the tough days, thinking about how much she needed me. I wish I could have done it for myself but when you don't care about yourself, how can you do anything for yourself? Then the day I start psychology is finally here, it wasn't the best start seeing that it was the 13th July, unlucky for some. I was just a moody bastard as I couldn't have my fix of cannabis which was now becoming a struggle and I didn't want this happening on my first day of counselling. If they would have known that I was smoking cannabis a week ago they would have cancelled it due to me not having a clear mind. I sat in the waiting room and my anxiety was through the roof as I'm now in a room with people I don't know and I trust no one. People were staring at me like I was some sort of weirdo, another sign of paranoia and psychosis kicking in and I hadn't even smoked anything. Then I get up and walk outside as my mind starts to go into overdrive and I start to panic, thinking to myself stay calm Stevie these people are only here to help you. I try to focus on something positive so I can go back in and wait for my name to be called, it works, there she is again, my beautiful daughter popping into my mind, coming to the rescue and then I start to calm down as I remember I'm doing this for her. You only do things for people you love and those feelings towards my daughter were stronger than ever. I make my way to reception and apologise for walking out then as I walk into the waiting room a lady comes out and calls my name, I put my hand up as I wasn't in the mood for talking and made my way to her room where she asked me to sit down. I was happy that she was female as if it was a male I would have walked out, one hundred percent. The first thing she said was 'we can stop at any time and we will take things nice and slowly'. If I'm honest, I just wanted to get on with it so I could get it done and get home as I couldn't deal with being out of my flat. Big signs that I was becoming a recluse and avoiding any and every situation that comes my way. She then explained how we will be talking about what happened to me as a child and how I was feeling. I start thinking to myself 'I live this every day and now I am expected to bring it all to the front of my mind which I can guarantee will bring the nightmares straight back'. Not sure whether this was a fact or was the cannabis playing tricks on my mind, just begging me to smoke a joint. Then she informs me that she will be waving a pen in front of me whilst talking about my feelings and emotions, and they have the front to call me Mental! What the fuck is this lady going on about? For now I follow what she says and she asks me to follow the pen, once in a rhythm she asks me what happened to me and within seconds, the tears are running down my face and I'm trying to hold my anger in. Then I stand up as I am shaking with anger and crying. All I can see in my head was him doing what he did to me that day, she then stops speaking and I break down even more, this is so hard to deal with. This is not what I signed up for. Yet again, I would think of my daughter which was the only reason that I was still in that room. I was fighting the sadness and anger and trying to get to the root cause of my pain, it was horrible and I didn't see how this was going to help. I felt ten times better when I was mentally torturing the sick bastard that had made me this way, that was my therapy and as far as I was concerned that was the only way. Then she said I think we will leave it for today Stevie you've done really well, I said 'you having a fucking laugh?' not in a horrible way but more of a sarcastic way, her reply was 'no, you really opened up and that's where we need to be'. I said 'really? I got somewhere I need to be' and then I walked out. As soon as I walked out of that place I would start to cry but they weren't tears of sadness, they were tears of anger. As you can guess, the sick bastard is due another visit so I make my way to my flat where I plan his next visit. I was driving myself mad again, fixating on that sick bastard. I wanted to forget but I couldn't as I had lived it for so long and still didn't have what I wanted more than anything and that was my justice. Before going to my flat, I did the craziest thing by making a phone call to order some cannabis. They want me to stop cannabis for that mental torture? Reliving what I already lived every single day. Now I feel myself rebelling against the mental health services as they were about as much help as the police and everyone else that had let me down. Yet again, the cannabis was playing tricks on my mind, making me see everything so differently. So, I thought 'fuck it, if in doubt, block it out', that's how easy addiction is and it was so much easier to block everything out than face my demons.

Into September 2017 and my 40th birthday is here, not that I would have anything to celebrate apart from living silently in hell. Even so, I made the effort and put on the mask for my family as in my mind, there was no point in celebrating as I was still in the same position that I was when I first came out with my demons and that kept me in limbo. I remember my mum saying 'life begins at forty my son' and me thinking 'you really have no idea how I feel do you?' But I just smiled, gave her a cuddle and pretended that everything was ok, just like I normally did.

I then spend the next month locking myself away from society, smoking cannabis but still attending psychology so no one would suspect what I was up to. With Halloween just around the corner, that can only mean one thing, it's time to pay that sick bastard a visit and cause some mental torture. This time I would need to do something different and play some more mind games, making sure he felt the full effect and making sure it caused him more torture rather than standing across the road pointing an air pistol. By now, I'm fixating more than ever thinking I was doing the right thing, not realising I was causing more pain to myself by carrying on the way I was but until justice was served, I didn't see any other way. I wanted to kill him but my daughter would be devastated if ended up in prison and I had already let her down so much in her life.

Halloween is finally here and it was the worst day to have psychology as I knew that sick bastard would be praying for children to knock on his door tonight. Well, not if I've got anything to do with it he won't and with that I called the hospital and cancelled my psychology appointment. It was the worst thing I could have done as all that anger I could've released in counselling will now be taken out on that dirty bastard. The kids needed protecting and that was enough for me to decide that he's getting a visit and that's all there is to it. Anything to stop him noncing other kids on a night that children celebrate, I wasn't having that on my conscious as I had already felt guilty for the amount of children he must have abused after me, due to me not coming forward sooner. As evening approaches I start getting myself ready to put some fear into that dirty bastard. I pack my rucksack, put on my black tracksuit and make my way towards Welling. The feeling I got when I knew I was going to cause him fear was immense and for once I was in control. He was fearing my next visit. Well, tonight was the night. Once in the field, I put on my scream mask as I wanted him to know it was the same person that visited him last time. I then take out my co2 pistol and make my way around to the back of his house from the field where I get myself a nice angle. I then pull out the pistol and fired three shots at the back of the house, making enough noise to disrupt whoever was in there, then I saw a shadow in the top window. I now have his attention so I reveal myself, not just so he can see me but actually reveal myself by taking off my mask, looking up at the window, firing three shots at the house then shouting 'now you know it's me, ring the fucking police'. I shouted that three times and then the shadow disappeared out of the top window. I had shown him exactly who I was and I was no longer hiding behind a mask, like I had for so many years. Now I had to get back to Belvedere as he knew it was me and it wouldn't be long before I got a visit from the police or maybe not. Not willing to take the risk, I get back to Belvedere. Once inside my flat I start to cry as I started to realise how much worse my obsession for this sick bastard was getting and I was so confused, he was still ruling my head and my life.

I so wished it was a real gun as that would have finished the job off and I could have my justice. As much as justice meant to me, my daughter would always come first as I really didn't want to lose her again and yet again I'm in limbo regarding my life and I couldn't take much more. My daughter was my rock, my world, my everything and I wanted to be a good dad but this bastard destroyed all that so how could I move on without justice? I just couldn't and I wouldn't let it happen. My daughter, my parents and everyone I knew in my life had suffered one way or another because of what that dirty bastard did to me and I can't and won't accept it, for as long as I'm breathing.

I attended my next counselling course a week later and am not in the best of ways as my cannabis addiction is now ruling my life and slowly but surely I'm becoming out of control. I was arguing with anyone and everyone, all because I was letting this anger inside of me take control and I was now associating everything around my demons. While in a busy waiting room my anxiety and paranoia kicked in as I'm thinking everyone is out to get me. It sounds terrible but I would still deal with all that as it was better than facing my past but until I did, I would look at the world totally different to everyone else. Not realising I was punishing myself more and more. When my name is called I jump up quick and practically sprint into her therapy room, she can see I'm in a state and am struggling to control my emotions and feelings. She then explained to me that this is what BPD (Borderline Personality Disorder) is and if you put in the time you will be able to manage your emotions and feelings but you have to let me in so I can help, followed by 'you need to be honest Stevie, otherwise how can I help?' I then broke down and told her I had been smoking a lot of cannabis to help me sleep and block out my problems. She then explained that the problem was always self-medicating and not dealing with things with a clear head. To which my reply was 'I walk alone, I push everyone away, how can I trust you? Why would you want to help me? I'm damaged goods'. For once, I see her eyes fill up as she could see what a state I was in but she remained hard and professional, even though she could feel my pain. Then when she realised how bad a state I was in, she agreed we should stop, this was making me worse, and then she explained I just wasn't ready. I'm thinking 'I know I'm more than ready as I've waited for over 30 years.' Her reply was 'if you were ready, you wouldn't feel the need to self-medicate all the time. Plus, your core emotion is anger and until you manage that and tell people how you feel they will not be able to help you'. Breaking down even more as yet again counselling had stopped down to my anger and emotions being all over the place and being unable to control them. No doubt the cannabis addiction had a big part to play in that, changing my perspective on life. Finally she says 'I really hope you get to where you need to be in your life Stevie and wish you all the best', my reply was 'I ain't got a life and thank you for your time'. I remember her saying I need to control my emotions and deal with my anger, plus I need to take myself off of cannabis and then the real fight to getting better can begin. Just because I was in the Mental Health services it doesn't mean it was easy, it was soul destroying. But, if I wanted to better myself, then I would have to work even harder and be more open regarding my feelings and emotions as until they knew about me, how could they help me. What I needed to do was accept what had happened. But, how could I as I had lived like this since I was 6 years old and I didn't know any other way of dealing with things.

I would have a few friends that would always give me a call and come visit me now that I lived out of the manor. Thanks to that dirty bastard I even struggled to be near Welling as my thoughts of revenge would increase the nearer I was to him. One mate would be there right when I needed him and always was, it was my mate from the furniture shop in Welling, the one who tried to help me from day dot. He would just come round out of the blue and say, 'right get the car, I'm taking you out today' followed by 'locking yourself away ain't gonna help you get your arse in gear. Keep fighting Stevie, you're doing so well' and with that I would go with him. He would spend most of the time trying to make me laugh and drag me out of the dark hole I was in. He never gave up on me even during bad times when first talking about my Demons and had been there for the last 10 years, even though we didn't see each other a lot as he was busy looking after his own little family. Unfortunately, he had lost his brother to suicide and I'm not sure he could cope with one of his mates doing the same, hence why he wouldn't give up on me. This is something I will always be thankful for as he is another reason that I have made it as far as I have. It was nice to see him and get things off my chest but then I also needed to realise that he was a good friend and not one of my councillors, not the best thing to do as he was always honest with me and sometimes I didn't like what I was hearing but that's only because I saw things differently which could sometimes cause arguments. So I would tell him I'm ok and tell him what he needed to hear, that way I wouldn't have to hear the truth coming from a good friend. Clearly I was in denial and tried to put on a brave face but sometimes I just opened up and cried. I just needed the feelings and emotions out which in turn would make him upset and that's something I didn't like to see, hence why sometimes it was easier to tell him I'm ok and just put the mask on, saving others from getting hurt. The problem I then had was that I was suppressing my feelings which would only build up into an outburst. People would then see that and then they would think I was proper crazy when really I was just trying to filter the anger I had within. If I'm honest, I was very lucky to have him in my life as I wasn't the easiest person to get along with at times. I was unpredictable when it came to my moods and emotions but that was understandable with a diagnosis of Borderline Personality Disorder, due to childhood trauma. I never knew how I was going to feel from one day to the next as my biggest struggle was trying to maintain some sort of stability in my life. Something a lot of people struggled to deal with as they never knew what they were going to get when I was around. The cannabis without a doubt, made things a lot worse, as not only was I dealing with my Mental Health but also dealing with paranoia and psychosis caused by my drug addiction to cannabis but anyone trying to tell me the drugs were making things worse I would cut them short or change the subject. Clearly I was sticking up for this drug and wouldn't have a bad word said about it, I was telling people who were drinking that hundreds a day die from alcohol but no one ever died from smoking cannabis. It was clearly a problem and was stopping me from moving forward in my life but I wasn't admitting that to anyone as I thought it did so much for me, blocking out all my shit. I wanted to stop it but my theory was 'if it ain't broke, don't fix it', not realising how broken I was inside and causing yet more self-punishment to myself. I always blamed myself for turning right that day, instead of left as I know it would never have happened and maybe, just maybe my life would be better than what it is now but people would say to me 'it ain't your fault, you were just a child'. I'm a realist at the end of the day. It doesn't matter how old I was, I did wrong and that's all there is to it. Just like it was my fault I was not moving forward due to my addiction and not being ready as 'not being ready' was a great excuse so I could keep hanging on to all my Demons. Hoping the longer I held onto it, the more chance of justice there was. I was just thinking that the police would knock on the door, just like that and say 'we got the bastard. That was how deluded I was at the time thinking 'hang on to this and the longer you do the more chance of justice there is', sad but very true. Now I'm starting to realise the way I am going is not helping anyone and all I am doing is hurting myself and the people around me. Why am I letting him win still and why am I letting him live rent free in my head and cause me more pain? Then I realised that things needed to change and decide to contact an old friend who had suffered in a big way regarding alcohol and cocaine, and was lucky to be alive. He managed to come out the other side, if anyone could help me it was him as he knew how out of control my cocaine, cannabis and alcohol was as I was out with him on a two day bender the day I broke my neck. He was really surprised to hear from me and he sounded like a totally different person and straight away I thought 'there is hope for me yet' as he was in a bad way just like I was, I couldn't help but tell him how I was feeling and pretty much broke down on the phone. He told me he could help but it ain't going to be easy and the journey had only just begun, I didn't take cocaine or use alcohol no more but being an addict the thought would always be there. He told me a bloke I could go and see but I needed to be honest and want to give up cannabis, his specialty was addiction and I was really hoping he could help with my cannabis addiction and also my bulimia which was now taking its toll on my body after a ten year addiction, yet again punishing myself rather than dealing with my demons. I spoke to the addiction specialist on the phone and told him exactly where I was at in my life, straight away he said he could help me but it wasn't going to be easy. I then said to him my life had never been easy so it shouldn't be a problem, thinking I knew it all, which is what I did when putting on my mask but he could see through my bull shit and must have heard it a million times. My mate, who put me in contact with him, said he would take me on my first time as I had trust issues and he knew I had spent the last 14 months locking myself away from society. To say I was nervous about the whole thing would be an understatement as I knew there would be other people there I don't know. That is something I had always struggled with inside. Plus, the paranoia from the cannabis had done me no favours whatsoever if anything it made things ten times worse, after all I was now a slave to my mind and once my mind got a taste of something it liked it wanted more and was very persistent until it got what it wanted. Welcome to the world of addiction, may your world be full of disappointment, rejection and all the other negatives that drugs provide. Then the day came that I tried to change my dark existence and come off the cannabis so I can face my demons head on. I called my mate to see what time he was coming as by now the cannabis had taken over my life and it was only a matter of time before things would get worse, unless I do something about it before it was too late. The thought in my head was 'don't go, it will be a waste of time', but the thought in my heart was 'my daughter and I needed to do this for her just like I did for my mum and dad with the cocaine'. Finally my mate and his partner arrived, I was in a right state and felt uncomfortable straight away as I didn't talk to many people at this point, and this was due to the paranoia from the amount of cannabis I was smoking. My old mate said straight away, well done mate you're doing the right thing but at the time it felt like the worst decision ever. Even though I knew him well, I hadn't seen him for a while and I didn't really know his partner but she seemed very friendly and willing to help, either way I was keeping my barriers up as being nice to me can only mean one thing, they must be out for something. All they wanted to do was help but I was in my own little world, suppressed by cannabis and prescription drugs looking at things totally different to everyone else. They could see the darkness within me and was both trying their hardest to make me feel at ease. The way I was thinking was so deep but so negative as well and I really couldn't see the point in anything anymore but that little bright light which was my daughter kept me going and trying to push forward with my life. I had only been in the car for five minutes and already I wanted to get out and go home. This wasn't because of my Demons as such but because my brain knew I was going to quit cannabis and already was playing tricks on my mind knowing it could no longer have its fix of cannabis. The thing about addiction that makes it so hard to deal with is that once you put a drug in your body, your brain likes it as it makes you feel good, it makes you feel immortal and it blocks everything out. In turn your brain likes what it is feeling and you have now created a void in brain, the problem you now have is that void needs to be filled and if it's not the brain will play tricks on your mind leading you back to one place and one place only and that's picking up the substance your brain now craves.

Getting back to the story, I now find myself at the group sitting in a hall with loads of other people sitting around me. I felt so lonely even though it was busy as I wasn't going to talk to anyone else that was struggling. I wanted to hear from the man himself and hopefully he could make me feel like I did when I was 6 years old, before everything went so drastically wrong. Then he enters the room and I think 'great, another male that is going to be telling me what to do. I don't think so. Why would he help someone for free? This bloke is up to something!' Then my brain whispers to myself, 'don't trust him, he can't help, he won't help us', signs that already my brain won't get its fix and is trying to change my mind set already. The feeling of being stoned enter my mind and when he was saying things I didn't want to hear I would come back with an answer, true signs I was an addict, sticking up for my self-medicating and backing the cannabis all the way, this bloke didn't have a clue or did he? Yet again my mind starts playing tricks on me. Then he points at me and says 'what you hear for mate?' He already knew why as my mate had pretty much told him what I had been through. Was he trying to mug me off? No, it was his way of getting me to open up and before ya know it I take it off the subject of why I was there and start talking about my childhood. He smoothly changes it back to cannabis and says 'if you can stop cannabis for ten days and follow my plan you will be free'. I wanted to laugh and say here we go again, another brainwasher, I ain't having this. I then say I smoke cannabis to block out my childhood and stop the feelings and nightmares, he replies with 'I know it's hard but you need to realise you're seeing the world differently. Not because of your childhood but because of the mind altering substances in your body'. No matter what I said he would have an answer for it, making me look like I was in the wrong. I found it very frustrating at what I was hearing as it involved me changing, which nobody likes and was even harder as addicts don't like change hence why they stay on drugs for many years but change was the only way and that's all there was to it. I would get anxious and angry a few times but that was due to people talking truth about addiction and at the time I didn't like what I was hearing at all. Finally the group ends and the bloke running the class came up and had a word with me, explaining that what happened to me as a child was wrong and a terrible thing to go through. I'm thinking to myself 'No shit Sherlock', but all he was trying to do was help but just like I did with everyone else in my life, I blocked it out and would push him away. All he was trying to do was help me and I just couldn't see why he would want to help me and yet again another sign that at this point my addiction was stronger than the words that came out that blokes mouth and if I'm honest at the time I thought 'this bloke is full of shit and thinks he is Jesus trying to change the world'. When I walk out the building, a sigh of relief runs through my mind and I think to myself 'thank fuck that is over. I ain't coming back to this place again', then I look at the church before getting into my mates car then laugh to myself thinking he definitely thinks he's Jesus as he has rented a hall next to a church. It's now confirmed in my eyes that this group was a load of bollocks and the person teaching the group hasn't even got a clue about the life I lead. Yet again, the way I was seeing things was totally different to him and that just goes to show the power of addiction. People want to help and you just don't see it as help but more of someone trying to stop you being happy, blocking out the pain and darkness when really it's the drugs that are making it worse. My mate then asked me how I felt about it and I said 'it was good mate, thanks for picking me up today it means a lot. Really, I was thinking the opposite but didn't want to let him down after all, he made the effort to pick me up plus I didn't want to say it was shit as he had recovered and would have said the same as the bloke in the group, that would have been the drugs talking mate, something I really didn't want to hear again. I got through my front door walked into the kitchen and started to roll a joint as if that group had never happened, ignoring everything the bloke said to me even though he was in the right, it didn't mean shit to me at the time. I wasn't ready to let go of my demons and I certainly wasn't ready to let go of cannabis yet as I was on the journey of obsession and self-punishment and the biggest problem of all was I couldn't even see it.

CHAPTER 9
ESCAPING THE NIGHTMARE

AGE: 40 - 41 years old
YEAR: 2018

January 2018 and I have had time to process what was said in the addictions group and I find myself cutting down on cannabis. What that bloke had said to me was starting to fight against the addiction and I found myself starting to beat it but I would still smoke one joint of an evening, it was a way of getting a little fix to feed my addiction plus, there wasn't any nightmares when I had. This was the biggest bonus of all and I saw it as a good thing as I wouldn't smoke any cannabis in the day time now but just of an evening to relax me and give me what little peace I had. My brain was always in overdrive with hundreds of thoughts of my demons in the front of my mind. No doubt psychology had played a big part in this as I was facing my demons in a deep way, trying to get out the anger and feelings I was experiencing on a daily basis. It had to be done as it was the only way to get all my feelings and emotions out, hence why it was stopped as I clearly wasn't ready but the truth was my addiction wouldn't allow me to continue. I was on the list for psychology for a third time as until I had dealt with this with a clear head, it would always be there. Something I just didn't want any more as I had already punished myself for over 30 years and something needed to change and that something was me. Easier said than done as I still really struggled with the fact that the sick bastard was still walking the streets, doing what he wants, when he wants. Destroying children's lives just to fulfill his sick fantasies and cause total destruction in his path.

Living in Belvedere had it positives and that's being as far away from that sick bastard as possible but that was something I struggled with as my life was in Welling and so was everything that I stood for. People would say hello to me every day as I had built a life in Welling being around the people I love and care about. Even the shop owners would come out of their shops in the high street just to say hello. Whereas living where I am now, I didn't know anyone, I trusted no one and wasn't willing to do so anytime soon. My point is that I was a somebody in Welling but was a nobody in Belvedere. That was down to my trust issues but also my paranoia from the cannabis addiction as I just couldn't interact or deal with society but with people I had known a long time there wasn't an issue and maybe it's because I had built up a little trust over many years with the people I knew.

Right getting back to the story and I now find myself attending the addiction group every Wednesday, trying to get as much information about addiction as possible. The more you know about your addiction, the more you can fight back and hopefully beat it. There was some stuff I didn't agree with as I was seeing things from an addicts point of view which goes to show the effect addiction had on my mind but I ignored these as I would end up making myself look silly arguing back every ten seconds, thinking I knew it all. That was mainly down to the fact I had cut down on cannabis and my brain didn't like it as it wanted its regular fix and I wasn't giving it what it wanted. The bloke who run the group saw me struggling and said 'keep going, you're doing well' as he thought I had totally stopped cannabis which is what I had told him but already I was lying and defending the cannabis as much as I could. This was a massive weakness as when you defend someone or something it becomes a passion and stopping a passion is a lot harder as passion gives you a nice feeling and who wants to stop a nice feeling. Because I had cut down on the cannabis my demons were slowly but surely creeping in and there was no way of blocking them out. How could I deal with them? If I did I would move forward but moving forward means no justice and I wasn't ready for that and don't think I ever will be.

Into March and I'm doing ok regarding smoking cannabis and only having the odd joint a day rather than a whole bag in one day. I'm slowly getting used to not being permanently stoned and trying to face my demons rather than bury them deep within. The only issue with that was that I suffered badly with Bulimia which is a type of self-harm, to me it was my release and once I had made myself sick it was like I was trying to get rid of my demons, it sounds crazy but it's the truth. Where I had been making myself sick four times a day for the last ten years, I would find it starting to affect my body more than ever, spitting up blood every now and then, waking up with chest pains, not bad ones but all the same pains I wouldn't have had if I didn't make myself sick. I was killing myself from the inside out but not giving a shit what it was doing to my body, it was my release and I felt better after it. I suppose it was the only thing I could control in my life. Not that anyone should be controlled because if they were meant to be controlled they would have come with a remote, like I have said before.

Then one night I went to bed without having a joint and unfortunately woke up after having the horrific recurring nightmare that I get with a clear head. I got up thinking to myself, don't let him win, get out of this flat and go get some breakfast. Once in the cafe, I ordered two of everything and a glass of milk. I must have eaten it in record time, followed by downing the milk. Then I made my way back to my flat where I ran into the toilet and put my fingers down my throat and made myself sick, just so I could have that bit of control in my life, not realising the damage I was causing myself. This was all down to my insecurities, maybe if I could deal with my demons I wouldn't keep making myself sick. Everything was crazy. I was crazy, my life was crazy, just crazy, crazy, crazy. Once I finished throwing up, I start to become dizzy and I am not feeling too good so I make my way to my bedroom, then lying on my bed, I'm struggling to breathe with my chest getting tighter by the second. Then I turned on my side to throw up again and brought up a load of blood. Then the panic starts to kick in so I ring my mate who has had major heart problems in the past and start explaining how I feel. It felt like a heart attack but he said it wasn't, I was still struggling to get my breath and was still coughing up blood so he advised me to ring an ambulance. I rang an ambulance and explained how I felt, I went to unlock the front door and just as I did I collapsed on the floor in my hallway. Shooting pains in my chest again, this was no panic attack as I had them on a regular basis plus, you don't bring up blood. Once the ambulance arrived I could barely hold myself together and would just break down crying as I had enough of living like this. Maybe I was killing myself slowly and even though my daughter always got me through, I was becoming tired of my life being in limbo and couldn't see any light at the end of the tunnel. Once in the ambulance they put an oxygen mask on me as I was struggling to get my breath. They would ask me questions and all I would talk about is what happened to me as a child. It ruled my life but when you hold a secret for over 30 years and you tell everyone, you hope that the more people you tell, the more chance of justice you can get. He had already done it to others and telling anyone and everyone would help me to find them. Even the ambulance driver wanted to cry. All I kept saying was 'please help me, please!' I was crying like a baby but I couldn't help it as I was having yet another break down, when will this all stop? I couldn't deal with it anymore. Once at the hospital both the paramedics said 'I really hope things get sorted for you Stevie, stay strong'. It was a lovely thing to say and it was nice to feel the empathy they had for my life story. I was then checked over by doctors and they had carried out various checks. They explained that making myself sick for so long was not good for my heart and that's why I brought up so much blood. He also added that it was very dangerous and many people have died from eating disorders. They were more concerned for my welfare as I was in a terrible state so they decided to refer me to the home treatment team, which are a group of trained people that help people when they can't look after themselves properly. A heartbreaking thing to admit but that was the truth of it, I needed help and I needed it now. They were only short term and would guide me in the right direction so they could try and help me recover. I wasn't holding my breath at the time but I had to take what help was offered as I had been a lone walker for too long and I couldn't do it on my own anymore. I had been broken again by my demons and cannabis addiction. I didn't know who I was all of a sudden and what day of the week it was. I had lost the plot again and it certainly wasn't third time lucky. I now realised I would have to put up the biggest fight as I was back with mental health services. If I didn't put up this fight and get the help I really needed my life would surely come to an end. I had to think of reasons to stay alive and there weren't many reasons at this point if I'm honest.

Once I had finished at the hospital my mate and his partner, the ones who took me to the addiction group and also told me to ring an ambulance, told me to call them when I was finished and they would come and take me home. I was in a complete mess and they could both see I wasn't in a very good place. While in the car on the way home he said 'you can't keep making yourself sick like that mate, it will fuck your organs in ya body up'. At the time I just agreed thinking 'what do you know', yet again someone trying to help and in my mind, I'm already pushing them away. The support and advice they both gave me was for the best but my mind was all over the place and I just needed to get home and have a joint. After all, I was living my life for cannabis not for myself. After all the cannabis was using me and I wasn't using it and still I would keep punishing myself. My mate and his partner said 'if ya need us, ring us, don't matter what time', another sign of someone who understands how I feel and what I'm going through. You think that would have been enough, knowing that he had come out the other side and had turned his life around for the better, why didn't I listen? I walked through my front door into my prison and there I am again all alone with only my demons to deal with and within five minutes my brain is calling for its fix. I roll a joint and the night time only joint went straight out the fucking window and I'll say it again, welcome to the world of addiction and welcome to the dark side. The next day I received a call from the home treatment team asking me to go to an appointment to have a health check and talk about my problems. This was something I wasn't happy about but it needed to be done if I wanted to escape this nightmare I was living and hopefully be free. I agreed to a time with the lady on the phone and felt anxious, yet more explaining and reliving everything! 'When do I get a break from all this and get the life I deserve?' I say on the phone. Her reply was 'you've suffered terribly in your childhood but without the help and support, things can't change', my reply was that 'I don't like change' I wasn't being sarcastic, just being honest. Her reply was 'if we don't make change, we stay where we are and I don't you think you've lived in darkness long enough?' Something I could answer but I didn't, still sort of pushing people away, staying locked onto my trauma, hoping for justice and I wasn't letting go until I got what I wanted and deserved. She then explained that once she had seen me, she could give me the help that I needed. I then say to her 'I bet you're thinking, why put yourself through such punishment and pain', I then started crying saying 'I can't let go until I get justice. He is hurting other kids and I can't accept that, please, I'm begging you'. She then said she is not the police but can help me feel better in myself, even she wanted to cry as she knew what I had been through in my life by reading my records. We ended the phone call without me flying off the handle and I just had to wait until tomorrow to hear what she was going to say regarding moving forward. I wasn't getting my hopes up as I had enough of trying and not getting anywhere. Not realising my cannabis addiction was playing a part in me not moving forward but also the thought of justice which was hanging by a thread, it wasn't a lot but it was better than holding onto nothing. Still, I would hide behind the mask even though everyone knew my story. I put that down to trust issues as I wasn't letting anyone in as I did it once and I won't do again. I ended up meeting with the lady from the home treatment team and was told to attend a group where there are others in my situation. I agreed but said I would like to do a course on how to deal with my emotions as once I could do that then I would be ready to deal with psychology and hopefully escape this nightmare. It was all there on a plate being offered to me, help again from two support networks and this time I was grabbing it with both hands as I knew this was the only way forward. Then my journey would really begin as I wanted to take all the knowledge I could and get an understanding of my illness and then I could keep my mind occupied at the same time. I was nervous about meeting others I didn't know but the fact there would be others there living the life I had been living would make me feel a little more at ease. All I ever said to anyone was that you don't understand as they couldn't unless they had been there. For the first time in a while I felt good about this group and I was intrigued as to how the group would work. I had nothing to lose and everything to gain. The support was there, more than ever, only a fool would refuse it.

Now into April and the journey and real fight began as it was my first day at my new counselling group. I was nervous as you like and straight away I decided to roll myself a joint and that way I could totally block out any bad feelings as I wasn't sure what way things would go. Yet again, not willing to deal with my feelings and emotions causing myself more pain and self-punishment. All I want is someone to understand how I'm feeling and make me feel like a 'someone' as being a 'no one' is very lonely and when you're alone that's dangerous as that's when you get time to think and thinking is something I hated doing. Things would only go one way and that's down. I get to the front gates of where my new group is, which is right next to a church, here we go again, another one who thinks they are Jesus! Straight away I start to think 'here we go, one of the poxy spiritual groups, this is all I need'. Thinking the worst as usual, I walk through the main doors and ask where the group is and a very lovely Scottish lady showed me the way. She made me feel very welcome at the start, happy days, and a female straight away. I felt at ease and things were going just fine. I then open the door to the group and this is an average size room and in the center of that room was a circle of chairs. Not having a clue what was going to happen next, I pick a chair, that being the one nearest to the door and sit and wait for the group to start, just in case I need to make a lively exit at some point as you never know what's going to happen in group therapy. Slowly but surely the chairs would fill, already I would start to feel anxious and my barriers go straight up as I don't know these people, they can't help me, they have no clue what's going on in my head, already putting myself into a negative situation. Then two ladies walk in the room and they are the facilitators for the group who keep things in order to stop things getting out of hand, so there is some sort of structure for us and everyone gets some allocated time to help with their problems. I was just hoping they could help me with mine as this group was an optional group to come to whilst I was awaiting more intense counselling. A way of keeping my mind occupied and preparing me for the tough journey ahead and even though it was a fight to get onto The Mental Health Services radar the real fight was only just beginning and it would have to get worse before it got better. Then the two facilitators would talk about how the group worked and then one by one we would check in, saying how we were feeling and why we were there. Then it was my turn and already my eyes are filling up and I was trying my best to stay strong but how could I as the thoughts were already controlling my emotions but for some reason I wanted to speak. I then went from not wanting to say anything, to spilling out my whole story but it was totally different to any other time I had told someone and that's because the others in the room understood me and were nodding their heads as if to say 'don't worry, we understand you'. Just like that I was relaxed and now surrounded by people that get me, that understand me but more importantly don't judge me. It was the hardest thing to do but also rewarding at the same time. I didn't feel alone all of a sudden and more like a part of something, something powerful.

Every other counselling session I had been to there was a qualified person that had learned from a book about how to help me. All of a sudden I'm being helped by people that are experiencing my journey or similar and some even with the same demons as mine and they felt my pain, felt my darkness and felt my feelings. Finally, people who understand me and people who had also suffered from a personality disorder due to childhood trauma and just like that, I suppose you could say, I would feel 'normal' but also part of something and even more importantly, somewhere I was welcome. The first session was definitely the hardest as I had to talk about my childhood and all the other negative stuff that was going on in my life. I cried like a baby if I'm honest and I felt like I was offloading all my shit onto people but they would give me support and that's something I had never been given before and in return they would all offload and be given support. Not many people could understand me but that's because until anyone had been through what I had, then how could they? They couldn't and it was as simple as that.

STEVIE - BEHIND THE MASK

All the worrying and anxiety was for nothing and all I wanted to do was ask questions to the others in the group. All of a sudden I was getting answers and the more the group went on, the more relaxed I became and my anger was so much easier to keep at bay. Plus, my thoughts and emotions were relaxed and I was buzzing but without a joint in my mouth. I was on a natural high for the first time in my life. It was a struggle to get through the first session but it was well worth it, as for the first time in a long time, I didn't feel alone. Once the group had ended I would check on how I was feeling about my first session and as you probably guessed, I was crying again but it was something I couldn't help as talking about my childhood was soul destroying but in the same sense, making me stronger as I was now facing my Demons rather than blocking them out. I was dumping all my shit and people were there to listen and showed nothing but support towards me. I still had so much I wanted to say and so many questions that I needed answers to. I only had to wait two days as this group was on a Monday and Thursday and already I had two things to look forward to in a week now. It doesn't seem like a lot to look forward to but to me it meant everything as that was all I had at the time and the thought of seeing my daughter every now and then of course. This child was my world, my rock, my everything and I was now doing this for her and as far as I was concerned that was a good thing.

Once home in my flat, I take time to process everything that had happened, then I run myself a bath as I feel so dirty after talking about what that sick bastard did to me that day. Yet again, fixating on my demons which were increased ten-fold due to my cannabis addiction, this would only make my OCD and cleanliness take over and before you know it, I'm bathing in bleachy water and scrubbing myself with a sponge. Not your everyday normal behaviour but the way I saw it, I was clean and if I was clean, life was easier. Just another part of the damage that sick bastard had caused to my life, making me see things differently to everyone else. After talking with people that understood me, I start to realise that the self-medicating of cannabis was good at first but now it has become an addiction and it was doing me no favours apart from helping with sleep and keeping the nightmares at bay. I knew it was wrong but what else was I supposed to do? The problem I had was that I was suppressing my feelings and emotions even more, not realising that yet again I was wearing another mask, making people think that I was ok.

I attended the group twice a week as it was the only place I could really get any peace in my mind and talk to those who were feeling my pain. The more I attended, the more I was determined to get myself out of this last addiction that was stopping me from moving forward. Maybe it was the cannabis stopping me from moving forward or was I just not ready? In my eyes, I was ready as I had waited over thirty years to be free from this shit. Why was I hanging on still? Because, at the time, justice was the only way forward for me so smoking cannabis would help with that painful thing I was clinging on to. I battled for many days, driving myself mad thinking 'yeah I'll stop', then two hours later 'why stop something that makes you happy?' I really I should be accepting the help again and stop pushing other services away, my trust issues rising to the forefront again. I didn't want to walk alone anymore, I wasn't strong enough.

Then after attending the group for three weeks I start to settle into the group, even though I'm still battling with the devil and the angel on each shoulder. Things were becoming easier as I had people there that was feeling exactly the same as me and giving me new techniques and tools to help deal with my daily struggles in life. In this place, sharing is caring and that's why I felt so at peace there. Then one day a new person started and she was very distressed and really struggled to open up in the group. This person would be another guardian angel in my life and before she even spoke I felt like we had something in common and there was a connection. I made it my duty to welcome her to the group and in time she would slowly come out of her shell and was wanting to talk. She heard my story one day as I was struggling and pretty much broke down asking why me? What did I ever do wrong to anyone? After that she opened up as she could see how I was feeling. It was a sad occasion but also one that brought our friendship closer. As she was talking more about her situation, it turns out she had exactly the same childhood as me but in my opinion, hers was on a whole new level. This poor lady had been raped and abused every weekend by her mum's boyfriend and would spend the week fearing when he was going to walk into her bedroom and destroy everything she stood for. What made this worse, in my eyes, was that he was practically family and it gets worse. Her mum knew it was going on the whole time, the dirty sad excuse of a mother. Her story brought me to tears and I would be there for her in her bad times and she would be there for me in my bad times. We knew exactly what the other was going through and it was this amazing, strong, independent lady that made me realise that I needed to put up a bigger fight than this if I wanted to move forward in my life. She would also tell me how she got justice and that he was in prison. My reply was 'well done you', but at the same time it was that word, justice, that I had longed for but I kept smiling in the hope it would make her feel better. She also explained to me how getting justice doesn't always mean you can move on as no matter what way you look at it, the sick bastard will always come out of prison one day. My reply was 'yeah, but at least they get some sort of punishment for their actions'. She replied 'they will never stop and there is only one cure for pedophiles and that's a 'gun to the head'. Now I'm liking my new friend even more as she definitely thinks the way I do as we are both crazy and hate pedophiles with a passion, perfect friendship in my opinion. Then from that day on I started to realise that I'm not alone and never have been, I just needed to open up a little bit, let people in and take the advice that was given to me. Easier said than done for someone who didn't trust anyone but it was my only option if I wanted to move forward. If I was going to trust anyone, it was her as she totally understood my pain and darkness. Only she knew how I was really feeling inside and from that moment of getting to know her, I did not feel alone when at the group. Even though at counselling I felt like I was me, I would still have to go home alone and deal with my thoughts at some point. Seeing that I suffered with borderline personality disorder it wasn't the easiest thing to deal with at times, especially now my demons were at the front of my mind. Some days were ok but the majority of the time I was in complete darkness and saw no way forward. After all, I had lost everything so many times and the thought of losing everything again would have finished me off as I always struggled to deal with my feelings and emotions. This was due to my childhood and what had happened to me, making me see things in a totally different way to others around me. The way I saw it, every child is brought into this world to seek pleasure and avoid pain but because of what that dirty bastard did to me, it was the other way around which in turn made me look at things so differently. So until I could maintain some stability in my life my only way forward was to start a 20 week Regulations Emotions group which would help me deal with my anger issues and help me control my emotions, keeping my demons and past at bay. Until that group started, I found myself slowly but surely getting back into my old ways of smoking cannabis. There was no deep one-to-one support while I was waiting for the new emotions group to start and I wasn't willing to have a clear head and face my demons without any support so it was easier to get through a day and block out my emotions, feelings and past. I had my group therapy where I met my 'sis from another miss but it's far from easy to talk about the real deep pain inside, that needed to come from a professional. I knew about my Mental Health and did as much research as

I could about my diagnosis as I felt the more I knew about my diagnosis the more chance of recovery I would have.

Soon the real fight for recovery would be here as one morning I received a call from the people who were running the course. I had been anxiously waiting for this call. The lady was very pleasant and informed me that the course would start in August. I was over the moon as once I could deal with my emotions and maintain some stability in life I could then move onto psychology for the third time and all I could think was 'third time lucky'! It works for everyone else doesn't it? Once I had finished the call to the lady, I walked straight into the kitchen and took my box with all my smoking paraphernalia in, then made my way to the rubbish bin where I threw my box down the bin shoot. Now I knew this course was coming up I needed to have a clear head. The Course would start in five weeks' time and cannabis took four weeks to come out your system, which would leave me with a clear mind and help me while fighting for freedom.

Until that course had started, I was not in recovery. This meant only one thing as far as I was concerned, time for some mental torture to that dirty bastard. After all, if I was living in hell then why shouldn't he? Not realising that all it would do is increase my anger and keep me holding on to my demons but at the time, I couldn't give a shit so I would start to think about how I would next fuck this dirty bastards life up, just like he had fucked up mine. I had to do it for my own peace of mind as there was no way he was getting off scot free, no fucking way! He needed to feel my pain and I wouldn't rest until he had. The thoughts that were going through my head about what I really wanted to do to him were off the chart and I would start to prepare what I was going to do in my mind but yet again my rock, my world, my everything would stop me from following through with these thoughts and that was my daughter. She was there in my mind, telling me how proud she was of me and how we are building a dad/daughter relationship. I still had to do something, just to keep him sleeping with one eye open and the only way was for me to make an appearance at his house. Making sure he knows I'm not going away anytime soon and him not having a clue whether it's his last day of breathing and existing anymore. This is what he had done to me and I was so obsessed with getting my justice, on my bad days of feeling darkness, my anger would build and build as I had no one and nowhere to filter my true honest feelings about how I felt about this sick bastard. This time round, I would not hide behind a mask and face him. I no longer have anything to hide and this dirty bastard saw my face for the first time the last time I went to his house and he needed to see me with nothing to hide whatsoever. I was no longer a victim but he was now mine, the tables had turned and he had no clue when I was coming back, living in fear on a daily basis just like I had for over thirty years. Only if the older brother comes forward and is honest about what happened that day can my justice be served, then all of this darkness and obsession can go away and I can start living my life. I knew that wasn't going to happen anytime soon as I couldn't go to his house shouting the odds and disturbing his kids it just wasn't right. So the only way to deal with things for now was to pay the dirty bastard yet another visit. I don't know about you but if someone did what I did to that dirty bastard on my visits to his house then surely you would ring the police? If you were innocent that is! Seeing a man wave, what you think is a real gun and that sounded like a real gun, then firing shots at your house. No, not this dirty bastard as he was guilty as sin which fuelled my anger even more, this made me decide my next visit would be the following day. The crazy thing is, I enjoyed what I was doing and it needed to be done to stop this bastard from hurting anymore kids. I felt bad enough not coming forward sooner and maybe I could have saved many more. To make things even more interesting, I was going to do it broad daylight. I clearly wasn't thinking straight but who gives a shit? This bastard needed to suffer and that was the whole point. Already not smoking any weed was driving me crazy and if I was going to take my frustration out on anyone, it would be the person that caused it all as that's why I smoked it in the first place, to block out that shit part of my life. Many people say cannabis is a gateway drug but I disagree, it stems a lot further back than that and that's because I believe it comes from your childhood. Whether you're raped as a child, bullied as a child, neglected as a child. I believe any childhood trauma makes you see the world differently and as you grow, you think about that trauma and that trauma eats away at you until you get to the point where you need to block it out and will do whatever it takes to get rid of them demons. That's what I think about the situation and that's all I can say about it as it's my journey and I come to this conclusion through experience and living it.

STEVIE - BEHIND THE MASK

The next morning I woke up after not much sleep because I was obsessing about my demons, no time for breakfast, and just enough time to get my clothes and trainers on then make my way to Welling. Once back on the manor, I make my way to the peados house where I stand opposite his house in broad daylight, calling him out. Not by shouting but calmly beckoning him out of his house. I knew he was in there as his car was there, I knew his number plate off by heart due to my obsession with getting justice. As per usual the top window curtain starts to move, now he could see me without a mask as I no longer feared him but more of a case of him now fearing me. The front door is opened and I'm nowhere to be seen, he then walks down the drive looking confused and puzzled to where I was? By then I was running to the back of his house via the football fields which backed onto his house. Then I would throw stones to get his attention at the back of the house and then the top window curtain starts to move. He can see who I am and I stand there tilting my head side to side freaking him out just staring at him and by the time he got to the back garden, I was gone again. I was hiding, watching his every move. He looked worried and very paranoid, exactly how I wanted him to feel and I fucking loved it! Play games with me you dirty bastard! We can all play games. He looked in fear, he looked worried, he looked like a victim and finally I would see that he was a no one and I was no longer a child. To see him in fear was a lovely feeling for me as this was my journey and I would do whatever was needed to make me feel like I was getting some sort of justice. Then I would feel at ease as I knew I was now in control and he could no longer hurt me, like he did that day in the woods. I wanted to hurt him but now I knew he feared me and was driving himself mad, I didn't see the point as if I hurt him or even killed him he still wouldn't feel much pain. But, if I left it at that for now, he would always have to look over his shoulder and also know that one day I would come back! What would drive him mad is the fact he had no clue when and if I was going to return. Finally, I had this dirty bastard right where I wanted him and there was nothing he could do about it. He wouldn't ring the police as he hadn't before and straight away I had one up on him as he had nowhere to turn. Just like me, that day in the woods. These sick bastards needed to know there are consequences for their sick acts and that all kids grow up. Then you get kids like me that have everything taken from them at such a young age but never forget and promise themselves that one day, they would find out who it was and get some sort of revenge and this was only the start. I then left and made my way to my mums, like nothing had happened. Making myself a promise that one day I will be visiting him for the last time and that won't be to shake hands. For now, my daughter needed me and that's the only reason that dirty bastard was still alive.

A week into August and my Regulation Emotion group has not started yet and I have already waited for this class for four months! I get on the phone to the mental health services and ask why I hadn't received my letter about starting my course yet. The lady on the phone didn't sound convincing and said 'I'm looking through the notes and it says the group is cancelled', I said 'what do you mean? I haven't even got my starting letter yet and now you're telling me it's cancelled?' Instantly I start to get angry, just something I couldn't help hence why I was wanting to do this course so much. Then unfortunately it's too late and I start shouting as nobody seemed to know what was going on. The lady asked me to calm down and I say 'Calm down? Do you know what starting this course means to me? Do you have any idea what I'm dealing with? I come out with all my shit to get better and now you're telling me there is no help?' I don't think she had a clue what this course meant to me as she was only doing her job but so was I doing my job and that was to attend courses and get better. She really couldn't see what it meant to me so I told her everything and then when she realised what I had been through, she would start to explain why it was cancelled and it was for a legit reason. As usual, I was thinking everyone was out to get me. No doubt because of my trust, paranoia and anger issues as I was no longer getting my brain break and fix from cannabis. Once I had heard why it was cancelled I accepted it but then I wanted to know why we were not informed of this, to which she couldn't give me an answer which to me meant they were taking the blame. People may think why create over something so small but this was no small matter to me as I now had a clear mind and wanted to move forward. After all, they said I needed a clear mind to continue therapy yet now I had, they wanted to cancel the support I needed. Before coming off the phone I informed them I would like written confirmation of when it would start, that way I would have written proof rather than trusting what comes out of their mouths and I would have them bang to rights. I got off the phone and all I could do was cry and straight away my feelings of getting better were being taken away from me and that's something I struggled with as I had already lost so much, this was just the same shit, different day scenario. I remember the lady saying the next course will not start until November and it's still only August, that was another three months away and I had already waited five months. Now you know what I mean when I say getting over a trauma is a fight and just because you're involved with mental health services it doesn't mean you still don't have to fight. You have to own at least fifty percent of the fight to allow services to work, if not, there is no point in wasting your time but at the time I didn't know this. Without the support, things were only going to go one way and that was down as now, with no professional support, I was straight back onto my brain break. It wouldn't be alcohol or cocaine as I had already dealt with that part of my life and was managing it, to the best of my ability, so it was just so easy and simple to go back to smoking cannabis and when I say I really didn't want to, I mean it but the power of addiction will always win especially when it comes to wanting to block things out. Even though I knew there would be many negatives to smoking cannabis like paranoia, psychosis and god knows what else, it was all worth it rather than have to deal with my head on my own. Yet again, just goes to show you how easy and powerful addiction is and within five minutes of coming off the phone I make a call to my cannabis dealer and ordered three bags. If they thought I was waiting for another three months with a clear mind then they were clearly mistaken and after ten days of hell and withdrawal from cannabis, I was back in the mix. Within two minutes of the cannabis arriving, I was outside smoking a joint, totally disregarding the ten days of hard work I put in getting myself off of it and yet again doing what I thought was best rather than listening to the help and support of others. Clearly I was deluded and in a very dark place but nothing was darker than dealing with a clear mind and deep thought process with no support. I would still attend my group therapy twice a week but all I would do is help out others that were struggling. I wasn't trying to be an angel as I was far from it but all the time I was helping out others I didn't have to think about my problems. I knew what pain was and if I could help someone out, in a way, it kind of made me feel better in myself as I knew I had made their journey that little bit easier, bringing a little comfort to myself and still managing to block out my own feelings and emotions. Probably the worst thing I could do as yet again I was still hiding behind a mask and not being the real Stevie. One thing I noticed this time smoking cannabis was that I would not let it control me like it did before. I made sure I would smoke more in the evening to help me relax thinking I was doing nothing wrong as I would have done anything to stop the nightmares. I found things easier this way as I would have more of a clear head when attending my group therapy, which in turn would make me open up more about my feelings and bond with other members of the group. I would only do this at group as I knew they all understood me and had all suffered with some form of mental health.

As I started to interact more with people at group, being more open and honest about my feelings, the more I start to like things about myself and the more I start to learn about my diagnosis. I always thought I knew what was right and was not up for any constructive criticism but the people at this group were changing my thoughts around this as some of their stories were absolutely heartbreaking and they were being honest and they were fighting for the truth and their freedom.

I now found myself spending more time out of my bedroom and more time going out walking. Mainly around where I live but I am no longer locking myself away from society and have had enough of all the self-punishment I had done to myself, all I could do was just hope that one day the older brother comes forward to allow me my justice. Finally, I was starting to open up and it was all thanks to every single person that attended this group therapy, also it was because I no longer feared that dirty bastard and now he was the one in fear, not me. I was in the driving seat now and the more open and honest I was about my feelings in group therapy, the more confident I would feel within the group which helped me to open up even more. No matter how negative I felt on some occasions they were always there to pick me up and in return I would help to do the same for each of them, I then realised even more that a problem shared with people that understand you is definitely a problem halved. These people were like family to me now and I loved all of them in their own unique way. Finally, I could off load all my shit and no one would judge me and everything would feel that bit more manageable allowing me to deal with my Demons and stop obsessing with that dirty bastard. The only thing I needed now was a clear head so I could prepare myself for my Regulations Emotions Group as that was my key to Psychology and hopefully the key to freedom. By opening up in group therapy it could only benefit me as unless the professional knew more about me, how could they help me? It was time for me to stop walking alone and try to move forward with my life as he was now running scared, just like I was in the fields that day.

Realising that my Regulation Emotions Group was starting in November I decided it was time to go visit the addiction specialist I saw before but now I was in a bit of a better place, being more open about my demons and feelings. I wanted his help getting off the cannabis and with my bulimia, which I now believe was becoming an addiction as well.

I made my own way to him via a train as I was ready to get out more and face society now my demons were out the bag. It wasn't an easy journey, suffering with severe anxiety if I'm honest but if I didn't put more effort into getting back out there I would end up spending another 3 years procrastinating in my flat, forgetting who I really was and I made sure I was one of the first ones there as there was no way I was walking into a room full of people as I would have just walked straight back out again. Not this time, I needed help and I wasn't going backwards. This time, if I did get help and help myself I'm not sure I would be here today to tell my story. I knew things were only going to get worse, I was becoming weaker and thinking on a whole new level about taking my life. That couldn't happen as my daughter needed her dad and I needed my life back after trying for over 30 years for freedom. He welcomed me with open arms and this time around I sat at the front like a good disciple listening to everything Jesus was saying drinking my holy water…! Jokes aside, this time it made more sense as I was putting more of an effort in trying to understand the true meaning of addiction and why I struggled so much. He informed me, the same as everyone else did, that was why I always pushed people away and always tried to do everything on my own, just because I didn't trust anyone and even if someone was doing a nice thing for me, I would assume they would always want something in return and always thought it was a bad thing. It was the damage caused, no doubt, by what that sick bastard did to me that day in the woods. Once the group had finished I didn't feel any different from what I did at the beginning. Why would I? I had been stoned for god knows how long and clearly didn't feel any emotions as that's what cannabis does, it destroys your personality and everything that you are, leaving you in a zombie like state, in a world of your own. This doesn't take away the fact that this guy was amazing at what he did and slowly but surely what he was saying was registering. Once back in my flat I would start to process what I could and started to realise that all this time, right back since I was 17 years old, I have been self-medicating and blocking out my Demons with alcohol and drugs. Not giving myself time to feel what real life was like. I didn't want to feel real life but if I wanted to move forward I would have to. I then walked out and into the kitchen for the umpteenth time, took my box with all my cannabis in and threw it down the bin shoot and I remember saying to myself 'this is the last time I do this, I am definitely not going back to smoking cannabis and blocking out my demons'. I'm not even sure if it was doing what it needed to anymore anyway as the addiction had now taken over and my brain needed it to function.

After a couple of days without smoking cannabis I became a totally different person as now I had to face all my thoughts and feelings with a clear mind. It would have been a good thing, according to others, not for me though as all the thoughts and memories of what he did to me that day would start to haunt me more than ever. At the time I didn't realise it but this was my brain playing tricks on me as my brain wanted its fix and I wasn't allowing it to get its way. I needed to fight it and fight I did as all these emotions would hit me and sometimes I just wanted to roll a joint and make it all go away but if I wanted to get better I would have to resist. I would talk to myself saying 'you don't need that poison anymore', then five minutes later 'yes ya do, look how good it makes ya feel'. Constantly battling with my brain, fighting with every part of myself trying to do the right thing. Some days were ok but most were soul destroying as I was also dealing with a personality disorder due to childhood trauma and that was a battle every day in itself. I would cry most days and smiling wasn't an option as there was nothing to smile about. I was facing my demons with a clear head and it was hell. I was being tortured by my past and all I wanted was peace but that wasn't coming anytime soon. You do the crime, you do the time! The crime being cannabis and withdrawal is the time but unlike others, I take ownership of my bad decisions and they need to be rectified by having a clear mind otherwise I would carry on living a life of being suppressed 24/7 and if that was the case then what's the point of being here? Feeling no emotions and having no personality was something I had while drinking alcohol and sniffing cocaine but with cannabis it's a totally different buzz which takes you away from society rather than fitting in to society. Many times I would think about drinking alcohol and taking cocaine but I now realised that if I went back there again then there would be no going back as I would be too weak to go through all that again. I am still an addict and I would be lying if I said I didn't crave alcohol and cocaine occasionally but the difference now is that I resist as even though it feels good at the time, the damage it causes physically and mentally is just not worth it. Plus, it was hard enough dealing with a cannabis addiction that now pretty much ruled my life. I just had to wait it out, locking myself away when I should be out there pushing forward but how could I the paranoia and psychosis were at an all-time high as still my brain would play tricks on me wanting its fix every minute of the day. Drugs shouldn't be taken anyway but when using them to self-medicate and block out trauma it only makes the addiction worse in my opinion as you are totally taken away from reality, making it harder to get back to reality which in turn makes the addiction process worse than it needs to be. The longer I went without smoking cannabis, the worse I would feel but I was doing the right thing. But why was I feeling like this? Surely I should feel better by now so why didn't I? This was all down to that dirty bastard. Now my mind couldn't have its fix it was trying to play tricks with me by making me obsess about that dirty bastard even more. It was his fault I was like this, why should I let him get away with what he had done to me? I am 41 years old and I am no one and nothing to society. I still live behind a mask and I don't know whether I'm coming or going and can never maintain any sort of stability in my life yet. All the thoughts in my mind that my brain was telling me were to make me feel worse so I would hopefully pick up a joint and give my brain its fix. It was so hard and at times it nearly broke me but I continued to get to 10 days which is how long it takes to get through any addiction before you stop feeling the withdrawal and start to feel a little better in yourself but things would get better as cannabis takes 28 days to get out of your system, making you feel better as time goes by. Now I had hit the 10 day withdrawal and I could still manage to sleep as I still had cannabis in my system which would keep my Demons at bay for now. My timing was perfect as my Regulations Emotions group was starting in a couple of days and that would help me, having support from others while I tried to deal with things with a clear head. Those two days dragged on like there was no tomorrow but finally the day of starting my group is here. Yet again I was a bag of nerves and was just hoping that the facilitators were going to be female as I needed to concentrate and couldn't do that if they were men as I still didn't trust men. While in the waiting room of the mental health services I noticed that everyone is the same as me, all wearing a mask, hiding their pain just hoping for a solution to their problems so they can try and maintain some sort of stability in life. Then out of a door came two ladies and straight away I'm thinking 'please call my name' and then my name is called and for the first time in a while, I smiled. I was thinking 'no male facilitators, happy days'. The ladies looked at me, as if to say, he looks fine or maybe that was still the paranoia I suffered with, due to the amount of cannabis I was smoking. Either way, I didn't care as everything was there for the taking as I was going to be educated on my thoughts and emotions to help build trust and start forming and retaining relationships with people. To top it off, I was now going to be educated by two females who I had more chance of believing and trusting than I would have if I was taught by males, just another effect of what that sick bastard did to me. Once in the room I noticed four females who are struggling and two facilitators who are females, this was good for me and would make me feel more at ease so I could be more open and relax. This group was my key to psychology and I was going to give it one hundred percent as I no longer wanted to live a life of misery and darkness and for the first time in a long time I didn't want to die. I wanted to live and I wanted to make my daughter proud but more importantly I wanted to do things for me as I was starting to like myself. Don't get me wrong, that dirty bastard was the last thing in my head before I went to sleep and the first thing on my mind when I woke up but now I was putting more effort into getting better. I could battle with him in my mind but I was becoming stronger and starting to maintain some stability.

When group started we would all start off with how we are each feeling, me thinking 'I know it all as usual, I try to put the world to rights expressing my feelings and emotions about society'. After I spoke I regretted it straight away and started apologising, which is something I have done a lot as I never really thought about things and how they affected others as I was used to dealing with my own thought process and nobody else's. The lady cut me short which is something people would have to do with me a lot as once I started I couldn't stop without being interrupted. She said 'I was just showing emotions and feelings but maybe with a little too much anger which is also an emotion', she wasn't being horrible she was speaking truthfully. I was an angry person and that's something I needed to deal with, I then started to get upset as I went past anger then started telling everyone what that sick bastard did to me. Again, obsessing about him again, not controlling my emotions one little bit. The lady then explained to me about my core emotion, which was anger. The reason why I'm always angry is because I need to deal with it, otherwise I will always be angry as that's what your core emotion does, and it takes over you, making everything in life based around your trauma. I hate to admit it but she was right and continued to explain that I have every right to be angry regarding my trauma but not to let it consume me and take over every aspect of my life. Normally I would start shouting the odds saying 'what do you know about trauma?' But I realised by being more assertive than aggressive you will get a lot further in life. It was hard to do as I was used to living a certain way for so long but without change I would stay where I was, so I embraced what she was saying to me and decided to put it into action. She finished off by saying that slowing things down a bit would help, I totally got what she meant by that as I was always one hundred miles an hour. Then, before she could say anything I said the reason I should slow down is so maybe I could think a little before I speak and she looked at me and smiled, which meant I was listening to what she was saying. It kind of felt good believing in what someone was telling me. The other ladies in the group all had their troubles but there was this one lady who I took a liking to, when I say liking, I mean in a friendly way, the reason for this is she was struggling, just like I was a few years ago and I felt it was my duty to help her, if I could. It may have been a lovely thing to do but straight away I was helping others which would stop me thinking about my problems. I was forgetting that when in services you have to think of yourself and your own problems otherwise you're defeating the object and are totally wasting your time. No doubt in time and with a bit of practice I can concentrate on myself but that's a hard thing to do when you have been in darkness yourself and remember the feeling that no one was there to help me. I just struggled to disconnect with other people's problems sometimes, I just wanted to help. At the end the lady mentioned that sometimes being kind to yourself and having 'you' time is ok. What I think she was saying, in a nice way, was 'I can't help everyone, that's down to them, not me'. Another thing I took on board before the class finished. I walked out of there feeling ok but was thinking about this core emotion stuff, which I found myself fixating on but I had no need to do that as I would learn more next week as it was a 20 week course. Then I decided it was time to slow myself down and think about my thoughts and actions. It was the only way I could learn more about myself and my emotions, it was time for change and that change needed to be now. No one likes change but anything was better than the life I was living, that's if you could call it a life.

After a month of attending my emotions group I was starting to learn a lot about myself and was managing some sort of stability in life. I was being open and honest about my feelings and emotions and no longer hiding behind a mask. I was also clear from cannabis and was dedicating my spare time to read up on my mental health, learning as much as I could to help me become a better person and move forward. The hardest part was taking ownership of what had happened to me as a child and realising that I had done everything possible to get justice but I would now have to face the fact that justice might not ever come, unless the older brother comes forward and like I said before, I couldn't see that happening anytime soon. It wasn't a lot to hold onto but it's something to hold on to as even though I had to move on now, I can still hope for justice one day and that's something I feel anyone in my position would want as well. I thought about it for a few days and realised that until I was in a better place, there was no point in fighting anymore. It would only be the end of me if I did as I was now fighting a losing battle because without the older brother coming forward it was like the police didn't even believe me and the CPS wouldn't entertain me without two bits of evidence for historical abuse. I had done everything in my power to get justice and realised I could do no more. The only one person that can change that is the older brother but I couldn't force him, so why punish myself anymore?

Another reason and the main reason I decided to now move forward was down to every single person at my group I went to twice a week. Showing me support and more than anything else, showing me that I'm not alone anymore. To move forward, sometimes you have to feel inspired and my 'sis from another miss was my inspiration, hearing her story and seeing how she fought for a better life and getting her justice, even though she struggles every now and then, she never gives up and is always there for others. What better inspiration can you get than that to move forward and join the rest fighting for a better future? After all, I had nothing to lose but everything to gain and for me to realise that was all down to her. Just to think, I spent all this time locking myself away from society, taking no advice from anyone and doing nothing but punish myself for something that clearly wasn't my fault. All I had to do was talk but at the time how could I when I had kept it quiet for so long? I was proving to myself that keeping secrets like that will only cause me pain and that's not where the pain belongs. The pain should be owned by that dirty bastard. Why should he lead a pain free life? I spent a few days thinking about where my life was going while in my flat and I decided that I can no longer obsess about justice and focus on myself. Things were looking brighter and I had to grab it while it was there. What made everything that little bit easier was that I was no longer alone and the support from friends, family and services was everywhere, only a fool would turn it down. All I ever wanted was support and understanding and now I had it. It was always there but I just wasn't ready and sometimes that's just how the journey goes. You know when you're ready and my time was now. Slowly but surely I was escaping the nightmare, getting rid of the mask and starting to be the person I've always wanted to be and that's not the free me but at least it's the real me.

My name is Stevie. You know my name, now you know my TRUE story, fighting for freedom…!!!

CHAPTER 10
THE FINAL MESSAGE

Thank you for taking your time to read my book...

I hope this now gives people an understanding of how some people live their lives after going through such a dark childhood trauma and how it can totally change someone's life in the blink of an eye.

I feel most who have been abused mentally or physically will totally understand my journey and for that I salute you all. You are very brave and a lot stronger than you think you are and if you are still holding in your trauma and have for many years then please don't do this anymore. It's not fair to you as you were only a child but now you are an adult, you have a voice and you deserve to be heard.

I'm not going to lie and say it's going to be easy fighting for your freedom but anything is better than living the life you're living today. You really don't have to punish yourself anymore as you were not to blame. You were a child and that pain and ownership belongs to the adult who thought it was ok to destroy your childhood.

I would also like to salute anyone reading this book who is battling addiction or suffering with mental health as you are also a lot stronger than you think as well. Hiding behind a mask is convenient for the people around you and will keep you feeling like everyone else for a little while but we are not robots and any human being will break after living a life hiding behind a mask and not being their real, happy self. It's ok to not be ok, we were all given feelings and emotions so let's use them in an honest way to help us live our lives to the fullest and helps us resolve our struggles.

To all of you that have not suffered any type of trauma in their life and are not dealing with addiction or mental health, but took the time to read my book to maybe understand what a friend or a family member are going through then I salute you too. Why? For being selfless and willing to try and understand other people's difficulties even though they might not affect you.

The more understanding and awareness that is raised regarding the above subjects, then the better things will become for those who are suffering, making them feel a little more at ease and helping fit back into society.

It goes without saying that I punished myself for many years knowing I was different and that society was struggling to accept the way I was but that's because all these subjects wasn't really spoken about so I had to hide things as there was no understanding and awareness. Now it's out there and that's why you no longer have to hide if you are struggling, help and support is out there and if you can fight like you already have so far then you have nothing to lose. You deserve to be happy and just because you feel different to many others it doesn't make you any less worthy. Just remember you may feel alone but you really are not, that's just how you're made to feel when you're struggling as you're protecting yourself and that's normal but so is reaching out and asking for help.

I'm living my life now to the best of my ability and I am very open about how I feel and what I've been through. I take ownership and I am not ashamed of my past, it has made me the person I am today. It has not been easy but now I can hold my head up high and try to lead a life with more happiness with my emotions and feelings now a lot more stable.

I know it will always be there but because I am being open and honest with my feelings and emotions people can see what's wrong and rather than hide it I now deal with it, giving myself a clearer head as I can now be the real me but unfortunately not the free me, yet.

All that being said, I am in a lot better place than I was living behind a mask, letting people think that I was ok, I wasn't being myself and that's not how things are supposed to be. After all, life is about seeking pleasure and avoiding pain isn't it?

I would just like to say to the two brothers that were there that day in the woods, I can totally understand why you want to keep quiet about that day but secrets only eat away at you and you know that's true as you can see what damage it has done to me, honesty is a much better option for mental stability. It must have been very traumatic for you both that day in the woods but we were only kids and if I'm honest, I was the one receiving all the pain and I was the one who experienced what child abuse and rape was on a whole new level. I'm not asking you, the older brother, to discuss anything about your life as I know you have a family but just put the boot on the other foot for one minute and I'm sure you will understand why you and only you can give me the justice I need and feel I deserve. You're not just doing the right thing by me but for all the other children out there who walk the streets not realising that sick bastard is walking free looking for his next victim. If you don't remember then I can't force you to but if you do remember then I am asking you to think about how it's destroyed my life and how you can prevent it happening to another child. Now I have my friends and family back in my life and look forward to living the life I should have had.

I've now got my daughter back in my life and she now has her dad back which was the most important thing to happen, making a positive situation out of a negative one. I have an unconditional love for my daughter so I must be starting to love myself again which just goes to show, you cannot love anyone in life if you can't love yourself.

You need to help and love yourself first, that's the key to your happiness and the rest should fall in place as long as you take full advantage of the help and support that is there, then one day you will be where you need to be.

And to all of you people out there that are suffering in silence, writing your feelings down on paper is a great way of expressing and learning more about yourself. It sounds silly but it is definitely worth a try as anything is better than how you're feeling right now if you're living in silence all alone.

I may not have my day in court now but I will hang on with hope that one day my day will come and justice will be served. For now, me sharing my story with the world and raising awareness is a sort of justice as we need to fight back to ensure this sick act that is being carried out on children all over the world stops and it needs to stop now!

I still battle with my addictions today but the point is, I am trying to better myself and I am fighting every day for a better future. Let's be honest with ourselves, it's much better to try than to do nothing at all.

Oh yeah, just one more thing you need to remember, you are not a VICTIM, you are not a SURVIVOR, you are a fucking WARRIOR…!!!

Acknowledgements

It goes without saying that I would like to thank my family and friends for all your support. It's been a tough four years and all you just being there has helped me more than you will ever know. Once you have read my book no doubt you will see how much you helped me, without even knowing.

I would also like to thank my two managers at the company I used to work for who helped me as much as they could and are still there today. To Laura and Andy, thank you for your support whilst working for you both, you really helped me get through a working week while I was dealing with my demons. You are both amazing human beings, bless you both.

Now time to thank all my close friends. I will start with a selfless and empathetic person who always wanted the best for me, but always knew there was something wrong and couldn't put his finger on it. So this is a big thank you to my mate Gunny for being there day and night whenever I needed you, also for your continued support it means the world to me. Thanks for being you mate.

I would like to thank someone who I have not mentioned in my book at all and that's not because I don't love him, but he knows what happens at Dan's (Big Jewish) stays at Dan's. On a serious note, thank you for being there Dan, you are a crazy man but have a big heart and I appreciate all you have done for me.

I would like to thank my best mate who is absolutely crackers and likes to be the hard man, but deep down is a lovely genuine caring person. He has a special place in my heart and was the first person I shared my demons with. So Scotty thank you for everything mate, your support over the last four years has been amazing, you have given me a bit of freedom to be the person I am meant to be and that's all thanks to you.

Now to my neighbour and younger mate Mamo, even though you have been through tough times yourself mate you are always there for a chat. Thanks mate, keep going and thanks for being you.

Next, I would like to thank the female friends that I have in my life who have been there for me within the last four years and they mean the world to me. Genuine, selfless ladies who have done so much for me and at times not even knowing that they are helping…

I would like to thank Tracey for giving me the confidence to carry on with my book.

STEVIE - BEHIND THE MASK

I would like to thank Angela, my next-door neighbour for being the first person to read my full manuscript and giving me the confidence to get it published.

Thankyou Anna for being there whilst trying to run your own business at the same time. What happened to us as children was very traumatic. On the positive side, it brought us closer together as friends and your support has been amazing, bless you mate.

I would like to talk about a lady I have known for three years. Karen, you are an amazing human being, meeting you and having you in my life has been amazing. Your support and advice means the world to me, you are a selfless, empathetic lovely lady and I will always be here for you in good times and bad. Bless you Karen.

This next thankyou is so deserved as I have spent the last year and a half on the same journey with you. You're my 'Sis from another Miss' and meeting you has made my journey so much easier. Emma, bless you and everything you stand for, your strength amazes me and I'm so happy to have you in my life mate. Thank you for being you.

Now I come to a person that has not only helped me get my story out there, but has supported me at my very lowest and has been there when most people couldn't or wasn't. From taking me to the mental health unit, to being there to talk to, you name it she would try her hardest to help and get me where I need to be. So Faye, never stop being you and thank you so much for all that you have done for me, you're an amazing person in every way. Bless you mate.

I would like to thank the three people that I have dedicated my book to, my Mum, Dad and Daughter. Without your love and support I can assure you that I would not be here today to share my story with the world. You have put up with me during tough times and have pushed me to where I am today. Mum and Dad I love you dearly and thanks for being you. To my strong, independent, beautiful daughter, you never cease to amaze me with your love and emotion for other people and helping others in times of struggles. I couldn't be prouder of you. I know I wasn't there in your earlier days but I promise I will be the best Dad I can and help you whenever you need me. Love you darling, Daddy.

Finally, to all my haters and enemies, thank you for being you as you made me the strong, independent Warrior that I am today.

In loving memory of
Julie Day
1974 – 2019
'Nothing is impossible'

Printed in Great Britain
by Amazon

41613214R00175